GREAT LAKES

Halifax

Cape Sable

Penobscot Bay

Boston
Cape Cod

Rhode Island
Long Island
New York
Philadelphia

Delaware Bay

Richmond
Yorktown
Norfolk
Chesapeake Bay
✕ Sept. 5ᵗʰ 1781

Pamlico Sound

Wilmington

Charleston

Savannah

Amelia Island

Mississippi
Delta

ATLANTIC OCEAN

OF MEXICO

Old Bahama Channel

Yucatán Channel

CUBA

Cap François

Windward Passage

CARIBBEAN SEA

JAMAICA

I. la Vache
Mona Passage

ADMIRAL RODNEY

Admiral Rodney as a young man.
After Reynolds; by courtesy
of the National Portrait Gallery

ADMIRAL RODNEY

Captain Donald Macintyre, R.N.

ILLUSTRATED

LONDON : PETER DAVIES

Copyright © 1962 Captain Donald Macintyre
First published 1962

Printed in Great Britain for Peter Davies Ltd
by The Windmill Press Ltd, Kingswood, Surrey

ILLUSTRATIONS

The endpaper map has been drawn by Jean Main and the battle diagrams by David Cobb, R.O.I., S.M.A.

I

THE blue waters of Villefranche Bay sparkled in the sunshine. Spread in neat lines on them lay a squadron of the British Mediterranean Fleet, the masts and yards of the ships making a graceful tracery in contrast to the squat black-and-yellow hulls from which they rose. The largest of them, a 90-gun three-decker with a huge red ensign floating from her ensign staff, the name *Namur* in gilded lettering across her square stern decorated with intricate 'ginger-bread', flew also a red flag at her foremast head. For she was the flagship of Thomas Mathews, Vice-Admiral of the Red and Commander-in-Chief.

From her side drew away a six-oared pinnace. The sailors pulling at the oars were uniformly dressed in checkered shirts and blue-and-white striped canvas trousers—unlike the motley-clothed majority of the men to be seen working about the ships—for they were the flag captain's boat's crew. In the stern sheets sat a slim young man wearing a red cut-away coat with blue facings, with gold lace at pockets and slashed sleeves, a gold-hilted hanger at his side. A black tricorne hat, edged with gold lace, with a black cockade attached to its left, upturned brim, covered his thick, rather long brown hair that was tied behind his neck with a neat black ribbon. At throat and wrist immaculate white lace showed.

It was not possible to tell from any arrangement of lace on the coat what rank the young officer held; for it was the year 1742 and the Admiralty had not yet decreed a uniform for the officers and men of the fleet, leaving them free to dress as they pleased. The boat threaded its way through the anchored vessels and made for one of the smaller line-of-battle ships, the *Plymouth* of 64 guns. In obedience to curt orders from the elegant young officer the boat was brought alongside her entrance ladder, a tier of wooden battens nailed to the side, leading up to the upper deck. With practised ease, gripping the side-ropes threaded through the eyes of short iron stanchions, the officer mounted, and, as he stepped on to the deck, lifted his hat and bowed to the older man waiting to greet him, behind whom a group of officers were standing bareheaded. The young man stepped forward and announced himself.

'George Rodney, sir, late lieutenant of the *Namur*, come aboard to relieve you in command. My commission from the admiral, sir,' and he handed over a rolled document.

'You are welcome, Mr Rodney,' replied Captain Watson of the *Plymouth*. Mr Crighton, here, your first lieutenant, will read out your commission and then we can complete our business over a glass of wine in the cabin.'

So George Brydges Rodney stepped for the first time on to his own quarter-deck as a captain. The assembled ship's company, taking stock of their new captain, noted his appearance of extreme youth, though he was in fact nearly twenty-five years of age. But in contrast to the sensuous, rather girlish mouth, they saw a square jaw and heavy chin and a long, thrusting nose, features which boded ill for enemies or incompetents. His clothes betrayed the elegant; the confident, rather haughty look he cast round, taking in at one sweep the state of the upper deck of the ship and resting for a brief, quizzical moment on the officers' faces, was that of a self-assured young aristocrat.

It was indeed into a family of ancient lineage that Rodney had been born in January 1718. The Rodneys of Rodney Stoke in Somerset had held their estates for upwards of 500 years when Sir Edward, the great-grand-uncle of George, on the death of his only son, allowed them to pass to his daughter. Rodeney Stoke thus became the possession of the Brydges family.

Henry, the father of the future admiral was the grandson of Sir Edward's brother George. After a brief military career as a cornet of horse, he retired and settled at Walton-on-Thames. Though probably far from rich, he possessed what at the time was equally important, namely 'interest' through his influential Brydges connections and those of his wife Mary, the eldest daughter of Sir Henry Newton, who was at various times

Ambassador to the Grand Duke of Tuscany and a Judge of the Admiralty.

1718 was a good year to have been born an Englishman. The country was at peace. Under its great Whig minister, Robert Walpole, it was to be kept so for another twenty-one years and to achieve a standard of prosperity never previously known. In the sunshine of material well-being the population was rapidly increasing and before the end of the century would have doubled its numbers. The Industrial Revolution had not yet begun to spread its pall of smoke over the green countryside. No squalid factory towns had yet sprung up. England was almost entirely agricultural.

Though the large cities had slums of appalling squalor which housed a population reduced almost to bestiality by poverty, this constituted a very small section of the country as a whole. The rest of the population was roughly divided into the landed gentry, the merchants and shopkeepers, the artisans and labourers. The country's wealth was in the hands of the aristocracy and the merchants; but the pinch of real poverty was not felt by the others. Though they handled little coin, they fed well, were well clothed and solidly housed. Furthermore they were lightly taxed. Above all, since the accession of George I and the consequent withdrawal of the monarch from active participation in government, they felt, however erroneously, that they were safe in the hands of Parliament from arbitrary injustice. They were thus, on the whole, content.

Government was, in fact, in the hands of the aristocratic landed gentry, mainly the wealthy Whig families which had first led the Bloodless Revolution of 1688 and later assured the accession of the House of Hanover at the death of Queen Anne. The Jacobite rising of 1715 had utterly discredited the Tories, leaving the Whigs to enjoy unopposed power which they continued to exercise for the next fifty years.

The eighteenth century was more than any epoch the age of 'interest' and 'place'. A gentleman could not soil his hands by dabbling in commerce. Financial rewards could only be sought in the perquisites of office. Such might be the salaries of genuine posts under the Crown or of sinecures of which there was an abundance. All were in the gift of the King himself or of some man of high rank or political power. To have the favour of such a personage meant 'interest' from which could come appointment to a desirable 'place'. In the struggle for advancement, 'interest' was the weapon; 'place' was the target.

Henry Rodney's interest came primarily from his Brydges cousin, the Duke of Chandos, an intimate of George I. Through him he obtained for himself a post in the Royal Yacht, used by the King for his frequent journeys across the Channel to visit his Electorate of Hanover. Being no sailor, Henry's post was no doubt an administrative sinecure; but it brought him the royal favour. When his second son was christened in February 1718 at St. Giles'-in-the-Fields, the King and the Duke of Chandos stood as godfathers, giving their names, George and Brydges, to the infant Rodney. (It may be mentioned here that the subject of this biography spelt his second name 'Bridges' for the greater part of his life, though it is as George Brydges Rodney that he has been known to historians.)

The royal patronage did not end at the font. When the boy was twelve years of age it was decided to bring his formal schooling at Harrow to an end and enter him in the Royal Navy. The King was approached with a request for a 'Letter of Service'.

The system by which the King's ships were officered in that day was typical of the age of 'interest' and 'place'. A father anxious to assure his son a career in the Navy might look around for a means of approaching a captain or an admiral, either directly, if he numbered such amongst his friends, or through relations or influential patrons otherwise, with a request to take him to sea. If such an avenue were found, the aspirant to a commission would be entered on the ship's books as 'captain's servant' in place of one of the genuine servants allowed. In reality he would thus be placed 'on the quarter-deck' in much the same capacity as a cadet of a later age.

The best patronage under which a boy could enter on a naval career, however, was that of the King himself. Furnished with a 'Letter of Service' signed by the King, he was entitled to a place on the quarter-deck and in due course would usually receive preferential treatment in obtaining his commission as a lieutenant.

The need for 'interest' working on his behalf continued to

govern the progress of a naval officer throughout his career. His rise from captain's servant or King's letter boy to midshipman depended upon a vacancy occurring; but it depended even more upon the favour of the captain who had brought him to sea. Qualifications for a commission as lieutenant were a term of years at sea, not all of which was necessarily in a King's ship, and the ability to hand, reef and steer, understand the rudiments of navigation and keep a log. He had also to be twenty years of age, but birth certificates to cover any deficiency in age could be arranged. But without a friend with influence in the right quarter to speak for him, vacancies in the fleet might always be filled by others more fortunate in this respect. A man might remain a midshipman all his days, a petty officer with no claim on the Admiralty for continuity of employment or salary.

Even having set his foot upon the ladder as a lieutenant, the same system governed his further advancement. Vacancies in command, to fill which he might be most suitably qualified and placed, might go to some protégé of a powerful politician working through a commander-in-chief who was indebted to him for his appointment; or they could go to protégés of the commander-in-chief's followers—captains who had long before hitched their wagons to the admiral's rising star and risen with him. The great explorer Captain Cook, whose origins were humble, was forty years old when he was commissioned a lieutenant and it was in that rank that he made his first famous voyage of discovery.

That the system was one of gross nepotism and favouritism cannot be denied. But in the circumstances of the age it was not without its merits. That officers should be recruited from the ranks of the gentry, or at least from the well-to-do, was very desirable; for, as a rule, only they could gain the necessary educational groundwork. That their entry and advancement depended upon the favour of a senior officer could lead to scandalous jobbery; but the captains and admirals knew that their own reputations and even safety could depend upon the fitness of the men they promoted; and in fact it was by no means rare, even in so class-conscious an age, for a man to be raised to the quarter-deck from before the mast. Thus while the First Lord of the Admiralty might remind the commander-in-chief that a protégé of his was serving under him and it would infinitely oblige him if he might have the first vacancy which occurred, it would be unlikely that the admiral would comply without ensuring that the protégé was reasonably competent.

Whatever the merits or demerits of the system—and under it the Royal Navy entered upon its Golden Age—it was inevitable in the stage of development reached by democracy in England of the eighteenth century—a democracy in theory, an oligarchy in practice.

With young Rodney's family connections, a King's Letter of Service was readily obtainable. It was actually the last of its kind ever to be issued, the practice being shortly afterwards abolished; entry as captain's servant continued to be the normal gateway for a long time, however. It was to the ship of Captain Medley, Governor and Commander-in-Chief of Newfoundland with the status of commodore, wintering as was the custom, in the Medway, that the boy of twelve reported in 1730.

Let us follow him as he is shown round by the gunner who has charge of the youngest of the 'young gentlemen', as the captain's servants, midshipmen and master's mates are collectively called. His first sight of a 74-gun line-of-battle ship in harbour preparing for sea after a refit must have been an astonishing and horrifying experience to the young lad fresh from the shelter of a gentleman's comfortable home.

They will have started their tour perhaps at the extreme after end of the ship, up on the raised poop-deck. Above their heads, from an ensign staff, floats a huge ensign, red, white or blue according to the grade in the hierarchy of admirals their squadron commander enjoys—or, if the ship belongs to no particular squadron, it would be red. At intervals down the midship line of the deck rise the three tall masts, mizzen, main and fore, with the yards to which the sails are attached slung squarely across athwartships.

From the masts, to which they are attached at various heights, stretch down to either side the stout tarred hemp hawsers of the standing rigging which support them—the shrouds and the back stays—secured at their lower ends to iron fittings in the channels; or 'chain-wales' or, briefly 'chains', heavy timbers protruding from the ship's side and running fore and aft. Joining the shrouds

6]

together horizontally at regular intervals, and so forming a ladder climbing to the tops and yards, are the hemp ratlines. Stretched forward and down from points aloft are the other main portions of the standing rigging, the fore-stays, heavy double hemp hawsers.

At each side of the poop-deck are guns, the smallest in the ship, nine-pounders, on wooden carriages. This deck, a vestigial remnant of the old after-castle of medieval ships, extends forward only as far as the mizzen mast. The next deck down, which can be seen stretching away to the bows of the ship, is not a continuously decked-in space, nor has it a single name. From the forward end of the poop, or the break of the poop as it is called, to the main-mast it is the quarter-deck. Forward of the mainmast it is cut away in the centre for about a third of its length, leaving the deck below partly exposed, to form the waist. The cut-away area does not leave the deck below totally open, however, for stretched fore and aft across the gap are the spare spars—topmasts and yards— known as the 'booms', and on them are stowed the ship's boats. Along each side a broad planked strip is left called a 'gangway', which leads forward to where the deck is again completely planked to make the forecastle.

The work of storing and provisioning the ship being com-pleted, the whole expanse gives an impression of the most precise neatness of arrangement with every rope's end coiled beautifully down into flat 'cheeses' and the deck planks gleaming white between the parallel lines of black tarred caulking.

Going forward from the poop, a ladder at each side leads down to the quarter-deck, the area sacred to the command, where only officers may linger and they only on the port side in harbour or the lee side at sea, if the captain is on deck. It is saluted by a lift of the hat by anyone stepping on to its immaculate, scrubbed and holy-stoned surface. At its after end, under the overhang of the poop-deck which gives some small shelter, is the big, double steering wheel from which the tiller lines of rawhide thongs run through guide blocks aft to the tiller. Forward of it is the compass binnacle, a wooden chest some four feet high and five long in which are fitted two compasses, one to each side, with a candle lamp to illuminate the card at night.

Before continuing on forward across the quarter-deck, as the captain is still ashore the gunner might take the boy aft into a space called the half-deck. To each side is a small space enclosed by portable deal walls, one being the cabin of the master, who is the navigating officer, the other forming that of the first lieutenant, second-in-command of the ship.

Beyond them, stretching right across the ship, is another removable bulkhead with a door in the centre. Here, normally, would be stationed a marine sentry; for beyond lies that holy of holies, the great cabin, where the captain lives in solitary grandeur and comparative comfort and space. Perhaps the gunner allows the youngster a peep inside.

The cabin occupies the whole space between the bulkhead and the stern where glazed casement windows stretch from side to side. Other windows open on to narrow galleries projecting from the ship's side, the quarter galleries. In the middle of the cabin is a round dining-table with chairs for half a dozen to be seated at it. Round the sides of the cabin are cushioned settees, which being hollow with hinged seats, serve as closets for the captain's effects. A space curtained off contains his swinging cot and a portable wash-basin on a tripod. A wooden dresser filled with china an glass for the table stands against the forward bulkhead. Amidst this almost homely comfort, it is a shock to see the black nine-pounder gun at each side facing its closed port.

The way now leads back through the half-deck to the quarter-deck. From here it is necessary to slant to the ship's side to make for one of the gangways. There the thick oak bulwarks, which form the sides of the quarter-deck, cease, giving way to canvas-sided troughs in which are stowed the hammocks of the ship's company, a protection during battle as well as a convenient stowage. Along the gangways there are no guns, what space there is being left free for the handling of the sheets, tacks and braces by which the sails and yards are managed.

Leaving the gangway, the forecastle is reached; here more nine-pounder guns are mounted at each side, and two long bow-chasers point forward on each side of the bowsprit. Amidships thrusts upwards an iron chimney to carry the smoke from the ship's galley, two decks below. Forward of the forecastle is the beakhead, to which ladders lead down; from there the bowsprit can be reached, and thence the spritsail yards, which carry two small square sails for use in a following wind.

Down now, by the companion ladder of the fore hatch, to the upper deck—upper gun deck, to give it its full name. Forward of it we come to a space surrounding the galley chimney piece. This is the sick bay. Warmed by the chimney and reached by fresh air from the waist, it would be the healthiest part of the ship but for one drawback. Beyond it, right in the bows, is the head, where the ship's company of 670 men repair to relieve nature when the weather is calm enough for them to get out and squat in primitive lavatories overhanging the side. At each forward corner of this deck is also a round house where similar arrangements exist for the 'young gentlemen'. In foul weather, seas will be apt to pass through the head and flow foaming into the sick bay.

As we turn aft we see on either side the long curving line of guns, eighteen-pounders on this deck, with their thick hempen breechings to take the recoil, with tackles to haul them out into the firing position again and others secured amidships with which they can be hauled inboard to be loaded or worked upon. Much of the remaining space is occupied by the workshops of the carpenter, blacksmith and armourer, and by pens for livestock which will be brought on board just before sailing.

It is here that a boy would get the first shock to his innocent susceptibilities as he sees the figures, male and female, which sprawl or loll in various degrees of undress and intoxication in every convenient space—not many on this deck, for there is but little room left for them. They are the overflow from the crowded lower deck whence the babble and song of men and women taking their drunken ease and pleasure can be heard welling up through the open hatchways.

The blushing boy would pick his way over and round the obstructions human and material, following the gunner past the waist where glimpses of the sky and a waft of fresh air come down from between the spare topmasts and yards stowed above, and on to the after end of the deck where a canvas bulkhead bars further progress. Through an open door in the middle of it is caught a glimpse of the wardroom, the mess of the lieutenants, the principal warrant officers—master, purser and surgeon—and the chaplain. Like the great cabin above, it runs aft to a line of stern windows. But there the resemblance ends. The room is long and narrow with canvas walls at either side behind which are the cabins of the lieutenants and other members of the mess. Down the middle of it runs a deal table with a soiled cloth at which some of the officers are lounging, tankards in hand, their red faces and dishevelled dress betraying their condition. One of them lurches to his feet and makes for a side door which opens on to quarter galleries which are fitted as lavatories for the officers.

Meanwhile the gunner will have led on down a companion ladder to the next deck—the lower deck or the gun deck as it is variously called. Aft of the ladder is the gunroom to which the boy has already been introduced; for here under the gunner's stern care he will mess together with several other young hopefuls whom Medley has agreed to take to sea. Like the wardroom above, its limits are set by portable bulkheads of canvas stretched on battens; but there are no stern windows. The space is lit by candle lanterns which give but a dim, gloomy light; no special arrangements are made for ventilation, and the air is thick with the foul smells which linger everywhere between decks, compounded of stale bilge water, the stickly odour of dry-rot in the timbers and of nearly 700 rarely washed bodies, with an overtone of stale cheese and rancid butter from the store rooms below. A more welcome ingredient which struggles in vain to disguise the others is that of the Stockholm tar with which the cordage is treated, and clothes and hats are made waterproof.

Here the youngsters sling their hammocks by night and pass what leisure they are allowed by day, or study mathematics and navigation if they are conscientious; though these pursuits are not strictly necessary for their further advancement. The gunner occupies a canvas-sided cabin leading off the mess.

Now, with scant consideration to the embarrassment of his young charge, the gunner would lead the way forward where, in the long expanse of the lower deck, under the low beams of the deck above, can be seen a milling throng of seamen and their women. Many of them are dockside trollops, though others are respectable wives who have come to join their men who are not allowed ashore so soon before sailing, even though in this time of peace they are all volunteers. Between the big thirty-two-pounder guns, mess tables are slung from the deck above. At them, on narrow wooden benches, sit men and women grasping tankards of beer to which has been added a generous portion of fiery spirits bought illicitly from the bum-boat women or smuggled aboard by the men's doxies.

As the boy follows the gunner, who walks with an habitual stoop from constant avoidance of the low beams overhead, his shocked eyes take in scenes of unveiled debauchery while his ears shrink from jokes and curses foul even by the standards of such a licentious age.

The gun-ports are open now, bringing light and fresh air; at sea they will be more often shut, the air will be thick and humid, the ship's side glistening wet. Nevertheless the lower deck is where the great majority of the ship's company eat, sleep and pass their leisure hours at sea.

At the forward end of this deck is found the brick-floored galley with its wood-fired cooking ranges and vast coppers in which the musty oatmeal issued by the purser is boiled into an unpalatable gruel known as 'burgoo' for the men's breakfasts. Another prominent feature is the tub in which the salt beef and pork is steeped in fresh water to soften it sufficiently for cooking and to extract some of the salt.

Right forward, up in the bows, are the hawse-pipes through which the hempen anchor cables are led inboard and down through navel pipes to their stowage on the deck below. At sea the hawse-pipes are plugged and caulked to prevent the ingress of the sea as the ship surges forward under sail; but in spite of the plugs, water still gets in, and to prevent it making its way aft into the galley, or on to the lower deck, there is a low wooden barrier or spurnwater, the space forward of it being called the manger; and indeed it is sometimes used to house livestock.

Once more the pair descend a wooden companion ladder. They are now below the waterline, and on this deck, known as the orlop, there are no ports or scuttles. It is only partly decked and below it are the main and after magazines, the hold, the various storerooms such as the fish room, bread room and spirit room. In the centre of the orlop deck the great hempen anchor cables are stowed in the cable tiers. Here live the boatswain and the carpenter, both warrant officers, in little canvas-screened spaces where they can sling their hammocks and be handy to their own particular store-rooms.

[11

The after end of this deck is given over to the senior midshipmen and master's mates who live in a dark, scantily-lit and odoriferous space called the after cockpit. At the age of fifteen they have been liberated from the surveillance of the gunner, and in the cavernous gloom of the cockpit are free to taste any form of depravity they fancy.

Such were the surroundings and the atmosphere into which the lad of twelve was plunged. They have to be borne in mind as forming the background to the professional life of Rodney, the naval officer, just as the system of political corruption and patronage was to flavour his conduct in pursuit of his personal ambitions.

II

SERVICE on the Newfoundland Station was a seasonal occupation, devoted as it was to the protection of the fishing fleet which worked the Grand Banks and dried their catches ashore in Newfoundland. The fishing fleet had to be convoyed across the Atlantic in the spring and brought back with its cargoes of dried cod to be sold in the Mediterranean in the autumn. For the next six years Rodney served with Medley, and at the end of them he was still only a midshipman. Not for another three years was he to make the crucial step into the ranks of commissioned officers when, on 15th February 1739, he was 'made', as the expression was, by Admiral Haddock, while serving under his flag in the Mediterranean.

For one who was to go so far it may seem a surprisingly long apprenticeship, if compared with the early career of his near contemporary, Admiral Howe. Howe, entering the Navy in 1740 at the age of fourteen, gained his commission in 1743 and his first command two years later. The fact is, however, that when Howe came to sea the long years of peace were at an end. The fleet was being put on a war footing, and vacancies were therefore plentiful.

It was also the quickening influence of war which brought Rodney to his first captaincy after three years as a lieutenant.

The Navy of 1743 had few captains of the calibre of Howe and Rodney, however. The long period of uninterrupted peace since the Treaty of Utrecht in 1713 had inevitably wrought a deterioration in the quality of the fleet and of the officers who commanded in it. Service at sea was a grim, harsh, dangerous way of life. Comfort was non-existent. On deck there was no shelter from the wind, the spray or the rain. Between decks the head room was so low that even the shortest men had to move about with bent shoulders; there was no warmth but that generated by the packed humanity occupying the ill-lit, evil-smelling space. The food was unspeakably foul, consisting for the most part of badly cooked, fat salt pork or beef, and weevil-ridden biscuit. It was washed down with doubtful beer so long as the supply lasted, for the water, stored in wooden barrels, was slimy and fetid. When the beer was exhausted, wine would be issued instead when available, or rum in surprisingly large quantities—sufficient to make drunkenness common.

Officers lived little better than their men. They ate much the same food. To compensate for its unpalatable nature they drank, often to excess in the fashion of the day, fearful mixtures of fiery spirits and sour wine. The miseries of gout at an early age were usually the result. They slept in hammocks. Cabins, where they existed, were temporary structures of wood or canvas which were dismantled on clearing for action. Only the captain, in a 'private' ship, or the admiral in his flagship, enjoyed the comparative luxury and privacy of the 'great cabin', right aft under the poop-deck. There he had his swinging cot, a dining-table at which he could entertain a few of his officers, brother captains or foreign officials on occasion. Washing arrangements were primitive even in the great cabin, rudimentary in the officers' quarters and almost totally lacking on the mess decks.

In addition to the sheer discomfort of life at sea, the management of a ship in the age of sail could be a matter of unremitting toil, watchfulness and danger. Warships were unhandy craft with little capacity to beat to windward. In coast-wise waters the repeated call for 'All hands' to tack or wear ship, to furl or reef sails or to spread more canvas, with every change in the force or direction of the wind, deprived officers and men of any regular rest. The sailors were driven to their duty by vicious application of rattans or 'starters' in the hands of petty officers and warrant officers. In the indifferently charted waters of those days, navigation was a constant anxiety. The poor weatherly qualities of the ships made every lee shore a peril. Even when lying to an anchor in harbour, a gale could bring mortal danger, the parting of the hempen anchor cables setting the ship helplessly adrift to be wrecked on a lee shore before she could be got under control. Professor Lewis, in his *Social History of the Navy*, has recorded

14]

that during the Napoleonic Wars, 1793–1815, of the 111 ships of all rates lost, 101 were lost through accident—wrecked, foundered or burnt.

Once clear of soundings, a ship could settle down to an ocean passage of weeks or months. Boredom and monotony would then descend on the close-packed company of men. Petty irritations would grow into bitter quarrels. The savage punishments of the day—flogging with a cat-o'-nine-tails on the bare back—by which an iron discipline was imposed, would increase in frequency and severity.

Dr Johnson, from the cosy comfort of the 'Cheshire Cheese', gave his view of life at sea: 'No man will be a sailor who has contrivance enough to get himself into a jail; for being in a ship is being in jail with the chance of being drowned. A man in jail has more room, better food and commonly better company.'

The effect on a boy like Rodney of twelve years of age of such an environment cannot be over-estimated. Professionally it must certainly have bred a seaman to the bone. Midshipmen went aloft with the topmen in all weathers and were expected to lead the race up the ratlines. They lay out on the yards to reef and hand the sails, punching the sodden or frozen canvas into obedience. In addition they had their regular watches to keep on the quarter-deck under the iron hands of tough, unsympathetic lieutenants who saw no reason why the brutal treatment they had themselves received should not be passed on to the next generation. Shortcomings were punished by hours at the masthead regardless of the weather or by thrashings with a rope's end, the victim bent over a gun-breech.

Off duty there was nowhere to go but the austere discomfort of the gun-room, the squalor of the after cockpit or, eventually, the wardroom and the companionship of the misfits and failures who made up the majority of its members. Cold, damp, and foul smells were the common lot of officers and men alike. Wet clothes remained wet in winter weather. Illness was treated by surgeons with a minimal medical knowledge and a meagre supply of medicaments. Scurvy to some degree was a commonplace, with no known preventative or cure. Typhus, brought on board by the unwashed scarecrows who volunteered out of destitution or to avoid jail, could sweep through a ship's company and decimate it.

It took toughness to survive, and courage—or insensitivity—to stick it out.

The young gentlemen were exposed from the start to the spectacle of a taste for vice amongst the residents of the after cockpit who included among their number a proportion of elderly midshipmen whom promotion had passed by through a lack of the right 'interest'. They learnt at an early age to escape from the gloom of their surroundings by deep draughts of cheap liquor, and their constitutions were often permanently undermined.

Edward Mangin, a clergyman who served for a few horrifying months as a chaplain during the Napoleonic wars seventy years later, described how his messmates passed their leisure hours in harbour. In the restricted space of the wardroom, games of backgammon, fencing practice, singing or playing various musical instruments went on amidst the continual comings and goings of midshipmen arriving for orders, the sergeant or corporal of Marines on errands, officers from other ships visiting, the stewards at work cleaning the mess, clearing up after meals or preparing for the next, officers' servants attending to their masters' clothes and boots.

At 2 p.m. the rolling of drums announced the dinner hour. After the meal, although some members of the mess off duty might mount to the poop- or quarter-deck to exercise, others would remain to drink wine and play at cards till 6 p.m. Then came tea which, according to custom, the midshipman of the last dog watch and one of the petty officers would be invited to join. The evening was passed in much the same way until 9 o'clock, when the last glass of grog went round; and at 10 the masters-at-arms entered to report to the first lieutenant that all lights and fires were extinguished, and it was time for bed.

Poor Mangin complained that it was in such surroundings, with the addition of the sights and sounds of the entertainment of women of the town, that he was expected to compose his sermons. It was not long before he resigned, preferring to take his chance of procuring a living ashore 'to the necessity of dwelling in a prison within whose narrow limits were to be found Constraint, Disease, Ignorance, Insensibility, Tyranny, Sameness, Dirt and Foul Air; and in addition the dangers of Ocean, Fire, Mutiny, Pestilence, Battle and Exile'.

The question inevitably springs to mind, 'What sort of men were they who chose such a life in a time of profound peace?

So far as the men of the lower deck were concerned, there were enough bred-in-the-bone seamen, who knew and cared for no other life, to form a professional nucleus. Their numbers were swelled sufficiently for the purposes of the reduced peacetime Navy by doubtful characters with good reasons of their own to get away to sea and by unemployed young men attracted by the lure of adventure or the tavern tales of old salts.

But for the young men of better-class families who became officers, prospects were hardly such as to attract the best. Promotion was slow and uncertain. Pay was small. Sickness and shipwreck took a heavy toll of their lives. Periods on half-pay were long and frequent. There was no prospect of prize-money, the great attraction for naval officers in time of war. A fair proportion of officers came from middle-class families of the traditionally maritime counties. The West Country provided many; others came from around Portsmouth. They had little influence in high places, but their fathers' Parliamentary votes were probably worth a letter to an admiral recommending their younger sons. Prospects were slim for younger sons in any walk of life, indeed, unless they were unusually bright. So it was quite customary to send the 'fool of the family' to sea; and of such were composed the majority of naval officers.

It is surprising therefore to find George Rodney amongst them. As we have seen, his father had the patronage of the King himself. He moved in fashionable and influential circles. A better career than the peacetime Navy could surely have been open if the boy had shown any talent. Yet George's schooling was brought to an end at the unusually early age of twelve and he was bundled off to sea. No evidence remains of his early promise or lack of it. What does emerge from his life story is that it was late in life before he reached the summit of his achievements. It is reasonable to surmise, therefore, that he was a late-developer and thus he may have lagged behind his schoolboy contemporaries and been taken for a bit of a fool earlier on.

If Rodney's qualities of brain and leadership did indeed develop somewhat late, nevertheless he stood out in other ways at an early age from the general run of his brother officers. Most of them were rough, tough, hard-swearing men who knew no other life than the sea. Many of them spoke in a sea jargon almost incomprehensible to landsmen, nautical expressions and similes being almost their only means of communication. Rodney when ashore belonged to the fashionable world of London. His friends moved in court circles or were prominent in politics. Beside the shabbily dressed 'tarpaulins' he was a be-laced and brocaded elegant. In moments of anger or stress, where they would explode in loud-mouthed invective, he would resort to the biting epigram and the icy rebuke. It cannot have been a quality to endear him to his fellows in the lieutenants' mess. He would have been far in advance of his time if he did not in return regard many of them with a class-conscious disdain. In later life he was to comment on their narrow outlook. 'It is their misfortune,' he wrote, 'to know little of the world, and to be bred in sea-port towns, where they keep company with few but themselves.'

Now he had moved on from their company to the solitary with-drawn existence of that awe-inspiring creature who occupied the great cabin. Armed with an authority which was by long custom, if not by law, almost absolute, the captain in his own ship received the homage elsewhere reserved for reigning monarchs.

On first assuming command he was received by a guard of Marines on the poop, all officers mustered with heads uncovered on the quarter-deck and the whole ship's company lined up. If a band was available it would play 'God Save The King' while the Marines presented arms. His commission would then be read aloud. All hats would be off in respect. On every subsequent occasion of leaving or returning to the ship, all officers would be mustered and boatswains would pipe the side in salute. Every head would be bared.

Any officer or man addressing the captain did so uncovered, and only if necessary in the course of duty would he presume to do so at all. If the captain stepped on to the quarter-deck all other officers would at once vacate the starboard side in harbour or the weather side at sea so that the great man was left to pace it in solitary pomp.

The captain rarely busied himself with the day-to-day running of the ship or its navigation. The former was left to the first lieutenant, the latter to the master. He could order the summary

18]

punishment of any man at his whim and, although he was restricted by regulations to awarding not more than twelve lashes with the cat-o'-nine-tails, this was regularly exceeded. He could arbitrarily disrate a midshipman or master's mate and turn him before the mast. Anyone who in his unsupported opinion committed an offence could be confined in irons for indefinite periods.

In the great cabin he dined in solitary state unless he cared to invite some of his officers to the often doubtful pleasure of joining him. The Reverend Mangin after such an experience asked why his fellow guest, a lieutenant, had been so silent during the meal and was told that it was 'not according to naval etiquette to converse at the table of a captain of a man-of-war'.

Such excessive respect and unbridled authority turned many captains into brutal megalomaniacs whose ships were floating hells. Unrestricted in their savage methods of enforcing discipline, they were far from amenable to it themselves.

The loyalty they owed to their country, their superiors and their fellow captains was often corrupted by their primary devotion to whatever political party they belonged to. Many of them were Members of Parliament. Whig or Tory, even in the presence of the enemy, kept a weather eye lifting for lack of support or even treachery on the part of a political opponent— sometimes not entirely without justification. Indeed the sight of such an opponent in difficulties could bring a certain satisfaction, and did not always call for their utmost endeavours to succour him. Personal quarrels were carried on with a relentless vigour which, when war broke out, was sometimes to sap the enthusiasm with which they attacked the enemy.

With captains of such a calibre—and admirals too—Britain's Navy was in poor shape to meet an enemy. War had been declared against Spain in 1739 as a result of clashes in the West Indies, where the Spaniards had been attempting to enforce their restrictive monopoly of trade with their colonies. Resentment had risen to a frenzy when a merchant captain named Jenkins, at the bar of the House of Commons, had told a tale of torture at Spanish hands and produced his severed ear which he said had been cut off by them to the accompaniment of insults aimed at King George.

In the War of Jenkins' Ear which followed, the role of the

British Mediterranean Fleet was confined chiefly to blockading operations, at first off Cadiz and later, when the Spaniards had succeeded in slipping out and through the Straits, off Toulon where they had taken refuge with their undeclared allies, the French.

Soon after assuming command of the *Plymouth*, Rodney was ordered home on convoy duty. He was therefore spared the ignominy of taking part in the disgraceful events which followed the entry of France into the war against us at the end of 1743. They were probably only surprising to him in the degree of ineptitude, poltroonery and even treachery they disclosed. A brief account of them is necessary, however, to give an idea of the state of affairs in the Navy at this time.

For indeed the situation in the fleet was such that shame and disaster were inevitable should an enemy of any spirit be met. The commander-in-chief, Mathews, was to show himself personally brave and considerably more spirited in action than the general run of senior officers of the time. His character, however, was such as to make him unfit for either of the two posts he held simultaneously—Commander-in-Chief, Mediterranean, and Minister to the Court of the King of Sardinia at Turin. An ill-mannered, illiterate man of violent temper, he earned amongst the Italians the contemptuous nickname of *Il Furibondo*.

In the fleet he carried on a bitter feud with his second-in-command, Rear-Admiral Lestock, whose recall he had asked for but which had been refused. A public reprimand for having failed to send a frigate to meet him on his arrival from England was his first exchange with Lestock. The coarse insults on this and later occasions made a sullen, malignant subordinate of the rear-admiral.

While the Spanish squadron skulked in Toulon, the British fleet lay idly at Hyères and Villefranche, ships' bottoms getting foul and crews losing their skill from want of practice. When the war became the War of Austrian Succession with the entry of France on the side of Spain, it became known that the combined French and Spanish fleet was preparing for sea. Mathews came down from Turin and hoisted his flag in the *Namur*. On 10th February 1744 the enemy were reported to be putting to sea with twenty-eight ships of the line.

By the morning of the 11th, the British fleet of twenty-nine ships of the line had struggled clumsily out of harbour and were in sight of the enemy. Both fleets were in the conventional line-of-battle ahead; but the English had not caught up with the enemy sufficiently to be abreast of them, the leading ship of Mathews' van being opposite the leading ship of the centre squadron of the allies. Furthermore, his rear squadron under Lestock was some five miles astern of the remainder. The previous evening it had already been out of station. When Mathews signalled for the fleet to lie-to for the night, he had also kept the signal flying for close order. To a loyal subordinate his intention would have been clear. While the leading squadrons lay-to, the rear squadron was to make the most of the opportunity to close up and form close order.

Lestock, probably with malicious intent, chose to obey the signal to lie-to. At daybreak he was still far astern, and in the light, fluky wind it would be hours before he could join his commander-in-chief.

Mathews, either impelled by impatient fury at Lestock, or confident of the superior fighting qualities of his ships, showed himself to be untrammelled by the rigid tactical ideas of the day. The Fighting Instructions laid it strictly down that when battle was joined, each ship of the British line must engage her exact opposite number in the enemy fleet, so preventing any overlap which might allow the disengaged enemy ships to double back and bring the British van between two fires. To do this now meant waiting for the tardy rear squadron; and meanwhile the enemy, fresh from dockyard, might sail away from the slower British ships.

Mathews decided to engage without delay. It might be possible to overwhelm the Spaniards in the rear squadron and the French in the centre before, in the light winds, the French van could double back to their rescue. Making the signal for action and keeping the signal for the line flying, he bore down with his flagship on the enemy.

Such unorthodox behaviour was too much for many of his captains. On the quarter-decks of the British ships there was much thumbing of signal books and of the Fighting Instructions as they strove to discern what was in the admiral's mind—an admiral whom few of them knew at all well and whose irascible, ill-mannered nature had discouraged any intimacy. Confusion in the British line inevitably resulted. Ships straggled down towards the enemy and might have been cut to pieces as they came one by one into action had their enemy shown any real spirit.

So far the keynote had been mere ineptitude, the consequence of inexperience. But now there were added examples of craven cowardice on the part of a number of the British captains. Instead of supporting their admiral they hung back, turning their ships up parallel to the enemy line at long range where their fire and that of the enemy were quite ineffective; one of the worst examples was Richard Norris of the *Essex* under whom Rodney had served for a time. The few exceptions showed what might have been the result of a spirited attack on the half-hearted enemy fleet, notably the *Berwick* of seventy guns, commanded by Edward Hawke, which forced the Spanish *Poder* to strike, making the only capture of the action.

At nightfall Mathews drew off his force to bring some order out of the general confusion. Little had been accomplished. When Lestock's squadron finally rejoined, Mathews might have gone in chase of the retreating enemy. Instead he bethought himself of his orders to cover the coast of Italy against the passage of enemy troop convoys and allowed the allied fleet to make good its escape. Lestock was placed under arrest and sent home.

When the news reached Parliament, Mathews was relieved of his command and brought back. The shameful story was debated in the Commons, Lestock and others being brought to the bar to give evidence while Mathews, a Member of the House, was heard from his place. The Admiralty being pressed to take action, a series of courts martial followed which advertised to the world the sorry state into which the Navy had fallen.

The cowardly captains were cashiered, with the exception of one who was given a lesser sentence because he was so old and nearly blind, and of Richard Norris who deserted in Spain on his way home rather than face trial, and was never heard of again. When Lestock came up for trial, however, he was able successfully to maintain that he had followed the letter of his orders, and he was acquitted. Mathews was therefore tried in his turn. It being shown that he had made a signal for line-of-battle and yet so acted himself as to make preservation of the line impossible, he was condemned and dismissed the service.

Technically the verdicts were correct. Mathews' audacity had led him to disregard the Fighting Instructions. Had he been successful he would have been a hero. Had he had the capacity of a true leader, he might indeed have been successful. But, betrayed by subordinates whose respect and confidence he had never tried to gain, he paid the penalty of unorthodoxy.

The result of the condemnation of Mathews was to put the tactical thought of the Navy into a strait-jacket which was to hamper it for decades to come. Rodney took no part in the sorry chain of events; but he was to feel their effect at a critical moment and to have victory snatched from him thereby thirty-six years later.

III

RODNEY's command of the *Plymouth* was but short-lived, as he must have anticipated; for she was a ship-of-the-line, too important for a young officer's first command. The normal ladder of promotion would have raised him from lieutenant to master and commander of a minor war vessel as the next step. But the *Plymouth* was a 'post' ship, one which rated a 'post' captain in command. If the admiral's commission were confirmed by the Admiralty, Rodney could skip the intermediate rank.

A successful outcome of his first assignment was therefore important. It was one to test his abilities. Under his charge was a convoy of 300 merchant ships of the Lisbon trade, homeward bound with full cargoes. An unwieldy body to control, it had also to be shepherded clear of the enemy privateers which haunted the western approaches to the Channel. When it was safely brought to harbour, the relieved merchants of London and Bristol were not slow to send the officer responsible their congratulations and thanks.

Certainly the Admiralty must have been satisfied, for Rodney was confirmed in his rank of captain before being shifted to a ship more suitable to his seniority, the 20-gun frigate, *Sheerness*. During the next four years he moved steadily upwards—to the *Ludlow Castle* of forty guns, in which he fought and took a large privateer out of St. Malo, gaining his first prize money, thence to the *Centurion* of fifty guns, and in 1747 to the line-of-battle ship *Eagle* (60).

During this time there was little action or glory to be had out of the desultory war at sea. The French and Spanish naval commanders were so incapable and unenterprising that our fleets cruised unopposed. It was perhaps as well. There was little to choose between most of the commanders on either side, as the British Government itself realised. When in 1744 a number of its store ships for the revictualling and supply of garrisons and warships in the Mediterranean were penned in Lisbon by a French fleet, the most suitable commander it could find to lead a squadron to drive off the blockading force was Sir John Balchen, a seventy-five-year-old veteran of the navy of William III. He had been long in retirement, holding the post of Governor of Greenwich Hospital, but was nevertheless persuaded to hoist his flag again at sea. He successfully accomplished his mission, only to be lost with his flagship the *Victory* in a great storm which lashed the Channel soon after his return.

Rodney's interest was evidently effective enough to bring him steady advancement during this inactive period, however. He had been taken up by the powerful Whig Prime Minister, Henry Pelham, and by his brother the Duke of Newcastle. Between them (Henry Pelham died in 1754) they were to govern England from 1745 to 1761—with brief intervals. No more useful patrons could have been found.

Pelham was a disciple of Walpole and was anxious to bring the war to an end. He succeeded in negotiating the Peace of Aix-la-Chapelle in 1748, a peace which solved nothing so far as the struggle between France and England for colonial primacy, dependent upon sea power, was concerned. But in the previous year the naval war flamed briefly into activity. A new spirit animated both sides. The French were preparing a large merchant convoy for India which was to be escorted clear of danger by a squadron of ships-of-the-line which were then to go on to American waters. Admiral Anson, ordered to sea with sixteen of the line to intercept, fell in with the enemy off Finisterre. The French escort, greatly inferior, gallantly accepting battle to save their convoy, was annihilated; but all but four of the convoy escaped.

That the old corrupt spirit had not yet been eliminated from naval affairs emerges from an incident connected with the assembly of Anson's force. The captains of two of the ships selected, Grenville of the *Defiance* (60) and William Montagu of the *Bristol* (50) had little relish for dull and probably not lucrative fleet work, and would have preferred orders to cruise independently where they might pick up prizes. Grenville's brother George was on the Board of Admiralty. He arranged for a sentence to be included in a letter to Anson, which the First Lord, the Duke of Bedford, was expected to sign without reading, directing that Anson should not keep the *Defiance* and the *Bristol* with him for more than seven days. The Duke noticed it, however, and refused to sign, growling that 'they should deserve to be hanged for it if it was done'.

Prize money, indeed, was never long out of the thoughts of naval officers of the day. Though they may not have intrigued in this fashion to avoid duty which offered little hope of it, they certainly tried to secure appointments in which the chances of prize money were good. Considering the sums involved, this is not surprising. By the rules which held good at this time the value of any prize taken was divided into eight shares. An admiral under whose command the ship which made the capture was serving was entitled to one of these eighths; so that an appointment to one of the well-known prize-money commands was equivalent to the gift of a great fortune even when there was a junior flag officer under him, who was entitled to one-third of the share. Thus it has been estimated that Anson himself and Admiral Saunders, who was to become famous as the naval commander at the capture of Quebec, each made between a quarter and a half a million pounds, equivalent to a staggering sum today. When admirals, including Rodney, are heard bewailing their luck in being deprived of opportunity for prize money, these figures have to be remembered, as well as the fact that the hope of such fortune was one of the inducements held out to encourage men to serve for paltry pay and under conditions of great hardship and danger.

Similarly, the captain of a warship might hope to make his fortune. For the next two-eighths of the value of a prize went to him. If several ships were involved he shared the proceeds with his brother captains. Otherwise the whole went to him; furthermore if he were sailing 'under Admiralty Orders' and not under those of a flag officer he was entitled to the full three-eighths. There were many examples of captains netting huge sums this way, perhaps the most notable being the capture of the Spanish frigate *Hermione*, loaded with treasure, off Barcelona by the

Active and *Favourite*. The two captains, Sawyer and Pownall, each received £65,000, as did their flag-officer, Admiral Saunders. Even lieutenants got £13,000 each and 'common seamen' £182. These were remarkable sums for the lower grades, who normally came out very badly in the matter. All lieutenants, masters and captains of Marines involved were lumped together to divide between them a one-eighth share. Another one-eighth went to master's mates, chaplains, lieutenants of Marines, the principal warrant officers and the admiral's secretary. Another eighth was to be divided between midshipmen, inferior warrant officers, principal warrant officers' mates and Marine sergeants. This left two-eighths to be shared out between all the rest.

While Anson was dealing with the French East India convoy, a second squadron under Captain Thomas Fox and including Rodney's *Eagle* was cruising in the Atlantic to intercept the homeward-bound French West Indian trade. The convoy of 170 sail of merchant ships, escorted by four warships, was sighted off Cape Ortegal. The escort, faster than the attackers, trailed its shirt all day to draw them off, but at nightfall the French commander decided he had done all that could be expected of him; he gave Fox the slip, leaving the merchant ships at the mercy of the British. Forty-eight of them were captured, richly laden with West Indian produce. Rodney and his fellow captains made a princely haul of prize money.

He was shortly to gain more; but this time he was to be made to fight for it by a gallant and skilful enemy. Learning that the French were assembling in the Basque Roads a great convoy of outward bound merchant ships, Anson, raised to the peerage and to the Board of Admiralty after his successful action, had despatched a squadron of fourteen sail-of-the-line to attack it in the roadstead. The force was under the command of Rear-Admiral Edward Hawke; one of its units was the *Eagle*.

It was at sea, off Finisterre, that Hawke came upon the French, however—a convoy of some 252 ships escorted by nine ships-of-the-line under Admiral Desherbiers de l'Étenduère flying his flag in the *Tonnant*. At daybreak on 14th October the French frigate *Castor* had signalled the presence of Hawke's force, but l'Étenduère imagined it to be some stragglers from the convoy which had lost touch during the night. Then the hulls of the British ships rose up over the horizon; the double rows of gunports showed the French admiral his mistake.

In spite of the odds facing him he had no doubts as to where his duty lay. Signalling the convoy to run for it and sending one of his force, the *Content* (64), to guard it, he formed line of battle with his remaining eight ships, placed himself between the enemy and the convoy and awaited the unequal combat. Hawke, down to leeward and at first unable to discern how many amongst the cloud of sails were men-of-war, had similarly formed line of battle and was tacking laboriously towards the enemy. As the situation grew clearer, however, and he realised the preponderance of strength in his favour, he hauled down the signal for the line and hoisted that for a 'General Chase'. Released from the requirement to keep station which restricted them to the speed of the slowest ship, the British captains crowded on sail. The *Lion* of sixty guns was quickly in the lead and soon after midday fired the first broadside of the action. At brief intervals the rest of the British ships came up. Before being overwhelmed the French gave a good account of themselves, not the least effective being the *Tonnant*, which was first engaged by the *Eagle*. The Frenchman's eighty guns so disabled Rodney's ship that she fell foul of Hawke's flagship the *Devonshire* and for a time the two ships lay entangled. Then they extricated themselves and plunged once more into the mêlée.

By the evening six of the French ships had struck after suffering heavy damage and fearful casualties. The *Neptune* (70) had no less than seven officers and 300 men killed before giving up. Enough had been done *'pour l'honneur du pavillon'*; furthermore the convoy had been given time to escape. The two French ships yet unsubdued were the *Tonnant* and the *Intrépide* (74). Hoisting what sails they could on their shattered masts they bore away down wind to escape.

Their move was seen by Captain Saunders of the *Yarmouth* (64)—he who was later to be the admiral at the taking of Quebec. Drawing the attention of Rodney and of Philip Saumarez of the *Nottingham* (60) to it, he set off in pursuit followed by the others. The *Nottingham* soon outstripped the *Eagle* and the *Yarmouth*, and as dark was falling she came up with and engaged

28]

the two bigger French ships. She paid for her temerity with heavy damage and many casualties including the death of her captain. Hawke had meanwhile made the signal of recall and the two French ships were able to escape.

The outcome of the battle had been certain from the moment that l'Étenduère had decided to sacrifice himself for the sake of his convoy. The French claimed that having achieved their object of saving their convoy, the honours were theirs, in spite of the loss of six ships of the line. Certainly their sailors had displayed a gallantry acknowledged by both sides. A young 'garde-de-la-marine', equivalent of a midshipman, taken prisoner with the crew of the *Monarque*, declared 'it was one of the most glorious actions which had been fought at sea'. The ardent young man was Bailli de Suffren—who, thirty-four years later as an admiral, was to prove a thorn in the flesh of the Royal Navy in the East Indies.

In England, where the revelations of the court martial following the Battle of Toulon were still freshly remembered, the action was also hailed as a notable victory. Though it might have been suggested that Hawke—and Anson earlier—could perhaps have afforded to reduce their overwhelming superiority somewhat in order to capture the French convoy, it was sufficient to know that a breed of officers who knew how to fight was coming to the fore.

The Battle of Finisterre was the last clash at sea before the Peace of Aix-la-Chapelle brought an uneasy truce between the combatants. With it, the *Eagle* was paid off and put into reserve. Rodney naturally gravitated to London, the seat of influence where a word in the right place could enable him to avoid that bane of a naval officer's life, half pay. Waiting upon the First Lord of the Admiralty, Lord Anson, he was taken to court and presented to George II. His very youthful appearance—though he was now thirty years of age in fact—took the attention of the King, who remarked on it. The austere and icy Anson, from whom words of praise were not easily earned, replied that 'young Rodney has been six years a captain in Your Majesty's Navy and I most heartily wish Your Majesty had one hundred more such captains, to the terror of Your Majesty's enemies'.

It was not surprising, therefore, that in March 1749 Rodney was appointed Governor of Newfoundland and captain of H.M.S.

Rainbow with the status of a commodore. Thus he found himself occupying the same position as his first captain, Medley, and back on a regular round he knew well. It was a responsible post, for across the Atlantic the peace was but little respected, clashes between the French and British repeatedly occurring wherever their territories touched. Both British and French had fishing rights on the Newfoundland Banks, so trouble was always on the cards.

Rodney had evidently already impressed the new First Lord, the Earl of Sandwich, with his reliability and discretion, for in June 1749 we find the latter writing to him, 'I am satisfied that your prudence is such as will not suffer you to make any injudicious use of the information you now receive. There are some people that cannot be trusted with any but public orders; but I have too good an opinion of you to rank you among them, and shall think this important affair entirely safe under your management and secrecy'.

Nevertheless it was in the winter months, with the *Rainbow* moored in the Medway, convenient to London, that Rodney was more particularly to advance himself at this time. It was the elegant habitué of White's and Almack's, the assiduous caller at my Lord Sandwich's apartments at the Admiralty or at the town house of the Duke of Newcastle, who was becoming well known rather than the post-captain and commodore. John Clevland, Secretary of the Admiralty, no doubt got to know him well. Clevland 'owned' the borough of Saltash in Cornwall. When an election was held in 1751, Newcastle, the Whig party election manipulator, must have approved Clevland's choice of that sound Whig and well-connected young naval captain, George Brydges Rodney, for the seat. Rodney had almost certainly let it be known by this time that his vote in the House would be at Newcastle's disposal.

It was all quite normal by the customs and standards of the time and only differs from today in that loyalty was given personally to the leader of a faction rather than to a party, and that it was necessary for a naval officer to further his career by such means. Years later Rodney was to write to his wife, 'A man in our country is nothing without being in Parliament.'

On return from Newfoundland in the autumn of 1752, the

Rainbow was paid off at Woolwich and Rodney's appointment lapsed. The ill-health, usually gout, which was to plague him for the rest of his life, is first heard of at this time; for he reported to the Admiralty that it had been necessary for him to go ashore at Portsmouth and put himself in the care of a physician while his first lieutenant took the ship round to the Thames.

He was not too ill, however, to take his seat in the House of Commons for the first time in October of that year. Nor, would it seem, was he absent from London social life where he set about the business of making a suitable marriage. In February 1753 he married Jane Compton, the niece of the seventh Earl of Northampton.

Marriage in the eighteenth century was a cold-blooded affair, as a rule. A gentleman without personal expectations would frankly seek a lady of fortune or influential connections or both. The 'ridiculous passion', as Swift called romantic love, was rarely allowed to influence the choice; nor indeed was the lady always consulted as to her views on the matter, the whole affair being arranged by her parents.

There is nothing to indicate that Rodney's first marriage was any different from the general run of such things. His father had died in 1737. As a younger son his inheritance cannot have been large. Life in London as a fashionable young man and a Member of Parliament was expensive. Prize money was no longer obtainable in peace time; Jane Compton's dowry no doubt took its place. The young bride was apparently no beauty. In his history of the Compton family, the Marquess of Northampton records that 'a small portrait in the Old Library of a dreadfully ugly woman has her name written on the back of the canvas'.

In spite of this a very real devotion sprang up between the two, particularly when Jane presented her 'dearest Captain Rodney' with two sons, George and then James, on whom their father doted. Rodney had begun in 1752 to build a handsome and stately home at Old Alresford in Hampshire on the site of an old Manor house, the estate being held by him on a 'three lives lease' from the Bishop of Winchester, lord of the manor. The grounds he had landscaped in the fashion of the day to plans by Capability Brown.

Rodney's influence was now sufficient to enable him to obtain appointments which kept him on full pay but avoided irksome and tedious sea service in time of peace. Portsmouth was handy to London as well as to Alresford and it was to the *Kent*, guardship in the harbour there, that he was first posted. For a time the Rodneys leased a house at Alverstoke across the harbour from Portsmouth. But leave was generous and frequent, the duties light. The fashionable dissipations of London beckoned and it was there that a naval officer's interest could be nursed. So there was also a house in Hill Street.

Until the end of 1754 the Rodneys enjoyed a period of contented domesticity. Then the war clouds began again to gather. Fighting indeed had never entirely ceased in America, where the French, ambitious to prevent any westward expansion of the British colonies, had advanced from Canada by way of the Great Lakes down the Ohio River where they had set up forts, notably Fort Duquesne on the site of the present Pittsburg. The Governor of Massachusetts appealed to the Home Government for aid to dislodge the French, and in 1755 a force under Major-General Braddock was despatched.

Both sides were in fact preparing for the war they knew to be inevitable. When a French fleet to carry reinforcements to Canada was known to be preparing, Admiral Boscawen with eleven ships of the line was sent across the Atlantic to intercept them. He was followed shortly by Admiral Holburne with six of-the-line.

All this entailed strenuous endeavours to find crews to man the British warships. Though large bounties were offered by the Government and by the merchants of the City of London to encourage volunteers, the results were quite insufficient. Conscription was necessary and the only form of this known to the eighteenth century was impressment with all its well-known cruelties and injustices. Rodney, as captain of the Portsmouth guardship, necessarily played a large part in organising the Press Gangs from that port, both on shore where any able-bodied man who fell into their clutches was swept off to sea irrespective of his trade or calling, and at sea where homeward-bound merchant-men were stopped and the greater part of their crews taken off for service with the Navy. It was a cruel business, but the fleet had to be manned. It was a heartless age, indeed, and eighteenth-century

England was not sufficiently organised to devise any more complicated system of conscription. Strangely enough it was the Englishman's passionate belief in the freedom of the subject which made impressment necessary in time of war. The French had an *inscription maritime* under which every man of the maritime population was registered and called up in his 'class' as necessary. The proposal to institute a similar system in England raised a storm of protest at such 'slavery', and it was hastily dropped.

In July 1755, a squadron of twenty-one sail of the line under Sir Edward Hawke was assembled. War had still not been declared, but Hawke was sent out into the Atlantic to await orders to begin hostilities. A French trade convoy from the West Indies under escort of a squadron of men-of-war was expected. Rodney, who, in common with the majority of people in England, did not believe that the strained relations with France would lead to war, had up to this time avoided being sent to sea. When at the end of 1754 the *Kent* was ordered to be brought forward to commission for service, there had been a possibility of his having to go with her. Mrs Rodney retired sorrowfully to Hill Street to lament the hard lot of a sailor's wife.

'I wish you had been a Parson or anything but a Sailor,' she wrote. 'Then I should have lived and not known the uneasiness of being parted from him I love better than Life.'

The pleasures of family life were calling to the sailor also. He did not believe that war was coming. So long as it held off, service held no attractions for him.

'I sincerely wish I had quitted before this Bustle came on,' he wrote to his 'dear Jenny'. 'However I will be wiser for the future and learn to live without a Guardship. 'Tis but staying so much longer in the Country to make up the difference in Expense. I have learnt when 'tis too late, that Ambition has lost its Charms to me and that to have a Wife and Children engrosses all my Attention and that where one's heart is, there the mind is also.'

Rodney secured a transfer to the new guardship, the *Fougeux*, only to find that she, too, in her turn was to join the fleet. In January 1755, poor Jane was writing:

'I am very glad you find all quiet and hope in God we shall have peace and quietness while I live, for was you to be obliged to go abroad, Misery to me must ensue. I have not Philosophy enough to support so severe a Tryal, nor would your coming home loaded with Riches make up for my Sufferings during your Absence. With what I have I am Content, provided you are with me, but without you life is not worth my care, nor would millions make me happy. . . . I hope you will, then, as soon as you possibly can, give up that vile ship that causes us so much pain.'

She was not the last wife to be jealous of her husband's ship. For the time being she was successful in getting the better of her rival; for a few days later Rodney wrote:

'To convince you that I don't intend going abroad in case the *Fougeux* should be ordered to sea, I have this day desired my Lord Anson to remove me into a ship of 90 guns that is in this harbour, and which it will be impossible to be ready for the sea at least in a year—long before which I hope all this storm will blow over.' Again a little later he was assuring Jane that 'love will get the better of Interest and her Influence has induced me to change the best sailing ship in the world (*Fougeux*) for the *Prince George* of 90 guns of which there is not the least likelihood that she will ever go to sea.'

Rodney had miscalculated, however, for the *Prince George* was ordered to join Hawke and soon his letters were bewailing the boredom and discomfort, especially as fat merchantmen were sighted daily but could not yet be captured. They brightened considerably when, under fresh orders from the Admiralty, Hawke's squadron began to snap them up—behaviour which the French, with some justification, dubbed piracy. With the passing of summer, however, Rodney was back again, and after some leave he was appointed in February 1756 to the *Monarch*, guardship at Plymouth.

Jane was expecting her third child and retired to Alresford to await the event.

Meanwhile open war was drawing closer and more certain. In America General Braddock had met with disaster and defeat at the hands of the Marquis de Montcalm. Boscawen had failed to prevent the French squadron from getting through to reinforce the garrison of Quebec, but by capturing two of them he had committed an act of war. At the end of 1755 [the French had marched an army to the Channel ports, and this had thrown the

British Government, under the bumbling guidance of the Duke of Newcastle, into a shameful panic. The French move was in fact a diversion, under cover of which an expedition was prepared which sailed from Toulon in April 1756 to invade the British-held island of Minorca. The island was soon in the hands of the enemy with the exception of St Philip's Castle guarding the naval base of Port Mahon, which was closely invested. Declaration of war soon followed.

In truth the French had no hope of mounting an invasion of England. Their fleet, starved of money during the years of peace, was in numbers little more than half that of the British. French lack of interest in their Navy had led to a deterioration in the quality of the personnel; rarely going to sea in peacetime, the officers were unpractised and unskilled.

On the other hand the British Government knew that the Royal Navy was by no means as powerful as published figures indicated. Years of neglect, corruption and misappropriation of funds voted for the upkeep of ships in reserve were having their effect. From time to time efforts were made to clean up the administration. But the system was too deeply entrenched to be easily uprooted and the ministers responsible were themselves often the chief offenders.

For example in 1749, during Lord Sandwich's first occupation of the post of First Lord of the Admiralty, he made a visitation of the dockyards. To his disgust he 'found the men generally idle, the officers ignorant, the stores ill-arranged, abuses of all kinds overlooked, the timber ill-assorted, that which was longest in store undermost, the Standing Orders neglected, the ships in ordinary in a very dirty and bad condition, filled with women and children . . . in short, gross negligence, irregularities, waste and embezzlement . . .'

Sandwich's justifiable wrath at such a state of affairs was all very well. But when the country was governed from top to bottom on a system of bribery and corruption, a system under which he himself did handsomely, his anger should have been aimed at people higher in the scale than the petty officials of the dockyards.

Thus, though the outbreak of the Seven Years War found Britain nominally greatly superior to the French at sea, there was in fact need for every available ship to be got ready, and this included Rodney's *Monarch*. As senior captain in the port, he was kept furiously busy.

'I have much on my hands,' he wrote, 'as the whole fitting of the fleet at this port depends upon me at present as Commanding Officer. The *Monarch* is almost ready, but I want 400 men.' She had been much neglected. When Rodney finally got her away to sea in July 1656 to join Boscawen in the Channel, loose timbers caused her to leak dangerously and she was ordered back to Portsmouth to refit.

He had been fortunate to avoid inclusion in the fleet under Rear-Admiral John Byng which had been sent to the relief of Minorca and which was to bring shame upon the Navy's reputation. Byng was the type of naval officer with whom Rodney was always exasperated; though physically brave, he was a moral coward, fearful of responsibility and in moments of doubt relying upon the letter of the regulations to free him from making a decision of his own.

Thwarted by the mistakes or the stupidities of officialdom, Rodney would not spare to castigate those responsible, but he would not allow them to deflect him from doing his utmost to fulfil the task before him. Byng, faced with the same situation, saw in it an excuse to avoid risk or positive action.

Failing to relieve Minorca, and withdrawing from any attempt to do so after an indecisive and half-hearted encounter with a French fleet of equal strength to his own, Byng was brought to trial by court martial. Though evidence made it clear that Byng showed no lack of personal courage, nothing could clear him of a lamentable lack of vigour both in his efforts to bring aid to the garrison of St Philip's Castle and during the encounter with the French fleet. The new Naval Discipline Act of 1749, Article 12, which had been expressly devised to enable greater severity to be inflicted on such culprits as those condemned after the Battle of Toulon, prescribed the one penalty—death—for 'every person in the Fleet who through cowardice, *negligence* or disaffection shall in time of Action withdraw or hold back, or not come into the fight or engagement, or shall not do his utmost to take or destroy every ship which it shall be his duty to engage and to assist and relieve all and every of His Majesty's ships or those of his Allies which it shall be his duty to assist and relieve'.

Byng's brother officers on the court martial carried out their duty unflinchingly in finding that through *negligence* he stood condemned under Article 12. No choice was left to them but to pronounce sentence of death. Nevertheless they never imagined that their recommendation to mercy would be ignored. But in the face of a public outcry for Byng's death, neither the Admiralty, nor the Government, nor the King himself had the courage to be merciful; and on 17th March 1757, Byng met his death with calm courage at the hands of a firing party of Marines on the quarter-deck of the *Monarch*. Rodney was no longer her captain when this occurred, though one of the last orders he had received before relinquishing command had been to receive the luckless Byng and his retinue as 'supernumeraries for their victuals only'.

During the winter of 1756, while the *Monarch* was under repair, Rodney had been able to get leave. Some of it he spent in London assiduously cultivating his interest. But in November the disastrous events of the opening months of war drove his patron Newcastle from office; in the new Government Lord Temple was nominated First Lord of the Admiralty, and Rodney wrote to Jane at Alresford, 'I am now going to Court to see the new Ministers kiss hands. I can assure my dear girl that I stand the best with them of any person in the Navy and am assured from the First Lord that I shall have whatever ship I please, and he has likewise done me the honour to assure me that my advice shall go a great way with him in conducting Naval affairs . . .'

At the end of September Jane had been delivered of a baby girl, who was given her name. Not recovering as she should, she remained in the country, complaining of fevers and receiving what skilled attention country doctors of the day could muster. But in fact she was slowly dying, probably from consumption. The end came in February 1757 and baby Jane survived only for a year longer. From her graveside at Alresford, Rodney had to hurry to Deptford, where command of the 74-gun ship *Dublin* awaited him.

If the *Dublin* was indeed Rodney's choice of 'whatever ship he pleased', it was a singularly unfortunate one, which was to deprive him of the chance to take an active part in the splendid victories which were to grace British arms in the next two years.

For it was not until September 1757 that the *Dublin* was ready for sea, and then she was detailed to form part of the squadron under Hawke which was sent on a combined operation against Rochefort.

In July 1757 the Government had been reconstituted with Newcastle as the nominal head, but confining himself to the management of Parliament and the maintenance of power by his faction, while Pitt, as Secretary of State, was left to run the war. The operation against Rochefort was one of the diversions launched by Pitt with the object of inducing the French to withdraw troops from Germany where they were threatening the King's Electorate of Hanover and his ally, Frederick of Prussia. Unfortunately, though the dashing Hawke was in command of the naval forces for the expedition, the general in command, Sir John Mordaunt, was old and spiritless. Under his ineffectual leadership the Army achieved nothing and the expedition returned to explain its failure to a court of inquiry.

For the *Dublin* the operation was especially unfortunate. Rodney first had trouble with her rudder, which caused him to lose touch with the fleet. Then the scourge of the navy of that era struck, as an epidemic fever swept through his crew till 150 of the men were confined to their hammocks on the fetid mess-decks and many more so weak they were unfit for work. Rodney was forced to obtain permission to return to Spithead.

There the *Dublin* lay through the winter under repair. With the spring of 1758 she was ready structurally, but it was not until May that Rodney was able to make up his depleted crew to full strength just in time to sail as escort for a convoy carrying troops and stores to Nova Scotia for the impending attack on Louisburg. In the *Dublin* travelled the general in command of the troops, General Amherst, and his staff. At last, it seemed, Rodney was to become involved in an important operation. But the ill-luck of the *Dublin* held. Typhoid fever broke out again and by the time she reached Halifax was raging to such an extent that, while the rest of the fleet was taking part in the successful siege and capture of Louisburg, Rodney was penned in harbour with a great part of his crew ashore in temporary hospitals constructed by the ship's carpenters.

Thus he missed taking part in the brilliant little operation, at which James Wolfe was first able to display his capabilities, which put Louisburg, the key to the Gulf of St Lawrence, in our hands. It was an essential preliminary to the assault on Quebec and the conquest of Canada which were to follow in the next year.

Rodney was now forty years of age. He had been sixteen years a post-captain. Except for the Battle of Finisterre, a heartening but by no means brilliant fight, he had taken part in no important action. He was comparatively unknown. Few would have prophesied a bright future for him at this time. After the Louisburg operation the *Dublin* was ordered home with a convoy and to give passage to the French naval officers captured from the ships taken in the harbour. Arriving in Spithead, Rodney applied for leave to attend to his health. He went ashore a senior but obscure captain. He had had little opportunity to display any capacity for higher command; but it is also not unreasonable to suppose that, as a late developer, he was only now discovering the qualities which were eventually to bring him success and fame. He was already gouty and a year at sea in the unhealthy *Dublin* was enough to put him out of action for a time, even during the war, which was approaching its most eventful period.

Nevertheless George Rodney had still that sheet anchor of a naval officer's career in his day—a seat in Parliament. He could be counted upon by that unscrupulous dispenser of patronage, the Duke of Newcastle, for his steady, loyal support. Though the war was being successfully managed by William Pitt, Newcastle was still officially the head of Government, maintaining his party in power by a ceaseless trade of votes for cash or office, of interest for place.

Rodney with his solid Whig background saw nothing shameful in placing his interest at the disposal of a Government which included Pitt and which was prosecuting the war with vigour and ability. That such support merited reward followed naturally, nevertheless. Furthermore, at the head of the Admiralty was Anson who, though he was ever uncompromising in his refusal to bend naval promotions or appointments to political ends, had perceived Rodney's qualities as far back as the Battle of Finisterre.

Thus everything combined in Rodney's favour at this time, and in May 1759, he was raised to the flag list as Rear-Admiral of the Blue.

IV

IT would be easy to see in Rodney's advancement to flag rank at the age of forty-one after a not noticeably distinguished career a typical piece of eighteenth-century jobbery. It no doubt obliged his influential friends and relatives and it helped to keep the flag list sound in its support of Newcastle's faction. Certainly 'knowing the right people' was essential to success then as it has always been. It must be remembered, on the other hand, that the people who mattered in naval affairs at this time had already weighed George Rodney in the balance and found him worthy of their support.

At the head of the Admiralty was Anson, the stern incorruptible who would not allow even a marine lieutenant's commission to go to an unsuitable candidate, not even to oblige the highest in the land. It was the same Anson, however, who had broken his icy reserve to recommend Rodney to the King after Finisterre. In command of England's principal fleet, that in home waters, was Sir Edward Hawke, Rodney's old chief at Finisterre. He would certainly have been consulted about the promotions to the flag list and would have strenuously opposed a purely political candidate.

It can be taken therefore that Rodney was professionally as well as politically qualified. In his first assignment as an admiral he justified his superiors' choice. The year 1759, the Wonderful Year of Victory as it was to be called, was to see the flowering of the schemes of William Pitt to defeat France by the application of sea power. In Canada, General Wolfe, brilliantly supported by a fleet under Admiral Saunders, was to capture the key fortress of Quebec. In the autumn Hawke was to destroy France's main fleet in a gale of wind amongst the rocks and shoals of Quiberon Bay. At Lagos, Boscawen would defeat another French fleet.

Chance was to deprive Rodney of the honour of taking part in any of these great events. Instead he was entrusted with the task of scotching the French preparations for an invasion attempt by destroying their fleet of landing craft assembled at Le Havre.

With his flag in the 60-gun ship *Achilles*, he sailed at the beginning of July with a squadron comprising four 50-gun ships, five frigates and seven bomb-ketches. The operation was one requiring skill rather than daring, though Rodney's report mentioned that 'the enemy's fire from their bomb-batteries was very brisk indeed' and that 'great numbers of their shot and shells fell and burst among the bombs and boats'. Better to super-intend the bombardment by his lighter-draught ships the admiral shifted his flag to the frigate *Vestal* commanded by Captain Samuel Hood. Thus for the second time he met one whose life story was to be entwined with his own; for young Hood, a Somerset man also, had been a midshipman in the *Ludlow Castle* with him. His captain's favourable report after the successful action with the St Malo privateer had no doubt helped him towards his commission, which he had gained shortly afterwards. Now he was again to be singled out for praise. 'Had it not been for the Captains of the *Deptford*, *Vestal* and *Juno*,' Rodney wrote, 'I should have found it extremely difficult and tedious to have anchored the bomb ketches properly.'

The two men were long to remain friends. They were to be together at the moment of Rodney's greatest triumph and were to share the laurels. Towards the end, the friendship was to come under a grievous strain, however. Hood's intolerance and lack of understanding of the other when age and much illness had im-paired his faculties and made him crabbed and unapproachable led him into acts of disloyalty. But at this time they were both young and buoyant, appreciative of each other's quality. If Rodney was contemptuous of many of his 'salt-horse' contem-poraries, the young Hood was probably not far behind him in such views.

Rodney's appearance at this time can be seen in the portrait by Sir Joshua Reynolds, where he is dressed in the uniform of a rear-admiral as laid down in the regulations of 1748. The blue coat with white facings, which George II had decreed for naval officers after seeing the Duchess of Bedford in a riding habit of those colours, is richly laced with gold as is the long white waist-coat. Though uniforms were now prescribed, they could vary greatly in cut and detail. Rodney's is plainly the product of a fashionable London tailor and of splendid materials. In the portrait Rodney wears his own hair and is evidently superior to the dictates of fashion by which a powdered wig would have been correct on such an occasion. The long, acquisitive nose, the haughty expression and the sensual mouth reveal the main features of his character better than words can do.

The French invasion fleet having been destroyed together with the magazines set up on shore and a good portion of the town of Le Havre, Rodney withdrew his squadron and was employed for the next two years on duty in the Channel. This did not prevent him, however, from being returned for the Parliamentary seat of Okehampton at the end of 1759. It was not even necessary for him to meet his constituents. The seat was in the gift of the Duke of Newcastle and from his flagship lying in Spithead he wrote 'My lord, I beg Your Grace will permit me to return you my most sincere thanks for the honour you have bestowed on me in chusing me a Member of Parliament for Okehampton. A steady adherence to Your Grace's commands shall ever distinguish me while I have a seat in the House.'

To a twentieth-century ear the phrases have a ring of sycophancy and subservience; but it was the style of the age when even His Grace of Bedford wrote in similar terms to His Grace of Newcastle on a political matter. Nor is a 'steady adherence to Your Grace's commands' greatly different from the acceptance of the Party Whip of modern times, except that in that age of absolute Whig ascendancy there could be within the Party various factions to whom a man's loyalty could be offered.

Nevertheless it was a shock to Rodney when, on the dissolution of Parliament at the death of George II in 1760, he found that his safe seat of Okehampton had been given to another; a particularly unexpected shock considering that he had taken the trouble to remind Newcastle of his continued loyalty and to throw in the scales some Parliamentary interest of his own.

'I must beg leave to acknowledge the very great obligations I lay under to Your Grace for all the preferments I have attained in the Navy. Obligations which I can never forget and which now call upon me most humbly to offer what little Interest I have in the County of Southampton to be disposed of at Your Grace's pleasure, as 'tis whispered in this County there is a likelihood of an Opposition at the ensuing Election.'

Perhaps Rodney's loyalty was considered so certain that he needed no longer to be courted so hotly—or it may simply have been one of the awkward dilemmas that Newcastle must have constantly encountered in his endless juggling with votes, places, Parliamentary seats and sinecures. Whatever the reason it produced an immediate anguished cry from Rodney in a letter to Mr James West, Newcastle's agent for such matters.

'For God's sake, Sir, what have I done to gain his Grace's displeasure. . . . I must entreat you, Sir, to represent my Case in the Humblest Manner to His Grace and beg of him not to let me suffer in the Eye of the Publick as a person obnoxious to him and unworthy his protection, which I shall infallably do, unless His Grace vouchsafes to let me have a seat in Parliament by his Influence. . . .'

His Grace's attention thus drawn to the matter, some further shuffling of names no doubt took place with the result that Rodney was recommended to Lord Falmouth, head of the Cornish family of Boscawen, as a suitable member for Penryn for which Admiral Boscawen had sat until his death in January 1761. The Boscawens and the Edgecumbes between them could usually command a safe majority there; but on this occasion there was an active opposition at work. Not, of course, for a Tory; that would still be unthinkable; but for another candidate who the opponents claimed had been chosen by Newcastle.

Rodney's report on the situation perfectly illustrates election practices of the day with their unabashed corruption and the complacent acceptance of them by otherwise honourable men.

'My Lord—I must beg leave to lay before Your Grace the present situation of affairs at this place where I arrived on Sunday last, and hence in company with Lord Falmouth and Mr Edgecumbe canvassed the town.

'We find at present but a small majority owing to the defection of several officers in the Customs and Salt Office, both here and at Falmouth, as likewise two men belonging to the Pacquets, who are all obstinate in opposition, the Agents of the other party

[43

having had the presumption to read a letter as from Your Grace, which has deluded these people so much that Mr West's letter signifying Your Grace's pleasure had not the least effect. I must therefore join with Lord Falmouth and Mr Edgecumbe for the Dismission of one Charles Robbins, a Tydesman, etc., at Falmouth, which may have the desired effect on the other officers.

'I must now take the liberty to point out to Your Grace a measure which I am sure will infallibly secure the election, and which I most earnestly entreat may take place immediately, as it will convince the people in general (whose minds have been poisoned with different notions) that I have the honour to be nominated by Your Grace as candidate.

'Captain Peard of the *Savage* sloop of war, a Freeman of this Town, whose friends have great influence, has been offer'd by the adversaries a bond of one thousand pounds, and that they will procure him a Post Ship; he has resisted the temptation, and continues firm.

'If Your Grace will make it a Point that it may appear here before the election that Captain Peard has post, I am sure all difficulties will be removed. My ship, the *Marlborough* has no captain appointed as yet.

'From Your Grace's firm friendship to me I cannot doubt but you will grant me this further mark of your favours, as I shall always continue to be with the utmost gratitude and respect, Your Grace's most obedient and most humble servant, G. B. Rodney.'

What a sorry picture of eighteenth-century democracy is given by this letter; and what a villain Rodney appears if the background against which he stands is not taken into account. But once again it has to be remembered that such electoral methods were going on in every 'Rotten Borough' in England, that it was the accepted thing that a naval officer with any ambitions should have a seat in Parliament, and that to contest a seat other than one in the gift of a patron was far beyond his means—as Rodney was to prove one day.

As for the injustice done to poor Mr Robbins who was no doubt duly dismissed, the fact of the matter almost certainly is that he had accepted the usual payment in advance for his vote for 'the adversary', but had backed the wrong horse. Captain Peard on the other hand had 'continued firm' and was no doubt duly rewarded with promotion; but the promotion must have been a sound one professionally, for Rodney offered to accept him as his flag-captain in the *Marlborough* in which ship he was soon to sail to take command in the West Indies.

The business of assuring himself of a seat in the Commons behind him, Rodney set about his preparations for foreign service as Commander-in-Chief of the Leeward Islands Station. The origin of the name given to this command, anomalous as it was, requires an explanation.

The West Indies, as a whole, lie fairly in the path of the north-east trade wind. In the age of sail this was a dominant feature and it was natural for a seaman to describe a West Indian island to the westward of another as 'to leeward'. For to reach an island such as Jamaica some 850 miles to the westward from Antigua in the Lesser Antilles, it took only seven days. To return would require at least three times as long. Similarly every island had a windward and a leeward side. It was a matter of hours to run down wind to the leeward side; it might take days to beat back again.

The sailing limitations of a ship-of-the-line or a cargo-carrying merchantman must be remembered in this connection. Beating to windward they could not sail closer than about seventy degrees off the wind. While doing so they made leeway as well as headway, of course; so that even in still water they made only very slowly to windward. A contrary tide or current had only to be moderately swift to cancel out any such progress.

Between the islands of the Lesser Antilles the constant trade wind sets up powerful westward-running currents; so much so that it was sometimes impossible for a ship-of-the-line to beat through the channel to windward—just as in the English Channel it was often impossible to beat out against a flood tide.

It might be imagined that the Leeward Islands referred only to the westernmost of the West Indies—Jamaica, Cuba, San Domingo and the Bahamas. But in fact the Leeward and Windward Islands were two portions of the Lesser Antilles divided by the little island of Marie Galante. Strung out in a crescent running north and south across the path of the trade wind, it is not so immediately apparent that the group to the north of Marie

[45

Galante is much to leeward of the others; but in fact, the most northerly part of it is some 150 miles down wind of Martinique, the largest of the windward group. In 1761 those of the Lesser Antilles which had been acquired from their native population, the Caribs, were divided between French and British (except for one small island under the Dutch flag), with the advantage lying with the French, not simply because they had established themselves in the two largest, Martinique and Guadeloupe, but because from their splendid harbour and naval base of Fort Royal in Martinique they dominated the windward position in the islands.

It was true that the British held Barbados, even farther to windward, but that island had no good harbour; so that they had to rely upon English Harbour in the leeward island of Antigua, which with St Kitts, Nevis and Montserrat constituted the British Antilles. It was nevertheless with some lack of precision that the Admiralty called the command in those waters the Leeward Islands Station.

Rodney sailed in the 70-gun *Marlborough* for his new command in October 1761, and arrived in Barbados the following month. Operations to capture the French islands had already been started, Commodore Sir James Douglas having commanded the naval squadron which took Guadeloupe without encountering serious resistance. Martinique was likely to prove a harder nut to crack and had, indeed, beaten off an attack two years earlier. By 24th December a fleet of thirteen ships of the line, four fifties and nineteen frigates, with an army of 14,000 troops under Major-General Moncton, had been assembled.

The French Navy had been too thoroughly swept from the seas to offer any resistance afloat. Rodney's ships could thus bombard and silence the shore batteries at their leisure, after which Moncton's army was landed unopposed without the loss of a man.

The siege and capture of Fort Royal were not by any means so easy. The terrain and the use the French had made of it in defence presented a formidable obstacle. Assault by infantry alone was impossible, and the transport of artillery seemed equally so to the general. But the two senior officers got on well together and this spirit was transmitted down through the ranks. To the soldiers' help came the sailors of the fleet, exhilarated at the opportunity to get ashore and out of the squalid congestion of ship-board life. An infantry officer, writing home, described the scene:

'You may fancy you know the spirit of these fellows; but to see them in action exceeds any idea that can be formed of them. A hundred or two of them with ropes and pulleys, will do more than all your dray-horses in London. Let but their tackle hold and they will draw you a cannon or mortar on its proper carriage up to any height, though the weight be never so great. It is droll enough to see them tugging along, with a good 24-pounder at their heels: on they go, huzzahing and hallooing, sometimes up hill, sometimes down hill; . . . . swearing, blasting d-m-ing, sinking, and as careless of everything but the matter committed to their charge as if death or danger had nothing to do with them. We had a thousand of these brave fellows sent to our assistance by the admiral, and the service they did us, both on shore and on the water, is incredible.' Perhaps it is not surprising that the sailors' escape from the cheerless, foul life of the lower deck, the deadly routine and pitiless discipline aboard ship should release a wild ebullient spirit at the feel of good earth under foot and the opportunity to display the ingenuity with rope and tackle which was the mark of the man-of-war's seaman. Reporting to the Admiralty, Rodney wrote: 'In justice to those I have the honour to command, the intrepidity and gallant behaviour of the officers and troops employed in this expedition could be equalled only by the eager and cheerful activity of the officers and seamen.' The general similarly reported on 'the harmony that subsists between the fleet and the army, and the cordial assistance we have received from Admiral Rodney in every part of the operations when his aid could be useful.'

By 10th February Rodney was able to announce to the Admiralty 'the surrender of the most important citadel of Fort Royal . . . . which has given His Majesty's forces possession of the noblest and best harbour in these parts of the West Indies'. The surrender of St Lucia, St Vincent and Grenada followed without fighting.

While an active enemy was in view and there was fighting to be done Rodney was single-minded in his purpose. The last

[47

French resistance overcome, however, he turned eagerly, like any other naval officer of the time, to the legitimate hopes and prospects of prize money. That the King of Spain had tardily decided to honour the Family Compact with the King of France by entering the war against Britain at a time when France was so beaten that she could do little to help was splendid news. Spanish trade with South and Central America and with her possessions in the West Indies was rich and voluminous. The Antilles could safely be left unprotected for the time being, while a report of a small enemy squadron having gone westwards to San Domingo could be construed as a threat to Jamaica. Jamaica was outside the area of Rodney's station, but such a threat entitled him to go there and take over the command from the senior naval officer on the spot, a post captain. It was also the perfect centre from which to prey upon Spanish trade in the area. He therefore reported to the Admiralty his intention of 'hastening to the succour of Jamaica, with ten sail of the line, three frigates and three bombs'.

Alas for Rodney's hopes; before he had gone far he was over-taken by the frigate *Richmond* bearing important despatches from the Admiralty in which he was 'strictly commanded to desist from any enterprise he might have in hand'. An expedition under the command of Admiral Sir George Pocock—an officer of considerable seniority and renown—and General Lord Albemarle, was on its way to the attack of Havana. All Rodney's efforts were to be devoted to preparing the way, and any force he could spare was to be released for service under Pocock.

With unhesitating loyalty Rodney obeyed to the letter, sending his second-in-command, Sir James Douglas, on to Jamaica with ten sail of the line to await Pocock's arrival. He himself returned to Martinique to superintend the embarkation of Moncton's troops and to have them ready to join Albemarle's army. When the expedition departed on 6th May, he was left with only three ships of the line and the unrewarding task of holding the inactive Leeward Islands Station. Pocock and Albemarle went on to capture Havana and booty worth £3 millions.

A more bitter disappointment is hard to imagine. The war was nearing its end and during it Rodney had seen brother admirals and captains amass a fortune out of prize money. He had thirsted for a taste of the same draught, only to have the cup dashed from his lips. No wonder he went down with an attack of 'bilious fever' which prevented him from paying his respects to Pocock while he was at Martinique. No wonder too that a discovery of interference by General Moncton in the distribution of what prize money was available inflamed him against his erstwhile colleague.

The interests of naval officers concerned were customarily left in the hands of regularly appointed prize agents. When Moncton, as acting Governor of Martinique, granted two of his own followers the arbitrary power to sell all prizes brought in and to retain for themselves a percentage of the sum raised, the prize agent naturally refused to accept such an arrangement which was clearly contrary to the Prize Act. The agent, however, was forced to submit under threat of imprisonment.

Rodney discovered other irregularities designed to line the pockets of officials appointed by Moncton. In a furious letter to Anson at the Admiralty he complains that, 'in short, my Lord, the whole is a scramble who shall cheat his Majesty and the nation most'.

This period of Rodney's career brings a useful standard by which his integrity can be judged and through which a line can be traced dividing what, in his opinion, might or might not be done by a man of honour under the rules of conduct of his day. His letter to the Duke of Newcastle reporting the capture of Martinique also pointed out to his political patron that the conquest 'puts it into the power of Your Grace to oblige many Friends by the Posts and Employments in Your Grace's gift, and which are very lucrative in this Island, particularly those relative to the customs and Secretary of the Island. This I thought my duty to represent to Your Grace that you might not be deceived in their values, which are computed at four thousand pounds a year each.'

Rodney did not suggest that any such post might fall to him; and indeed it could hardly do so unless he retired from the Navy. On the other hand it is clear that he saw nothing wrong in pointing out the personal advantages to be gained by his patron by manipulation of the fruits of a national success. He went on to remind Newcastle of the author of his access of fortune:

'If . . . my conduct in this expedition meets with Your Grace's approbation, I shall be extremely happy, as among Your Grace's many friends none is more truly so than him who has the honour to be with the most profound respect and gratitude etc. etc.'

Rodney's success brought him promotion, at least. In October 1762 he was gazetted Vice-Admiral of the Blue. This was in effect a triple promotion; for at that time there were eight grades of admiral. From Rear-Admiral of the Blue, an officer normally progressed to Rear-Admiral of the White and thence to Rear-Admiral of the Red, Vice-Admiral successively of the Blue, White and Red, Admiral of the Blue, Admiral of the White— there was no Admiral of the Red.

But Rodney was ever dogged with ill-luck in the matter of plunder. As a reward for his part in the reduction of Martinique he was made a grant of 3,000 acres of land in one of the captured islands, as was General Moncton. But whereas the general had had his grant confirmed before the end of the war, Rodney had not; so that when the islands were returned to the French at the Peace of Paris in 1763, he could claim nothing in compensation.

In contrast he had seen Admiral Pocock gain no less than £122,697 10s. 6d. as his share of prize money after the capture of Havana. Such sums as this and others quoted earlier, which but for the luck of the draw might have been his, have to be borne in mind when charges of cupidity are levelled at Rodney and when his conduct in furthering his ambitions is judged.

By the terms of the peace treaty the islands of Martinique, St Lucia and Guadeloupe were returned to the French. It is fairly certain that if a seaman had had any say in the matter there would not have been such an abandonment of the windward position and of the two best harbours in the Antilles—Fort Royal in Martinique and The Carenage in St Lucia. But the young King, George III, and his chosen Minister Lord Bute, were determined to have peace. Though the Seven Years War was perhaps the most successful ever waged by Britain, the Government allowed themselves to be bargained out of the islands in compensation for the French cession of the whole of Canada. Their loss was to be keenly felt when war came again.

With the end of the war Rodney returned home and hauled down his flag.

V

THE political scene to which Rodney returned was one of rapid
and drastic change: George III had come to the throne in 1760
determined to re-assert the authority of the monarch, which had
lapsed under the first two Georges.

The first obstacle to this had been his powerful War Minister,
William Pitt. The majority of the Whigs, under Newcastle, had
been in favour of bringing the war to an end even though it meant
deserting England's ally, Frederick of Prussia. Pitt, determined
to press the advantages England had gained by his application of
sea power, had rejected French proposals of peace—against the
wishes of Newcastle and the Whigs.

In 1761, learning of a treaty between France and Spain, which
bound the latter to declare war on England before the end of the
year, Pitt had proposed striking first. Newcastle, supported by
the King, had vetoed the proposal and forced Pitt to resign.
Spain had been thus enabled to gather in the annual treasure
convoy from South America before declaring war, but it had not
prevented her from losing Cuba and the Philippine Islands.

For the King to achieve his ambition to rule as well as reign it
was necessary to break the power of the Whig party. Though it
had been the chief supporter of the House of Hanover, it was also
fixed in its determination to have a constitutional monarchy and
rule by parliament. The King had struck at the Whigs with their
own weapon—patronage—which he took into his own hand.
Newcastle had found that places and appointments which had
been in the gift of the Prime Minister were being given away by
the King, who did not even consult him in his choices. His
position had quickly become impossible, and in May 1762 he had
resigned.

George III had at once installed his favourite, the Earl of Bute, with instructions to negotiate a peace as soon as possible. So eager had they been to end the war that they had accepted peace terms by which Cuba and the Philippines were given back to Spain, and Martinique, St Lucia and Guadeloupe to France to compensate her for the loss of Canada. The storm of indignation which had broken over his head when these terms were announced had forced Bute to resign. The King had then called upon George Grenville to head a ministry of court favourites.

He had found, however, that he had misjudged Grenville, who was not at all inclined to play the part of a puppet. On the contrary, he believed in the supremacy of Parliament over King as well as people. Frustrated in his designs to keep power in his own hands, and in sharp conflict with Grenville, the King in desperation had appealed to Pitt, only to be told that Pitt would not consent to take office except in concert with the principal Whigs —the very thing he wished to avoid.

For the moment therefore the King had been checked in his ambitions and Grenville had been left free to assert Parliament's supremacy. It was to lead him into conflict not only with the King but with the public in England and the colonists in America.

Such, briefly, was the situation when Rodney returned home and hauled down his flag at the end of the Seven Years War. His old patron, Newcastle, was in eclipse, but at the Admiralty once again was John Montagu, Earl of Sandwich, and in the Government was the Duke of Bedford whose Duchess led the fashionable world of society to which Rodney belonged. In January 1764 he was made a baronet for his distinguished services in the late war.

Rodney was now forty-six. He had emerged from the war as one of the most promising young flag officers. Though he had not managed to make a great fortune out of prize money as so many others had, he was comfortably off. He could resume his place in fashionable society. A handsome, elegant widower with the romantic aura of the sailor home from sea, something of a hero as a result of his exploits at Le Havre and Martinique, and with the cultivated manners unusual in a naval officer of his generation, he was welcome in the drawing-rooms of the great. Sought after by mamas with eligible daughters, he was greatly in demand at fashionable routs and assemblies. Welcomed in the boudoirs of the far from strait-laced ladies of society of the age, the enforced celibacy of life at sea was not likely to leave him backward in response. Tittle-tattle of his various amours went the rounds.

An easy conversationalist, he was equally at home in the coffee-houses frequented by politicians and men of affairs and at their dining-tables. Coming from the lonely austerity of the great cabin of a man-of-war, he relished good food, good talk and the companionship of his social equals. This entailed, inevitably, in the fashion of the time, the consumption of huge quantities of liquor, rich and heady port followed by deep draughts of brandy and other spirits. Drunkenness was not a matter for any shame nor was it any embarrassment for a gentleman to be put to bed by his friends. The habit made inroads on the store of health of men in every walk of life. Gout and the stone were common ailments amongst the gentry, and Rodney was no exception.

The universal recreation of his class, however, was gambling. The gaming table was always the centre of attraction whether at the elegant resorts of Bath and Tunbridge Wells or in the exclusive London clubs. Fortunes were dissipated at cards and dice. In a letter to Captain (later Admiral Sir William) Cornwallis, known to the navy of his day as 'Billy Blue', a Captain Blankett in December 1771 wrote, 'Extravagance, luxury and gaming are the fashionable vices of the town, and it will astonish you on your return to see the vast improvements of the age. The Lottorie, Macaroni, White's, Almac's, etc. are in the most flourishing state and cards in all companies are the only things worth living for. A man of taste must play all the morning, or, at least, four or five games before dinner, which is shortened to give time for the exquisite pleasures of Quinze or Vingt-Un.'

Rodney was as much a gambler as any. It was partly on this account that his financial affairs were to become so involved and eventually even disastrous. The editor of his *Life and Correspondence*, his son-in-law, General Mundy, refers to them in phrases which so happily bring the flavour of the times that they must be quoted in full.

'It is to be lamented,' he wrote, 'that natures the most generous and ingenuous, from an honest zeal which flows through all their conduct, can seldom bring themselves to bear the dry methodical labour of arithmetical calculation, nor to bestow that attention to their financial concerns, which is, to a certain degree, indispensable in every condition of life. Sir George, it is to be apprehended, was one of this class. Possessing a pleasing and handsome exterior with the courteous manners and address of the accomplished gentleman (qualities not particularly valued by the navy in those days) he had, at all times, when on shore, been received into the highest circles of fashion, where he took his draught of pleasure, as others did; and his heart being warm and generous, he not infrequently found himself involved in pecuniary difficulties. . . .

'In those days, that curse of society, and bane of happiness, the passion for play, prevailed to a degree one can now have no idea of in assemblies of the great. The votaries of fashion, of all ages, and of either sex, were carried down its stream, and ingulphed in its vortex; and it has been asserted, that this gallant officer, so wise and circumspect whilst afloat on his country's service, was unable, although a skilful mariner, to steer altogether clear of its seductions.'

Having implanted this picture in his readers' minds, General Mundy seems to have recalled his role as a worshipper at the shrine of his father-in-law and goes on to say he does not believe a word of it. A memoir-writer of the time, Sir N. William Wraxall, whose words probably reflect the gossip of the day, says of Rodney,'Throughout his life, two Passions, both highly injurious to his repose, the Love of Women and of Play, carried him into many Excesses.' Whatever may be the truth of it, there can be little doubt that Rodney was soon in need of money to keep up his style of living, or that he found it in 1764 in the dowry of the woman who became his second wife. She was Henrietta, daughter of John Clies, merchant of Lisbon.

A bride from so different a social circle from his own must have had special attractions. No evidence exists that great beauty or charm on her part, or love on his, went to the making of the match. Not were they necessary ingredients in that age. But a handsome fortune would have been almost essential for a merchant's daughter to marry into the aristocracy.

In the year after his marriage Rodney secured a further access of income in the shape of the post of Governor of Greenwich

Hospital for Seamen, worth £1,000 a year. The appointment was one regularly given to admirals as a reward for good service, its perquisites including a handsome house which formed a part of Christopher Wren's noble riverside palace. During Rodney's time the administration of the hospital had for a long time been riddled with corruption typical of every public office of the day. The funds which should have gone to the care of the seamen pensioners were regularly diverted into the pockets of a mob of placemen and petty officials, while the seamen themselves were ill-fed and neglected.

By the standards of a later age, Rodney should have stripped and waded through the muck to cleanse the Augean stables. That he did not do so must, by the same standards, be held to display a despicable side to his character. But a man must be judged against the backdrop of his era. From the humblest doorkeeper to the highest offices of the state, bribes were taken in one form or another and public money diverted to private use. As besmirched with corruption as any man was Lord Sandwich, through whose good offices as Secretary of State Rodney had obtained the lucrative sinecure. It would have been asking him to ruin himself professionally and financially to expect him to delve into the ordure uncovering heaven knows what widespread rottenness leading inevitably to the door of his patron. Rodney was not of the stuff of martyrs.

General Mundy attempts to show that his father-in-law's heart was nevertheless in the right place and that, true gentleman as he was, he had the pensioners' welfare ever in mind. He relates how Sir George, taken to task by the Lieutenant-Governor for being over-generous in approving applications by the pensioners to be issued with greatcoats, rebuked his subordinate, who had reached the quarter-deck from before the mast, in the following majestic and cutting words:

'I have the greatest respect for you as a man who, by the greatest merit, has raised himself from the station of a foremast man to the rank of an admiral—a circumstance which not only does you the highest honour, but would have led me to have expected you as an advocate instead of an opposer to such a necessary indulgence. Many of the poor men at the door have been your shipmates, and once your companions. Never hurt a brother sailor. And let me warn you against two things more: the first is in future not to interfere between me and my duty as Governor: and the second is, not to object to these brave men having great coats whilst you are so fond of one as to wear it by the side of as good a fire as you are sitting by at present. There are very few young sailors that come to London without paying Greenwich Hospital a visit, and it shall be the rule of my conduct as far as my authority extends to render the old men's lives so comfortable that the younger shall say when he goes away, "Who would not be a sailor to live happy as a Prince in his old age." '

The authenticity of the story has been questioned, but it is certainly in character and may be left at that.

For the next five years Rodney, dividing his time between the Governor's house at Greenwich and his handsome country house at Alresford, watched a second young family grow. In the summer of 1766 he suffered a dangerous illness at Alresford and for a time the doctors despaired of his life. In his post at Greenwich he had acquired a secretary, the Reverend William Pagett, who was to continue to serve him in that capacity in his various naval appointments. From letters which Pagett wrote to Lord Northampton apprising him of Rodney's illness, it would seem to have been malaria, perhaps picked up in the West Indies.

'They began to-day,' he wrote in one bulletin, 'to give him the Decoction of the Bark which sate very well upon his Stomach. He is now asleep in a fine breaking Sweat.'

During these years Rodney was still Member of Parliament for Penryn. From his place in the Commons he watched the political ferment which developed as the arbitrary powers of Parliament were attacked on three sides—by the King, by the people of England and by the people of the American colonies.

The first of these Grenville was able for a time to hold off. The popular clamours at home and in America, however, were two aspects of a desire for a more broadly-based democracy which was to grow on the one hand into a movement for parliamentary and electoral reform, on the other into a demand for independence by the American colonies.

At home attention was focused at first on a demand for parliamentary proceedings to be made public and for free comment to be allowed in the newspapers. The leading personality was John Wilkes, who, though a profligate and rake, was to emerge as the leader of a movement for parliamentary reform. Arrested and sent to the Tower for his attacks on the Government in his journal *The North Briton*, Wilkes, as a Member of Parliament, was released by order of the Court of Common Pleas; but on being threatened with prosecution for seditious libel, he fled to France. He was to return five years later to raise a furore by standing for and being elected to Parliament for Middlesex while still an outlaw.

No evidence remains of Rodney's attitude in these commotions, but it can be fairly sure that he would have been on the side of authority. He was no forward thinker in political affairs. Furthermore Sandwich, as Secretary of State, had been responsible for the prosecution of Wilkes, and Sandwich was replacing Newcastle, who was in eclipse, as Rodney's patron.

The dispute which had arisen with the American colonies was in essence whether the Government in London had the right to levy taxes on the colonists without their consent, as had been claimed in the preamble to an Act of Parliament. It began with American resentment at enforcement of customs duty on trade between America and the Spanish colonies which had so long been disregarded that it had come to be considered inapplicable. Indignation next flared up at the introduction in 1765 of a tax on the colonies in the form of a stamp duty. Impassioned protests were made in colonial Assemblies, memorial of protest were sent to London, rioting and disturbances broke out, and there were attacks on property.

Before news of these reached London the quarrel between the King and Grenville over the former's interference through his 'Friends' both in the Commons and in the Ministry itself had come to a head and Grenville had resigned. It was a new Ministry formed out of the main body of the Whigs, now headed by the Marquis of Rockingham, which had to deal with the matter.

The Whigs as a whole were seriously divided on the question of America. One group, headed by the Duke of Bedford and Lord Sandwich, was fierce in its belief in coercion of the colonists. George Grenville and his faction, while less violent in their attitude, were committed to the fiscal policy so objectionable to the colonists and disapproved of by the Rockingham faction who believed in conciliation with the colonies. A lone wolf was Pitt who, though a Whig in all else, disliked government by party and was therefore an obstacle to Whig unity. Largely owing to his advocacy, the Stamp Act was repealed in March 1766.

The news of the repeal was received with enormous enthusiasm in America and was looked on as an admission by the Home Government that no taxes would in future be levied on the colonists without their consent. Even a defiant and insulting protest, signed by a number of Members of the House of Lords, and the passage through the Commons of a Declaratory Act affirming the Government's right to impose taxes on the colonies, failed to spoil the effect.

To the King, determined to keep the colonists in subjection, the repeal was an act of unforgivable disloyalty to the Crown. It confirmed him in his determination to break the power of the Whigs. Though he detested Pitt, the idol of the people, he shared with him a hatred for the powerful Whig magnates. In 1766, therefore, Rockingham was dismissed and Pitt, raised to the peerage as Earl of Chatham, formed an administration.

The Great Commoner was no longer the man he had been. Racked with gout he remained in seclusion much of the time leaving the Duke of Grafton to lead the Government in his place. So little was he in control that in his absence a series of resolutions was passed imposing duties on a number of commodities entering the colonies. All that he had worked for was thus destroyed. The active resistance of the Americans which was to grow into open rebellion can be said to date from this time. In 1768 Pitt resigned, leaving Grafton in nominal as well as effective leadership.

Such was the political scene when the General Election of 1768 became due. Rodney, still convinced of the need for a naval officer to have a seat in Parliament, in the shifting sands of the struggle for power no longer had the steady beacon of his old patron to guide him. Newcastle had retired from affairs and was to die in that same year. The men in power had other, more useful candidates for the safe seats in their gift.

Yet a seat Rodney had to have. His brother-in-law, Spencer, Earl of Northampton, 'owned', in conjunction with the Earl of Halifax, the borough of Northampton. It returned two members.

By long-established custom they were always 'the men' of the two earls. Rodney's second marriage had not affected his friendship with the Comptons. Northampton readily agreed to oblige him; Halifax's candidate for the second seat was Sir George Osborne.

This cosy arrangement was upset by the appearance of a third candidate, Sir James Langham, put up by the recently created Earl Spencer, a *nouveau riche* of the county who had just inherited £100,000. Such effrontery was not to be borne! Northampton and Halifax determined to defeat the Spencer candidate by any means, fair or foul. Spencer was happy to meet them on these terms and, at the opening of the poll, both sides agreed that the customary oath as to bribery should not be administered to any of the voters. As a contemporary account has it, 'each voter that would, had 12, 14 or 50 guineas, some £100, to £500.'

At one stage the electors trooped in an army to Horton, the country house of Lord Halifax, to be regaled with his entire stock of port. When that was exhausted they were offered the best claret. This they took to be simply inferior port and in disgust they moved on to Northampton's house of Castle Ashby.

To corruption was added intimidation. Lords Northampton and Halifax, accompanied by their friends, the two candidates, and the Mayor, paraded the town by torchlight. On meeting the opponents similarly employed, fights ensued, heads were broken and the windows of the rival headquarters smashed. It was too much for Sir James Langham—or he was bought over. He suddenly withdrew from the contest. Lord Spencer was not so easily dealt with. A Mr Howe—brother to the famous Admiral Lord Howe—stepped into the breach and the contest continued. At the close of the poll the Mayor declared that the two Sir Georges had a majority over Mr Howe of seventy-three. The irregularities were so flagrant—169 shoemakers of Northampton polled on both sides, having presumably been equally well bribed by each—and the partiality of the Mayor was so patent, that, on Spencer's appeal to the Commons, the election was investigated by a committee of the whole House. No doubt encouraged by the lavish hospitality offered at Spencer House in London, the Members decided that Mr Howe was elected. The two Sir Georges then 'tossed five guineas in a hat to decide which should occupy the other seat'. Rodney won; but it was a truly

c

Pyrrhic victory. Halifax and Northampton were both ruined. The former had to sell his estates and leave the county. Northampton's share of the £160,000 that the election was computed to have cost compelled him to sell all the timber on his estate for £50,000 as well as the contents of his two country houses and to retire for the rest of his life to Switzerland.

As for Rodney, his seat had cost him the staggering sum of £30,000 and saddled him with an insufferable load of debt. The prospects of paying it were remote while the lean years of peace continued; but in the following year the outlook from Rodney's point of view brightened as a possibility of war with Spain arose.

France had never resigned herself to the position of inferiority at sea she had been forced into by the humiliating defeats of the Seven Years War. Even before that war was over her great War Minister, the Duc de Choiseul, had succeeded in dispelling the French apathy towards maritime affairs; under his skilful guidance the discipline of the Navy had been restored and its strength rebuilt to forty ships of the line. In the years since the Peace of Paris he had continued the work. A determination to have revenge on the British Navy animated the French seamen, and Choiseul's preparations for it would reach maturity in 1770.

By 1769 he was encouraging Spain to hostile acts against Britain. Her opportunity came in a dispute over the dominion of the Falkland Isles which had been annexed by Britain in 1766. Since then a settlement had grown up at the principal harbour of the islands, Port Egmont, regular visits had been made by flotillas of minor warships and a guardship was usually stationed there. In 1769 a Spanish ship was found surveying the coast. The following year, in June, a squadron of five Spanish frigates appeared at Port Egmont, fired on the little guardship, a 16-gun sloop, the *Favourite*, and compelled the small garrison to surrender. When the *Favourite* reached England in September, carrying the dispossessed garrison, there was a fierce outcry. Chatham came out of retirement to thunder against Spain in the House of Lords. War fever mounted.

For the moment, however, Choiseul was not ready to come to Spain's aid if war broke out. He wished to see the year's trade safely home first, and induced the Spaniards to delay matters. By December he was ready and the Spanish attitude stiffened. The

British Ambassador was recalled from Madrid. War seemed imminent. The British Government ordered a mobilisation of the fleet and forty-one ships of the line were commissioned.

At the last moment Louis XV discovered Choiseul's machinations, which he had apparently been conducting unknown to the King. Less confident than his Minister of France's readiness for war, he dismissed Choiseul and Spain was advised to keep the peace or to expect no help from France. On 22nd January 1771, therefore, the Spanish Ambassador was authorised to promise the restitution of Port Egmont, and the dispute was for the time being settled.

Things were still tense, however, when during the first days of 1771 Rodney was offered the command of the Jamaica station by Lord Sandwich. His old service chief had just returned to the Admiralty as First Lord in the administration which had been formed in 1770 under Lord North. The resignation of Chatham and Grafton and their adherents had left available for office only the faction under the Duke of Bedford and the growing body of politicians who were prepared to accept the King's directions without question. They were gathered under the leadership of North into a Ministry which was in fact a cloak for the direction of affairs by King George himself. It was to remain in office for twelve disastrous years.

Sandwich had been a good friend to Rodney in times gone by. No doubt he was happy to find a senior naval officer who did not look askance at him and his unsavoury reputation. Rodney was certainly delighted at the prospect of command in the West Indies at a moment when war with Spain seemed imminent. The lure of prize money must have gleamed irresistibly to the debt-ridden admiral.

War was not yet certain, however. There were few attractions in a peace-time command abroad on an unhealthy station when £1,000 a year could be earned without leaving the comforts and domestic contentment of the Governor's house at Greenwich. Rodney, product of an age of unashamed sinecures, saw no reason why he should not retain the governorship while away at sea.

In the sprawling script which flowed from his gouty hands he addressed a stately remonstrance to Lord Sandwich:

'Your goodness, in thinking of employing me in the West

Indies, which in all probability will be the field of action should a war commence with Spain, lays me under the greatest obligation, and flatters my ambition, that I am thought worthy by the King and your Lordship of a command of such consequence.

'Pardon me, however, my Lord, if I feel myself a little disappointed in one circumstance which fell from your Lordship. I flattered myself that when his Majesty was most graciously pleased to honour me with the Government of his Royal Hospital at Greenwich, it would not be expected I should resign it on my being employed, but that I should enjoy it in the same manner as three out of four Admirals, who had been Governors thereof had done; viz., Lord Aylmer, Sir John Jennings and Sir John Balchen, all of whom were employed and commanded fleets during their government of the Hospital.'

So much for precedent. Rodney continued by giving vent to the disappointment which must have been eating out his heart ever since Admiral Pocock had swept through his station at the Leeward Islands and gone on to net £122,000 in prize money.

'My case is more peculiar,' he groaned, 'as I had the misfortune of being superseded in the command of a successful fleet, entrusted to my care in the West Indies, at the very time I had sailed on another expedition against the enemy's squadron at the island of St Domingo, and was thereby deprived of pursuing those conquests which so honourably attended upon another, and which secured him such great emoluments. . . .'

But Sandwich's heart remained untouched. There were other admirals with calls upon the patronage which was by now largely in the King's hands. Rodney had to hope for war with Spain if he was to satisfy his pressing creditors. Just how pressing they were can be judged by the fact that when the time came to join his ship, to avoid the bailiffs waiting for him he was constrained to have his barge sent to meet him by night at the water-side house of his brother-in-law, Henry Drummond.

It was a distinctly grumpy gentleman, therefore, who climbed aboard the *Princess Amelia* of eighty guns on 13th May 1771, to the ceremonial roll of drums and the shrilling of boatswains' whistles. The white flag with a St. George's cross was broken out at the foremast head, signifying his rank as Vice-Admiral of the White, to which he had been promoted in October 1770.

Rodney, the admiral afloat, was a very different person from Rodney the courtier ashore. The elegant habitué of White's and Almacks, the courtly payer of graceful compliments at the Duchess of Bedford's gatherings with a reputation as an easy, voluble conversationalist, became a withdrawn, taciturn chief whom subordinates found by no means easy to approach. The baronet with a strict sense when ashore of his respectful place in the aristocratic hierarchy that ruled Britain, firmly grasped when afloat the almost despotic power belonging to him as his sovereign's representative and upholder of the honour of the national flag.

Thus when two weeks later the port admiral at Plymouth, hearing of an impending visit by the First Lord aboard the yacht *Augusta*, inquired of Rodney as to how he proposed to receive him, he received a stiff, uncompromising reply:

'In case the yacht which brings his lordship into the port carries the Admiralty flag, I shall not only salute it with nineteen guns, but likewise give particular orders to all the captains of the squadron I command to do the same; but in case the yacht comes with a pendant only, I shall expect the captain of her to do his duty by saluting the King's flag entrusted to my charge; and should he neglect to do so, I shall send a proper officer on board to place him in arrest for disrespect to the King's flag.'

It is not therefore surprising to find that when, soon after his arrival at Port Royal, Jamaica, Rodney learnt that a small warship of his command, the schooner *Hawke*, had been arrested off the Spanish Main and taken into Carthagena, he reacted vigorously. The 60-gun ship *Achilles* was sent with a sharp protest to the Spanish Governor and a demand that the officers responsible be disciplined.

Rodney's action was by no means excessively provocative. The high-handed behaviour of the Spaniards was more than could be tamely accepted. Nevertheless the international situation had remained delicate since the conclusion of the Falkland Islands dispute. The British Government at that time had woken up to the serious lack of readiness of the Royal Navy. A Navy List impressive on paper was found to consist of a high proportion of ships whose timbers were rotten, having been built in haste of unseasoned oak during the Seven Years War.

Enough men could not be found to man such ships as were fit for sea.

Thus the Government was desperately anxious to preserve peace. When Sandwich received Rodney's despatch on the Carthagena affair he was assailed by fears that his over-zealous admiral might provide a spark to the explosive situation. Rodney's financial straits were, of course, known to him, and indeed they were no secret. If the admiral's ethical standards were on a level with those of Sandwich and many of his political friends, he might well be tempted to provoke a war which would be sure to line his pocket. Stories had reached the First Lord that in London Rodney had made indiscreet remarks within hearing of foreign ministers that he would be happy to see war break out with Spain.

Sandwich hastily penned a solemn warning, amounting almost to a reprimand: 'I cannot help cautioning you, as a friend, to be upon your guard and to avoid, by every justifiable means, the drawing of this country into a war, which, if it come on too speedily, I fear we shall have cause to lament . . . those who, at this time, take any hasty steps to draw us into a war, will deserve to be considered as the worst enemies of Great Britain.'

Lest avarice should overcome Rodney's loyalty and good sense he went on to hint that war would not bring him the financial rewards he might expect. On the contrary the disappointment of 1762 would be re-enacted:

'I will add one word more; and that is, that upon a declaration of war, larger squadrons must be sent out, and, very probably, senior officers, to most of our stations in foreign parts.'

Whether or not Sandwich's words caused Rodney to modify his conduct of affairs in the West Indies in any way is impossible to judge; but his actions were soon meeting with the First Lord's and the sovereign's approval. In March 1772 Sandwich wrote, 'I am very happy to have it in my power to assure you that the contents of your letter (which I have communicated to the person you would most wish to oblige), has met with entire approbation, and I do not think that there is any of our commanders-in-chief, who stand at present upon a better footing than yourself.'

Rodney had taken to Jamaica with him the usual band of young gentlemen recommended to him by their patrons, hopeful of preferment to posts which might become vacant, ashore or afloat. One of them was a Mr Marr, a protégé of Lord Northampton. A letter from Rodney to his brother-in-law throws a light on the management of such affairs; reporting his appointment in the place of an officer who had died, he wrote:

'. . . . the only officer that has made a vacancy by death since I arrived in this Island. You may judge by this how Healthy this place is, for many of my Captains and Lieutenants have lived very Free indeed; but the fifty Midshipmen I have on my Quarter-deck begin to despair. However if the Officers pursue the Course they followed lately, there will be some hopes for them among which Marr will give them a Chance, as the little Dog has been very Free with himself but is so Low Spirited after it for ten days that I almost pity him. However he seems to have taken a Resolution to withstand all Invitations to Feasts which are very customary here. I believe in a few days I will give him a Place worth between three and four thousand pounds for Mr —, as the Person who occupies it is given over by the Physicians. 'Tis the Navy Storekeeper whose salary is only £300 per annum but Perquisites are very considerable. The moment it becomes available I shall appoint Marr and write to Lord Sandwich in hopes he will confirm him; but should I apply before, he will have time to enquire the value of the Place and make a Merit of it to some Corporation or other. 'Tis entirely in the Gift of the Admiralty.'

As the international storm blew itself peacefully out, Rodney contemplated with dismay the end of his three-year tenure of command and the inevitable return to face his creditors on half-pay. In England and America events were following the dismal course which was to lead to the rebellion of the colonies. In 1773 came the Boston Tea Party, and in March 1774 the closing of the port of Boston. The appointment of General Gage as Governor of Massachussetts and of Vice-Admiral Samuel Graves to command the North American Station indicated the intention of the King to use force to coerce the colonists. The meeting of the first Congress at Philadelphia in the same year showed that the colonies were united in their determination to resist. None of this, however, was looked upon by men of affairs in England as a prelude to war. It seemed just a local disturbance which would be easily settled with the use of the peace-time establishment of the armed forces. The outlook was indeed grim for the fifty-five-year-old admiral.

Even without his embarrassments the prospects for naval officers in time of peace were so slim that many had gone abroad with permission to offer their services to foreign navies— particularly the Russian, where a Scotsman, Samuel Grieg, was for some time Commander-in-Chief of the fleet.

Rodney's age and background were against such a solution of his difficulties; so when the Governor of Jamaica, Sir William Trelawney became ill and seemed likely to die, he wrote to Sandwich asking for the appointment. An encouraging reply came back, but when Trelawney died in February 1773, Rodney's faith in the First Lord's support received a rude shock from the news that Sir Basil Keith had received the post instead.

It was a disappointed and a bitter man who came home in September 1774 and hauled down his flag, probably for the last time as it seemed. Rodney was in truth out of his depth in the political scene which had taken shape since the Whigs had been dislodged from their solidly entrenched position by the intrigues of the King. Sandwich, to whom he had looked as his patron since the death of Newcastle, was a most doubtful friend. Loyalty was never a strong quality with him, as had been demonstrated when he took the lead in the persecution of Wilkes, an erstwhile boon companion and fellow member of the Hell Fire Club. His conduct then had earned him the nickname of Jemmy Twitcher, after the character in *The Beggar's Opera* who betrayed Macheath.

An ageing admiral, in doubtful health and heavily embarrassed by debts, had nothing to offer in return for any boon that Sandwich might confer. He could be safely dropped in favour of other more useful clients. The facts of the situation were borne in on Rodney on his return. Polite regrets, graceful compliments, were all he could extract from the Admiralty where his old associate John Clevland had been replaced by a new Secretary, Philip Stephens.

In 1771, however, besides being promoted to Vice-Admiral of the Red, he had been nominated Rear-Admiral of England. The latter entailed no duties except ceremonial ones on state occasions and was a survival from the times when a Lord High Admiral commanded the fleet. The post carried with it a salary of £332 a year.

Added to his half-pay it might have been enough to keep Rodney and his family in quiet retirement, but never in the style to which they had been accustomed. Besides, there were the creditors whose patience was exhausted. Imprisonment actually threatened, his agents and advisers hustled him off to France. Until something turned up to help him out of his difficulties, it was wise to go into voluntary exile abroad where he was out of reach of the tipstaffs. Life should be cheaper in Paris and there he could perhaps without shame lead a less extravagant existence. So the Rodney family packed and followed him to settle in Paris in 1775.

VI

'HE then lived in very straightened circumstances until better days came; and to the credit of that gallant nation it must be mentioned that they treated the English Belisarius with the respect and sympathy due to his fame and to his misfortunes.' Thus General Mundy gracefully records the years in Paris. What a picture it evokes of shifts and stratagems to stretch a modest income to cover the expense of keeping up with his social equals in the aristocratic capital of Louis XVI!

The aristocracies of Europe had always been linked together by tenuous bonds of self-interest and a mutual sense of superiority, maintaining a sort of freemasonry of blue blood which national rivalries and wars failed to dissolve. Thus Rodney was naturally received into court circles and the houses of the great. Any idea he may have entertained of living quietly and economically was doomed from the start. No doubt there was a carriage to keep up. The fashions of the day, particularly among the French nobility, were wildly extravagant. Though the Rodneys were not likely to emulate the flights of fancy of the courtiers of Versailles, the brocaded, ornamental coats, the silk stockings, ruffled shirts, and silver-buckled shoes of a gentleman and the voluminous satin, fine linen, and huge feathered hats of his lady would account for a considerable income. There would be hospitality on a lavish scale to return. It would be difficult, probably impossible, to economise without retiring altogether from polite society—which was unthinkable. An English 'milord' was, of course, assumed to be wealthy. Credit was forthcoming and debts soon mounted.

Meanwhile the world situation, which had seemed so disappointingly peaceful when Rodney had decided to go into exile, was coming once again to the boil. By the use of arbitrary dismissal from official appointments of opponents to his will and their replacements by his adherents, George III had installed a Government which, under the leadership of Lord North, was ready to carry out his orders. These were that the American colonies were to be coerced into acceptance of the dictates of Westminster. In spite of appeals and warnings by Chatham and Burke in Parliament and by the City of London, the King remained adamant, while in America the colonists were arming themselves to resist.

In April 1775 the first shots were fired at Lexington where sixty-five were killed and 185 wounded out of a British force returning from an expedition to destroy military stores collected by the colonists. A few days later the important posts of Ticonderoga and Crown Point were surprised and captured by rebels. In May a British army of 10,000 troops arrived at Boston and the struggle had begun which was to end with the emergence of the United States of America on the world stage.

The confused, disjointed campaigns in America and Canada which resulted were not looked upon in England as calling for an all-out effort; there was little support in Britain for what was derisively called 'The King's War'. The naval estimates for 1775 were indeed a reduction on those for the previous year. But lack of success against the colonists gradually spurred the Government into greater activity. To reinforce the Army Hessian troops were hired, a step which embittered the Americans beyond hope of reconciliation. A large increase in the naval estimates for 1776 was voted and a number of ships ordered to be put into commission. To man them a larger bounty for volunteers was offered. When this proved ineffectual a General Press Warrant was issued and once again the press gangs scoured the streets of seaport towns.

The naval operations in North America were not, however, such as to make Rodney feel that his services were called for. They consisted largely of convoy escort and landing operations in support of the Army. The fleet allocated for the purpose was a small one, too small to require an admiral of Rodney's rank and seniority to command it. On the other hand, moving in court circles as he did, it was not hidden from him that the French desire and determination to have revenge sooner or later for the humiliations inflicted upon them in the Seven Years War had never flagged.

The pre-occupation of Britain with her troublesome subjects across the Atlantic might well offer the opportunity for which the French were waiting—a particularly attractive prospect in that it had been the elimination of the French threat in North America which had removed the colonists' need to rely upon the Mother Country for protection and so left them free to seek their independence. Rodney, sniffing war with France in the air, began to look around for a means to get back to London to offer his services. Employment would give him a chance to pay his debts; but in England the duns awaited him and even imprisonment. On the last day of 1777 he wrote to his eldest son, George, now a young man of fashion under the patronage of his uncle, Northampton, and an officer in the Guards.

'I beg my Dear Son you will call upon Mr Macreth and enquire of him if he has applied for me to the Gentlemen of the Board of Greencloth that I may be protected within the Jurisdiction of the King's Pallaces should I return to England. If I can be safe under their Protection, I think I ought not to stay here longer than I may have to satisfy the few Debts I owe here. Don't delay letting me know Mr Macreth's sentiments. Times are very unsettled and a War may come on sooner than expected. No news has lately arrived from America relative to General Howe and Washington, but the Americans here give it out that Howe will soon be in the same Situation as Burgoyne. Tell your Uncle Mr Drummond that all the vessels loaded with Goods bound to America which had been stopped in the Ports of this Kingdom have been permitted to sail since the unhappy news of Burgoyne's Defeat and the day before yesterday that old Rascall Franklin at dinner at the Hotel Militaire, had the Impudence to give as his Toast, the Perpetual Friendship and Alliance between the United States and France. One old Gentleman who was at the Dinner told it to me as a Matter of Fact and with great Indignation at the Behaviour of the old Traytor. French Ministers act now more openly and the American Deputies have free Access to them at all Times.'

In February 1778 a Secret Treaty of Alliance between the two countries was indeed concluded. The following month its terms

70]

were conveyed to London. Once again France and England were at war.

The outbreak found Rodney still in Paris in a fever to be away, but securely tied by debts which he could not pay. He had for some time been sustained only by 'all those great families from whom I received so many civilities, and whose attention in paying me daily and constant visits, in a great measure kept my creditors from being so troublesome as they otherwise would have been'. But by now, so clamorous had his creditors become that it was only the good offices of the chief of police that kept them at bay. Even he could not answer for the consequences if the admiral were to try to leave the city. For some time Rodney had been trying to raise the money to free himself. The talk of French naval preparations and the swaggering in the streets of Paris of American naval captains, including the famous Paul Jones, had clearly foretold the approach of war—a war which would certainly be fought out across the Atlantic. There was no one more suited, he felt sure, for the command in those waters than he, who knew the area so well.

On the 7th February 1778 he had written to Lord Sandwich offering himself 'to go on any enterprise whereby I may shew my attachment to his Majesty and the State. I am ready at a moment's warning to go on any service your Lordship may please to employ me in. . . .'

The curt, official acknowledgment which was all he received in reply, did not surprise him. He knew Sandwich too well not to realise that he would shrink from obliging an impecunious suitor who had nothing to offer in return. The First Lord had a sufficiency of rival claimants for command, younger and less, liable to be prostrated by the gout. Nevertheless, if only he could get back to London, Rodney felt sure he could demonstrate his superior claims.

Lady Rodney had crossed to England to see what help could be found amongst relations and friends. Young George Rodney, too, was assiduous in pressing his father's case to Lord North in private and at the levées which such personages held. Both were unsuccessful and the admiral's situation was soon desperate.

It was particularly galling to him in that the Navy Board had withheld his salary as Rear-Admiral of England since he had

[71

gone abroad; as he pointed out, if they would 'deliver but half of what is due to me it would be sufficient to satisfy everybody, and there would be money to spare besides'. Unfortunately the Navy Board was itself one of Rodney's creditors. He had authorised various bills on them during his tenure of the Jamaica Command to defray expenses of gathering intelligence of Spanish ports in the West Indies and the Caribbean. The Board refused their approval and reimbursed themselves by stopping the amounts out of the admiral's pay.

To add to his distress at this time came news of the death of James, his second son by his first marriage, who had been lost in the sloop *Ferret* in the West Indies.

Then help came from an unexpected quarter. One of the great men of France, the old Maréchal de Biron, hearing of Rodney's predicament and declaring that 'all France was sensible of the services Rodney had rendered his country and that the treatment they all knew he had received was a disgrace to the nation and to its ministers,' offered to advance 'whatever sum he might want, even to £2,000'.

The chivalrous gesture touched Rodney's heart. While hope of relief from other sources remained he refused to take advantage of it. But on 6th May, after the offer had been made for a third time, he wrote to his wife, 'I have this day accepted of the generous friendship of the Maréchal Biron, who has advanced one thousand louis in order that I may leave Paris without being reproached.'

The Maréchal's act of faith in Rodney was matched by the banking house of Drummonds. At its head was Henry Drummond, husband of Jane Compton's younger sister Elizabeth. Hearing the circumstances, he at once advanced the sum and repaid the debt. Amongst the Rodney papers in the Public Records Office lies the cancelled acknowledgement of the debt and the following graceful letter from Biron. 'I was really delighted to have an opportunity to oblige so distinguished a gentleman as you, and whose reputation is known all over Europe. I had the honour to assure you that I hoped you would not concern yourself solely about this little debt when you reached London and the hastiness with which you have discharged it has disappointed me. If your affairs in Paris had required a greater sum I would have been happier and, I vow, without making any time limit. I am in the situation of not having need of it; I only wished to be useful to you and, your having paid me so promptly, I have not been able to render you any service.'

Biron's chivalry was in later years to strike a responsive chord in so insensitive an organ as the heart of a Chancellor of the Exchequer. During the Terror of the French Revolution, Biron's daughter fled to England. To the assenting cheers of the Members of the House of Commons, it was proposed that a pension of £80 a year should be paid to her for life.

Mademoiselle de Biron returned eventually to the family house in the hills near Vichy. She lived on into the 1880's and every New Year's Day until her death the British Consul at Vichy climbed the steep slope through the snow to present the old lady with eighty golden sovereigns.

Back in London, Rodney lost no time in bringing himself to the notice of the Admiralty with a paper pointing out the crucial importance of the West Indies in the war about to begin and urging the immediate capture of St Lucia to provide a windward base for the fleet. He had protested, at the end of the previous war, at the return to France of both Martinique and St. Lucia. He now gave his opinion that possession of the latter, with its splendid harbour, the Carenage, and its advanced base at Gros Islet Bay, was the more important, owing to the devastation which had been caused to Martinique by a plague of African ants; but he concluded by saying that he was convinced 'that either of these islands in the hands of Great Britain, must, while she remains a great maritime power, make her sovereign of the West Indies'.

The advice was sound and would be acted upon when the time came, but by the hand of another. The various fleet commands had already been allocated and for the moment there was nothing for Rodney. By now he was thoroughly disillusioned as to what support might be expected from the First Lord of the Admiralty. Sandwich, following the rising star of the imperious young King, had broken with the Whigs, the main body of whom under Rockingham (and supported by the oratory of Edmund Burke) was in opposition to the King's determination to suppress the rebellion in America by force. Rodney, who until now had been stamped with the Whig seal, had no doubt that coercion of the colonists was the right course of action. He did not hesitate to say so on every occasion. Thus he soon found himself expelled from the Whig camp but by no means accepted by the Tories. Indeed his absence abroad had withdrawn him from the heat of party politics, and his sword was at the disposal of whatever government was prepared to prosecute the war with vigour. This, in fact, meant the King himself and it was to him that Rodney appealed directly in an audience at the Palace.

With his flag list full of admirals of the Whig persuasion who had made it known that while they were ready to fight the French they were by no means happy at the idea of turning their guns on their American cousins, the King was delighted to find one of Rodney's known capacity to whom an enemy in arms was someone to be fought relentlessly, whatever his blood. He promised him appointment at the first opportunity, and meanwhile promoted him to be Admiral of the White, the highest active naval rank that existed, on 29th June 1778. Nevertheless, it was to be another eighteen months before the King was to be able to fulfil his promise.

In the meantime Vice-Admiral the Hon. Augustus Keppel was commanding the main fleet in the Channel, Lord Howe was in North America, while in the West Indies there was only a small squadron of two ships of the line and thirteen smaller craft under Rear-Admiral the Hon. Samuel Barrington.

The situation as between the British and French Navies was very different from that which had existed during the Seven Years War. The British fleet which had been built up then under the stern, incorruptible Anson had been allowed to shrink and decay under his successors. The evil practices against which he had set his face crept back when George III, to defeat the Whig oligarchy, had used against them their own weapons of interest and corruption. To retain the support of a majority in Parliament, the King and his Ministers had had to close their eyes to abuses from which so many politicians and their hangers-on profited.

The ramifications of the system were so widespread, so ubiquitous that any serious effort to abolish it would have raised an outcry against which no administration of the day could have stood. So far as naval administration is concerned, some idea of the astonishing irregularities which went on at the bottom end of

74]

the scale is given by a letter from Captain Price of the sloop *Viper* on the North American Station.

'I am very much distressed for Petty Officers as well as Warrants. My Carpenter infirm and past duty, my Gunner made from a livery servant, neither seaman nor gunner; my Master a man in years, never an officer before, made from a boy on board one of the guardships, he then keeping a public house at Gosport. Petty Officers I have but one, who owns himself mad at times. A Master's mate I have not, nor anyone I can make a Boatswain's Mate. I have not one person I could trust with the charge of a vessel I might take to bring her in.'

No doubt the fees paid for Warrants issued by the Navy Office to Price's carpenter, gunner and master lined the pockets of a whole string of clerks, who had themselves obtained their posts by bribery of officials above them. At the other end of the scale peculation was on a vast scale so that a large proportion of the money voted for the Navy vanished without trace. Thus when war came in the summer of 1778 the Admiralty was unable to find fifty ships of the line fit for sea in spite of huge sums voted annually. Records show that, as an example, three such ships, the *Namur*, *Defence* and *Arrogant*, had had enough money allocated to their upkeep to build three *new* ships; yet they were not fit for sea.

The blame is commonly laid squarely at the door of Lord Sandwich who had been First Lord of the Admiralty since 1771. That he did handsomely out of the perquisites of his office goes without saying. He would have been a most unusual man of his epoch had he not done so. William Pitt, the elder, had been unique in refusing to profit from his first ministerial post, that of Paymaster of the Forces. Had Sandwich done the same as First Lord and set about cleaning up the abuses in the administration of the Navy, he would certainly have ensured his own dismissal and probably that of the Ministry he supported.

Sandwich was a much hated politician. He had first earned his unpopularity and the nickname of Jemmy Twitcher, as far back as 1763, as a result of his prosecution of his erstwhile friend, Wilkes. His desertion of the Whig cause to join Lord North's Government as First Lord of the Admiralty brought him the mistrust and execration of the whole Whig oligarchy. The shrill accusations levelled at him have consequently to be accepted with some caution. A study of his correspondence reveals a capable and shrewd administrator with the good of the Navy at heart. The opinion of Horace Walpole is also worthy of attention.

'The Admiralty in which he had formerly presided with credit was the favourite object of Lord Sandwich's ambition, and his passion for maritime affairs, his activity, industry and flowing complaisance, endeared him to the profession, re-established the marine and effaced a great part of his unpopularity. No man in the Administration was so much master of business, so quick and so shrewd, and no man had so many public enemies who had so few private; for though void of principles, he was void of rancour, and bore with equal good humour the freedom with which his friends attacked him, and the satire of his opponents.'

The fact remains, however, that when the rupture with France came in 1778, the Navy was quite unprepared for a major war. Few ships were fit for sea and for them the trained crews could not be found. Many experienced, but disillusioned officers were serving in foreign navies and out of reach of recall, or were serving in merchant ships. Dockyards were empty of most of the necessities for equipping and rigging ships brought forward from reserve.

In France the situation was very different. Even before the end of the Seven Years War the work of rebuilding the Navy had begun under the inspired hand of the Duc de Choiseul. When peace was concluded in 1763, a fleet of fifty-five fine, new ships of the line had been built. In comparison with British ships of war of the day, they were superior in speed, sailing qualities and fire power. The expansion of the fleet and revitalising of the dock-yards had come to a halt with Choiseul's fall from power in 1770. The accession of the young Louis XVI to the throne of France in 1774, however, gave her a sovereign who took a real interest, unusual in a Bourbon king, in naval affairs. With such encourage-ment, his Minister of Marine, M. de Sartine, was able to take up Choiseul's work again. He found the dockyards empty and hardly a ship ready for sea, so that, fortunately for England in her un-readiness, much still remained to be done when war came in 1778. Nevertheless the French enjoyed a clear start in the race for naval re-armament. With seventy-three ships of the line,

76]

many of them new and admirably built and designed, they had a superiority which should have been overwhelming when they were joined by the navy of Spain in 1779.

Material superiority is not decisive, however, unless backed by a personnel, ranging from the high command to the 'common seamen', who know how to use it technically, tactically and strategically. An examination from this aspect of the British and French Navies during the War of American Independence is therefore necessary.

The French Navy began the war in a condition of efficiency and high morale it probably never before and certainly never again achieved in the age of sail. Its ships were manned by a high proportion of skilled professional sailors obtained through the *inscription maritime* which swept the great majority of her seafaring population into the service of the state immediately on outbreak of war. England, on the other hand, had to rely largely upon the haphazard operations of the press gangs which filled the ships' complements with disgruntled landlubbers, homeless vagabonds or tavern scum. Ships were thus often woefully inefficient for some time after putting to sea.

Time, however, was on the British side. France had little or no reserve of sea manpower. Losses through capture, battle wounds, or disease were irreplaceable. As the war progressed, difficulties in manning increased. Coastguards and soldiers could take the place of common seamen; but when skilled topmen and petty officers were lost there were no reliefs available. And losses from disease even in the home-based French fleets were enormous.

The British Navy, for all its reliance upon the press gang and jail-releases to make up the numbers of its ships' complements, could rely upon a larger maritime population from which to find the key personnel. Furthermore, wastage from disease was not so high in British ships where thought had begun to be given to hygiene and the prevention of scurvy. In Rodney's fleet in the West Indies in 1782, where the climate had hitherto been considered extremely unhealthy, out of twenty-two ships of the line there would not be twenty-two men who could not come to quarters. A naval officer writing in 1788 attributed this good health to the more humane and intelligent system of man-management which had developed.

'The old system of enforcing discipline,' he wrote, 'was without method, by main strength and the frequent use of the rattan, without which no officer from the captain down to the youngest midshipman, ever went on deck. . . . In the last war (1778–83) there is no doubt that the internal discipline of His Majesty's, ships in general was brought to as great a degree of perfection almost as it is capable of receiving; I say in general. There were indeed imperfections; but in captains bigoted to the old customs, and whose ships might always be distinguished by their awkwardness and inactivity and by the indifferent figure they cut in action though commanded with bravery.'

We must not be led by this panegyric to exaggerate the improvements which had been made in conditions afloat. If the men were less frequently beaten to their duty like herded cattle, they could still be flogged unmercifully at some brutal captain's whim. Though efforts were made to keep the bilges sanitary and the between-decks spaces 'sweet', the mess decks were still evil-smelling, dank, unhealthy places. Though fresh food was obtained and issued as often as possible, the usual diet was still salt meat and ship's biscuits, issued on the principle that the oldest in store must be used up first.

Furthermore, while the discipline the writer applauds so wholeheartedly may have been good once at sea and away from the home ports, there were repeated examples of mutiny in ships about to sail from Portsmouth and Plymouth whose crews refused to unmoor or make sail until grievances about their pay were satisfied. Nor did the improvement prevent a high rate of desertion whenever opportunity offered, at the risk of being hanged if recaptured. Sir Samuel Hood in the West Indies in 1781 was to complain that if he sent a ship to Antigua to refit the crew always deserted. Writing to his brother in the previous year when he was Commissioner at Portsmouth, Hood lamented that: 'There is a wonderful spirit of discontent in almost every ship which I am afraid is encouraged; this I am well assured of, proper exertion to prevent it is not used. Such a want of Discipline and Order throughout the Navy was never before known, or such a want of regard and attention to the good of the King's Service. The negligence of officers in general is really astonishing, and God only knows to what extent the mischief will go.'

78]

The leadership and example of the officers was indeed the crux of the matter, more particularly in the British fleet where even the severe disciplinary code of the Articles of War could not of itself impose unquestioning obedience upon men who for generations had enjoyed a degree of democracy and who stoutly defended their rights as free men. Frenchmen, on the other hand, still lived under a feudal system with an unbridgeable gulf fixed between the aristocratic officers and the common sailors, so that there was less possibility of orders being questioned or inalienable rights being claimed.

In neither navy was the conduct of officers a good example to those they commanded. The French *Corps de la Marine* was the preserve of the aristocratic families of Brittany and Provence. Unspoiled by the decadence of court life, the provincial *cadets de famille* who chose a naval career retained all the courage and spirit of their race; but they suffered from an overweening pride of birth which detracted from good discipline. In contrast to the absolute authority of rank in a British ship, where the captain, remote and omnipotent, was given almost divine honours and respect, though socially he might be a humble 'tarpaulin', and lieutenants were regarded by midshipmen with terror, in a French man-of-war an officer's grade in the nobility could decide his status more certainly than his naval rank.

'This devilish spirit,' as an observer who went to sea under d'Orvilliers in 1779 commented, 'General, captain, ensign, midshipman, all mix together; they "thou" each other like comrades and when a manœuvre is ordered by a superior officer, the subaltern sometimes replies that something else would be better; he gives his advice and the irritated chief, if the matter is not too important, prefers to defer to him rather than increase the number of his enemies.'

Jealousies existed also amongst the officers—between *Bretons* and *Provençales* and between their own, aristocratic corps, the *officiers rouges* and the bourgeois *officiers bleus* from the merchant service who swelled their ranks on outbreak of war. Such a state of affairs was unlikely to conduce to good discipline amongst the ships' companies.

Similarly in British ships, though strict obedience at all levels was enforced by the savage penal code, real discipline and respect were often undermined by the deplorable behaviour of senior officers, particularly the undisguised political or personal squabbles between them, and the fierce partisanship of captains for or against rival admirals on political grounds or in acknowledgement of patronage. As in the previous wars, captains and admirals in battle were ever on the look-out for incompetence or cowardice on the part of their brother officers. The round shot had hardly ceased to fly before mutual accusations and recriminations took its place. While discipline was far from good in either fleet by modern standards, therefore, at the beginning of the war it was probably less unhealthy in the French.

In technical efficiency, also, the French had made great advances since the Seven Years War which had been so disastrous for them at sea. A thorough training in seamanship and tactics had developed a professional pride in the officers to take the place of mere amateur enthusiasm. Books on the subject of naval tactics, evolutions and signals by Bigot de Morogues in 1763 and Bourdé de Villeheret, published soon after, were given serious study. As a result the French Navy had a code of signals greatly superior to that of the British, while French officers had an appreciation of tactics denied to their opponents whose ideas too often went no further than an ambition to lay their ship alongside a presumably acquiescent enemy and fight it out at point-blank range.

Practical training was introduced in peace-time to emulate the superior seamanship displayed by the British in the previous war. Following the British example, midshipmen were sent to sea-going ships to learn their business at an early age instead of receiving instruction mainly in guardships or ashore. In 1772 a training squadron of three ships of the line, six frigates and three corvettes was sent to sea under the Comte d'Orvilliers to practice manœuvres and carry out gunnery exercises. The experiment was repeated in 1775 and 1776.

Besides firing practices at target hulks, training was mainly concentrated upon signalled manœuvres and evolutions, the aim being to enable senior officers to control squadrons and fleets with a parade-ground precision. It was admirable and essential training. French squadrons attained a very high standard of flexibility and precision in manœuvre. But the spirit in which it was carried out was such as to discourage captains' initiative in favour of strictly ordered drill aimed at preservation of the desired formation, invariably the line. Thus the Comte d'Estaing, one of the foremost French sea commanders of the day, though originally a soldier by profession, wrote: 'If all Captains are perfect at manœuvre, one can guess what they will do, because one will be sure that it will be what they ought to do. The route for each ship is known, the dance is arranged, and if no change of wind or other navigational happening occurs, things will go passably well. This is good enough for us with our present organisation.'

Both navies adhered to the basic doctrine of the preservation of the line in the closest possible order whereby a concentration of force was achieved and ships mutually supported one another. It was indeed the very heart and backbone of naval battle formation and an admiral faced by an approximately equal foe abandoned it at his peril. Once battle had been joined, however, ships were liable to be damaged in varying degrees, breaking up the close order. Brought to a standstill by the loss of their masts they might become isolated and in danger of being overwhelmed unless their neighbours came to their rescue. In the dense smoke of battle from hundreds of guns using black gunpowder, admirals could see little of what was going on outside the immediate vicinity of their flagship. British Fighting Instructions, while insisting on preservation of the line during the approach to battle, wisely left captains free to exercise their own judgment as to how they fought their ships once battle had been joined. The French orders deprived captains of all initiative. A captain might not attempt to board his opponent without informing his admiral. He might not, 'for any reason whatsoever, unless his ship is extremely endangered, disabled and in no condition for fighting, leave his position in the line, under pain of Court Martial', nor could he 'during the action, leave the line to succour a vessel in distress, unless the Admiral signals him to do so'.

Such orders must effectively prevent advantage being taken of a situation arising from an enemy's mistake or distress which might otherwise lead to a decisive victory. They were, however, in accordance with French strategical doctrine which had discarded any idea of seeking a clear-cut decision at sea. A fleet would go to sea to achieve a definite object, the safe passage of a convoy, the landing of an army or to attack an enemy convoy. Battle with an equal or superior force was to be avoided and in any case to be broken off at the earliest opportunity.

To ensure an ability to do so at will, French broadsides were aimed at the masts and rigging of an opponent who would thus be disabled from pursuing when it was desired to break off the action and continue with the object in view. Similarly, the tight control of the movements of individual ships even after battle had been joined, would enable an orderly retreat to be made at the desired moment. The truth of Bigot de Morogues' dictum that 'there are no longer decisive actions at sea' was thus not merely accepted but actively ensured.

It was here, that, in the long run, the British Navy held a clear advantage, not only in the field of strategy but in the deep-seated morale of its personnel, from admiral to powder-monkey. Its object was always to find a means to destroy the enemy's fleet in battle, after which all the advantages of sea-power would automatically accrue.

The British method was to fire at the hulls of their opponents, inflicting such casualties and wreaking such structural damage that they could force a surrender. The enemy would thus be permanently eliminated, not simply left disabled and free to fight another day. To do so, however, they had somehow to get within decisive range of their unwilling enemy before their own motive power aloft had been destroyed.

Even then, if the enemy could preserve his line intact, the battle developed into a hammer and tongs, mutual bombardment which morale and courage being equal, might end in both sides being equally crippled and no decision secured. Thus Morogues' pronouncement was echoed by Captain John Jervis (later Admiral Lord St Vincent), but with a modification. 'Two fleets of equal force never can produce decisive events,' he wrote, 'unless they are equally determined to fight it out; or the Commander-in-Chief of one of them misconducts his line.'

The British, by leaving a degree of freedom of manœuvre to individual captains or inferior squadron commanders once battle had been joined, were in a position to take advantage of such a happening. The French system was too rigid to allow them to do so, even had they so wished. The fact that they did not seek to force a decision in battle and that their admirals were usually hampered by instructions to risk nothing when faced by an approximately equal force, led to a defensive outlook which gave their opponents a permanent moral ascendancy.

Control of the situation in an encounter between sailing ships lay initially with the side which was to windward of the other—held 'the weather gage'. The windward fleet could refuse battle simply by keeping close to the wind, or it could choose its own moment to bear down to the attack. It could then decide the range at which to fight, either by hauling close to the wind again when still at long shot, restricting the battle to an indecisive skirmish, or forcing its way into point-blank range to try to force a decision. The leeward fleet depended upon the willingness of its opponent to bring on an action at all. It could refuse action only by bearing away down wind, turning tail in fact, and leaving the field to its enemy. It must then sacrifice any hope of achieving whatever object it had in view.

The lee gage nevertheless held certain advantages. If it were blowing at all hard and ships heeling to the wind, the windward ships not only would have difficulty in elevating their guns sufficiently to reach their target until at very close range, but they might not be able to use their lowest—and heaviest—tier of guns at all. Finally, as it was the windward ships which ran into the attack and the leeward ones which awaited the onset, the former approached at least partially head-on and exposed themselves to being destructively raked by the enemy's broadsides while unable themselves to bring their guns to bear.

It will be seen, however, on every occasion of an encounter between French and British fleets, that the opening stages are invariably a contest of wits as to who shall hold the weather gage. The French will want to gain it or retain it in order to avoid a decisive clash but not to be deflected from their ulterior object in pursuit of which they have come to sea. The British will seek the weather gage in order to force their unwilling enemy to a battle à l'outrance. Thus the opening moves of the two fleets are tactically similar, but with an opposite strategical aim.

The naval war which was about to begin was to test the two strategies against each other. Application of the French conception of sea-power was to contribute largely to the victory of the Americans. The persistence of the British in seeking to force a decisive fleet action resulting in a crushing defeat of the main French fleet, was to save the rest of the Empire from the hands of the French.

VII

THE moment chosen by France to embark on her war of vengeance could hardly have been better chosen. To oppose her splendid new Navy of well-designed, well-built ships under officers proud of their profession and fired by a burning desire to humble the hereditary enemy, Britain had a fleet composed largely of rotting survivals from the previous war for which neither crews nor equipment could easily be found. Many of her experienced officers, embittered by lean years on a beggarly half-pay, had quit the service and were no longer available; others were unwilling to serve under an administration they distrusted and despised.

This latter consideration applied particularly to flag officers, most of them of the Whig persuasion and unwilling to serve if it meant fighting in America where they had no sympathy for the Government's policy. Thus Vice-Admiral Lord Howe had accepted the command in North America only because he was at the same time appointed a Joint Commissioner with his brother, General Sir William Howe, empowered to restore peace.

When it became clear that all hope of reconciliation with the colonies had gone, he threw up his command and came home, asserting that he had been deceived into it and vowing that he would refuse to serve again 'so long as the present Ministers retained office'.

Similarly Admiral the Hon. Augustus Keppel, a staunch Whig, offered the main fleet command in the Channel, had accepted on the understanding that he would be employed only against a 'continental' enemy. Even so he had had misgivings at serving under Sandwich's Board of Admiralty. His friend the Duke of Richmond had written to him, 'I cannot wish you joy of

[85

having a fleet to command, prepared by the Earl of Sandwich, with new men and officers, unacquainted with each other, to risk your reputation and the fate of your country upon, against a French and Spanish fleet who are, I fear, much better prepared.

'No one can be surprised that you should suspect a minister whom you have constantly opposed, of not giving you all the help he might do to a friend, without suspecting him of treachery. If he has but a bad fleet to send out, 'tis doing Lord Sandwich no injustice to suppose he would be glad to put it under the command of a man he does not love. . . . If we meet with a misfortune, he hopes to get off—he was not to blame for having giving the command to a relation or friend. He chose the man the nation called for. He hopes to secure himself against the attacks of opposition, because he hopes to blend himself with you in the operations carrying on, and if blame is to be borne, he will endeavour, by every art he is but too much master of, to throw if on your shoulders.'

It had certainly been an astute move on the part of Sandwich to choose an admiral from the heart of the opposition, and one who enjoyed great popularity in the country and with the men of the fleet. Keppel had gained renown as a young commodore towards the end of the previous war, when he had captured Belleisle in the Bay of Biscay, and as second-in-command at the taking of Havana for which he had received promotion to flag rank—and £25,000 in prize money. His popularity brought volunteers flocking to serve under his flag, easing the difficult manning situation, and was a useful buffer between the public, seeking culprits for the disgraceful state of the Navy, and the Government whose fault it was.

The first news of impending naval action by the French was of a squadron of twelve ships of the line and five frigates preparing to sail from Toulon under the Comte d'Estaing. Its destination must obviously be either North America to bring promised aid to France's American allies or Brest to join the thirty-three ships of the line there under d'Orvilliers. A British squadron at Gibraltar and another off Brest was the classic counter; but this was far beyond Britain's resources in the spring of 1778.

Keppel had gone down to Portsmouth in March to take command of a promised twenty ships of the line. Richmond's warning must have been in his ears when he found just six ready for sea, and they gave 'no pleasure to his seaman's eye'. When, at the beginning of May, his twenty ships were at last approaching completion and news came that d'Estaing had sailed, it was too late for him to go to Gibraltar. Vice-Admiral Byron was therefore directed to take a squadron of thirteen of the line to America to reinforce Lord Howe's small force. His squadron existed principally on paper. To make it up Keppel was told to surrender nine of his ships. To get the remainder ready, stores and equipment even down to running rigging had to be taken out of Keppel's ships to fit out those for Byron. Even so Byron was unable to sail until 9th June, nearly two months after d'Estaing.

Beset by incessant destructive storms, 'Foul-Weather Jack'— as Byron was justly nicknamed—was not able to re-assemble his fleet at New York until the end of September. Nevertheless the knowledge of his arrival on the American coast was enough to immobilise d'Estaing until, with the end of the campaigning season in the north, at the onset of winter, both fleets sailed for the West Indies.

Meanwhile the naval war in European waters had got but haltingly under way. On 13th June, four days after Byron, Keppel was able to sail with a squadron of twenty of the line. War had not yet been declared, but his orders made it clear that he could open hostilities provided that any opponents he met were not 'manifestly superior'; should they be so, he was to return to Spithead for reinforcements whose preparation for sea would be hastened on during his absence. Capturing a French frigate, Keppel learnt that the French fleet in Brest numbered thirty-three of the line. In accordance with his orders he returned to harbour, anchoring in St Helen's Roads on 27th June.

By 11th July the promised reinforcements were ready and Keppel was again in the mouth of the Channel, this time with thirty of the line. Commanding the rear division was Vice-Admiral Sir Hugh Palliser, who had gained a reputation as a good officer and a brave man in the previous war. He was an old acquaintance and shipmate of Keppel; but politics had put a barrier between them. Palliser was a Tory and a 'King's Friend' who had left a seat on the Board of Admiralty to take up his command.

The French fleet under d'Orvilliers was encountered off Ushant on the 23rd July, roughly equal in numbers. With Keppel anxious to bring on an action while d'Orvilliers wished to avoid one, the two fleets manœuvred for three days within sight of each other before a shift of wind gave the British admiral his wish. A brisk cannonade occurred as the two lines passed on opposite courses, after which, with several ships drifting disabled and others with their rigging damaged, Keppel's fleet was in some disorder, with Palliser's division separated from the remainder, astern and to windward.

Seeing this opportunity d'Orvilliers signalled for his fleet to reverse course by wearing in succession. His leading ship, the *Diadème*, either failed to see the signal or her captain preferred to ignore it, so that d'Orvilliers' chance to fall upon a part of Keppel's fleet with the whole of his own was missed.

Keppel, too, wished to fight again as soon as his line was re-formed. But in spite of his signals to form line and a message to the same effect sent to Palliser by frigate, the rear division hung back. Not until Palliser's ships were called forward one by one by individual signal did they make a move. By this time evening was drawing on and it was too late to renew the action. During the night d'Orvilliers quitted the scene and made for Brest, at which Keppel also turned for home.

The first battle of the war had been an indecisive skirmish and was of importance only on account of its aftermath. The ugly and demoralising spirit of faction was once again evoked in the British fleet by the questionable behaviour of Palliser. Keppel had magnanimously made no criticism of it in his despatch after the battle, but an account derogatory to Palliser was published anonymously in the newspaper the *Morning Intelligence*. A furious letter from Palliser to Keppel with a demand that he should publish a version written by Palliser met with Keppel's refusal to add anything to what he had written in his despatch. Palliser therefore wrote to the *Morning Post* a letter not only exculpating himself but charging Keppel with mismanagement of the battle.

A madness seems to have seized Palliser who rushed blindly on to his own destruction, aided and abetted by the Admiralty, who agreed to court martial Keppel on charges brought by Palliser.

Public feeling rose to fever-pitch in Keppel's favour when the court assembled in January 1779 at Portsmouth; the accused travelled there in company with the Royal Dukes of Cumberland and Gloucester, the Dukes of Portland, Richmond and Bolton, the Marquis of Rockingham, the Marquis of Granby, and Burke, Fox and Sheridan. At his acquittal five weeks later the same company and sixty naval captains escorted the hero of the hour back to his house to the sound of bands blaring 'Rule Britannia' and 'See the Conquering Hero Comes'. Palliser, in contrast, barely escaped with his life from the Portsmouth mob. In London his house was wrecked and his possessions burnt in the street, while the houses of the Prime Minister and Lord Sandwich were invaded by a mob and the windows smashed.

The Freedom of the City of London followed for Keppel amidst scenes of fantastic enthusiasm, his carriage drawn by sailors who rigged a huge blue ensign over it. London went mad in honour of 'Little Keppel'. Rodney, kicking his heels at his house in Cleveland Row, St. James's, must have been a witness of much of it. Politically he was by now, like Palliser, a Tory and a 'King's Friend', but he had always set his face against the intrusion of politics—of 'faction'—into the Service. Keppel, seven years his junior and with a similar aristocratic background, had been a life-long friend and was to remain so in spite of opposing political allegiances. The sight of the Navy split into two warring political camps can only have disgusted Rodney. He was one day to express himself furiously at signs of a similar spirit in a fleet under his command. Nevertheless the widespread mistrust of the administration and of the Admiralty by senior naval officers was eventually to act to his advantage.

Meanwhile he was to be seen and heard at every gathering of the fashionable and influential, holding forth at length on matters nautical and on the correct strategy with which to confound the King's enemies. Wraxall noted that Rodney 'talked much and freely upon every Subject; concealing nothing in the course of Conversation, regardless who were present; and dealt his Censures, as well as his Praises, with imprudent Liberality; qualities which necessarily procured him many Enemies, particularly in his own Profession.' Whigs he antagonised by his attitude to the American colonists whom he looked upon as rebels to be chastised without scruple, while the Tories were by no means convinced of the soundness of one who had so recently been in the opposing camp.

While the dissensions at home were advertising to the world and to Britain's enemies the low state of morale in the Navy, across the Atlantic Byron had suffered a defeat in which only d'Estaing's incompetence saved the British from disaster.

News of the declaration of war had not reached either the French or British commanders in the West Indies until the beginning of September 1778. The French had no man-of-war bigger than a frigate in those waters, but the Marquis de Bouillé, Governor of Martinique, had at once embarked 2,000 troops and captured Dominica, taking the weak garrison by surprise. With Martinique, St Lucia and Guadeloupe already in their hands, this gave the French possession of the whole chain of windward islands and of all the best harbours in the Antilles.

The news of war reached Barrington, the British commander, at Barbados. He had two ships of the line only and with the news came instructions to stay where he was until the arrival of Commodore Hotham from North America with an expeditionary force.

It was not until 4th November that Hotham sailed from New York with five ships of the line and 5,000 troops under General James Grant. On the same day d'Estaing had left Boston with his squadron of thirteen battleships and had also steered for the West Indies, arriving at Fort Royal, Martinique on 9th December. The next day Hotham reached Barbados. There was not a moment to lose in implementing the Government's plan, following Rodney's advice, of seizing St Lucia before d'Estaing could interpose his superior force.

On 12th December the expedition was on its way, and the next day anchored in the Grand Cul de Sac, a small but secure harbour two miles south of the larger Carenage. Troops were landed at once. So rapidly and vigorously did they act that by the afternoon of the 14th they had captured Morne Fortuné, the fortified French headquarters, and were in control of the shore line from the north side of the Carenage to the Grand Cul de Sac.

The French standard had hardly been lowered when a frigate under a press of sail was sighted approaching. As she closed it was

90]

seen that she was the *Ariadne*, flying the signal for 'enemy approaching'. Her captain brought news of twelve enemy ships of the line and a number of frigates. It was d'Estaing who, on his way to attack Barbados, had changed direction on hearing of events at St Lucia.

Though threatened by a greatly superior force, the British commanders, naval and military, awaited the enemy's attack with the greatest confidence. D'Estaing, finding the batteries commanding the Carenage in British hands, led his squadron to attack Barrington who had anchored his seven warships in a line across the mouth of the Grand Cul de Sac, covering his transports farther up the bay. Twice d'Estaing's line sailed past the British exchanging broadsides. It was to little effect. Impatiently d'Estaing, who had made his name as a soldier and only recently turned his talents to the sea, decided to land his troops at Gros Islet Bay, some six miles north of the Carenage and attack the British positions from the rear. On the 16th he led his men personally to the assault, delivered with courage and élan, but repulsed three times with crippling casualties.

Driven off by sea and by land, d'Estaing sailed away in despair, leaving St Lucia with its splendid harbour of the Carenage and an advanced base at Gros Islet Bay in British hands for the rest of the war.

During the winter and the following spring both sides reinforced their squadrons in the West Indies, the British by the addition of ten ships of the line under Byron, who took over the command from Barrington. By the end of June 1779 the French had built up their strength to twenty-five of the line against Byron's twenty-one. With this superiority d'Estaing set out to capture the smaller British islands of the windward group. St Vincent was captured at one stroke, whereupon the French admiral moved on to Grenada. This, too, had fallen after a brief defence when Byron arrived off the island on 6th July.

At daybreak he sighted the French fleet emerging from St George's Harbour and forming line as they drew clear, one by one, from the huddle of ships in the anchorage. Byron, who wrongly believed himself superior in numbers, equally wrongly thought he had caught the enemy unawares and in confusion. Seeing the signal for 'General Chase' broken out at the masthead

D

of Byron's flagship, the British ships surged forward and sailed into action piecemeal against a superior enemy in line. The result was inevitable. The first four British ships to come into action suffered severely and were disabled. Three of them drifted helplessly to leeward and only an unaccountable lack of enterprise on the part of d'Estaing prevented them from being captured. Byron was glad enough to break off the action and shepherd his cripples back to harbour, leaving Grenada in French hands.

Byron's defeat helped to bring Britain's naval prestige still lower, though it had by no means plumbed the depths yet. These were to be reached as a result of events in home waters. There, England was about to be faced by a renewed alliance between France and Spain. Keppel's and Byron's lack of success was encouraging the Spaniards to believe that Britain's sea-power was on the wane. The opportunity had come, perhaps, to recover Gibraltar and Minorca as well as to humble the Navy which had so often defeated them in the past. By 4th June they had declared themselves ready and the French fleet at Brest (still commanded by d'Orvilliers) sailed, thirty of the line, to join up with a Spanish fleet of thirty-six.

The combination would make a force numerically overwhelming in opposition to the thirty-five ships of the line available to form Britain's Grand Fleet, and a grandiose scheme of invasion had been prepared. The alarm which spread in England amounted to panic. Early in July a Royal Proclamation ordered all horses and cattle to be driven inland; booms were placed across the entrance to Plymouth Harbour and ships prepared to be sunk in the harbour mouth. To add to the fear of invasion there was anxiety for the safety of 200 merchant ships on their way home in convoy from Jamaica and another rich convoy from the East Indies. The Grand Fleet was at sea cruising in the mouth of the Channel; but it was, on paper, inadequate to deal with the huge Franco-Spanish fleet which appeared in the Channel at the end of July and there cruised unopposed for six weeks in sight of the English coast.

The British Grand Fleet meanwhile had taken up a position some fifty miles to the westward of the Scilly Isles. It was commanded by Sir Charles Hardy, sixty-three years of age but old for his years, brought out from slippered retirement as

92]

Governor of Greenwich Hospital. Keppel, after his court martial, had refused to serve further an administration which had put him on trial for his life at the instigation of an officer junior to him. Howe had taken the same line on his return from North America, as had a number of other admirals. Barrington, returning as a wounded hero after his brilliant operation at St Lucia and the valiant part he had played in the Battle of Grenada, had been offered the command; but he, too, declined to serve as a Commander-in-Chief while Sandwich was at the head of the Admiralty.

Admirals of pronounced Whig sympathies were in any case barred by the King's insistence that any candidate for office or command was expected wholeheartedly to support the war against the colonies. Rodney certainly qualified from this point of view. He never ceased to press his claims for command. Sandwich's lack of response embittered him against his one-time friend and patron for a time. But the First Lord laboured under very real difficulty in the matter, on account of Sir George's financial bankruptcy. In that age every holder of an office under the Crown was expected to feather his nest by manipulation of accounts. Not the least forward in such activity were naval captains who regularly drew the pay of imaginary members of their ships' companies or of those who had died but were kept on the books for pay and victuals. How much more opportunity, then, was there for a Commander-in-Chief on a foreign station through whose hands might filter large sums for the supply of stores and victuals! The temptation for one so desperately in need as Rodney might be irresistible. A minister with so many enemies seeking for any means to discredit him cannot be blamed for hesitating. As Sandwich wrote to Lady Rodney:

'If Sir George will consider the thing impartially, he will see that, though his merit as a sea officer is undeniable, there are reasons that make it impossible for me to prevail on His Majesty to appoint him to the command of a foreign squadron . . . as a man in office, your husband has deprived me of the power of being useful to him.'

Sir George evidently did consider the thing impartially after this. He set about clearing up his financial tangle. In return for an annual payment he borrowed a large capital sum and was soon writing to a friend:

'As my annuitants have made a proposal which I have reason to think will in a great measure relieve me from my present situation . . . . it will be the means of all my creditors being amply satisfied . . . . the sooner it takes place the sooner Lord Sandwich's reasons for not employing me will cease.'

Nevertheless, for the time being there was no opening at home. The Biblical axiom that 'a prophet is not without honour, save in his own country', was borne out at this time by a letter Rodney received from a friend in Paris, a Monsieur de Clonard.

'Though as a Frenchman,' it read, 'I ought to be sorry at finding you employed at the head of a numerous squadron because, without flattery, I am convinced no man would execute the trust reposed in him with more valour and ability, yet I own to you I cannot help looking with an impatient eye at every newspaper in hopes of reading that Admiral Rodney has hoisted his flag at Spithead. I begin to find that my good wishes for your welfare outweigh my patriotism on this occasion. It gives me pain to find you unemployed, but indeed we have no right to be astonished at any thing that happens on your side of the water—your Court-Martials, your accusations, the manner and time of forming them, are all of a piece with the rest. I have been told your friend Jemmy jockeyed you out of the East India command and that his endeavours will be against you upon every other occasion.'

This was unjust to Sandwich. Apart from the difficulties in the way of helping him to a command, Rodney had probably made it clear that he was prepared to wait for an opening in the West Indies. He had pointed out in a paper called for by Sandwich in March 1779 that, 'In all probability the great stress of war will be carried on in the West Indies and on the coasts of America.' He had gone on to demonstrate how, by taking advantage of the seasonal cessation of campaigning weather in North America and the West Indies, the one beginning as the other ended, an economy could be made in the number of ships needed on the other side of the Atlantic, thus strengthening the fleet in home waters. It involved a certain risk and, no doubt, if the plan were to be implemented, the Admiralty would prefer to have its instigator do so and take the blame if it went wrong.

Meanwhile Hardy was proving himself sadly unfitted for the command at home at this critical moment so reminiscent of 1588 and the arrival of the Spanish Armada in the Channel. As Chief of Staff he had Richard Kempenfelt, probably the most astute and thoughtful naval officer of the day, whose comment on the situation shows how d'Orvilliers might have been handled in the same way as Medina Sidonia. Kempenfelt reported regularly to Charles Middleton, later Lord Barham, who in 1778 had begun his long career in naval administration as Controller of the Navy. To him he wrote, 'Twenty-five sail of the line, coppered, would be sufficient to hazard and tease this great, unwieldy, combined armada, so as to prevent them effecting anything; hanging continually upon them, ready to catch at any opportunity of a separation from night, gale or fog; to dart upon the separated, to cut off any convoys of provisions coming to them.'

Alas, Hardy was no Howard of Effingham or Francis Drake. While the Franco-Spanish fleet lorded it off Plymouth he held to his position to the westward until the end of August when, beating its way past the Scillies, the British fleet was sighted and shamefully chased up Channel.

Fortunately for Britain, however, d'Orvilliers' fleet shared other similarities with that of Medina Sidonia. It was short of water and provisions. It was largely manned by landsmen and soldiers who were ravaged by sickness and dying at a frightening rate. A mixed force of French and Spanish ships, it was difficult to manoeuvre. It lacked pilots with a knowledge of the English Channel so that it sailed 'more or less by chance and without knowledge of the dangers and currents along the coast; the Spaniards complain about this even more than we do and grumble unceasingly'. A westerly gale could drive the clumsy-sailing battleships far up the Channel whence, like the Armada before them, they might be unable to return. D'Orvilliers complained that many of his captains were 'mediocre'. 'We must centre our hopes on bravery and firmness,' he wrote. 'The combined fleet will be too numerous and of too little experience to expect good manoeuvring.' The invasion plans, to implement which he had gone to sea, were first delayed beyond the season suitable for such an operation, then changed and eventually abandoned.

On sailing from Brest on 4th June, d'Orvilliers had expected to be joined at once by the Spanish squadron. Disappointed, he had sailed south to a rendezvous off Cape Finisterre. It was not until 23rd July that the Spaniards had appeared and then it had been found that, contrary to pre-arranged agreement, they had no knowledge of French signals. Six weeks of summer weather had been wasted in uneventful cruising while the crews were being ravaged by an epidemic. It was thus not until 14th August that d'Orvilliers had entered the Channel—too late to intercept the Jamaica convoy, and with a fleet 'losing in efficiency from day to day'. Soon after the ineffectual chase of the British fleet, d'Orvilliers was ordered back to Brest, where the combined fleet anchored on 14th September.

The threat to England's shores was over for the time being. Elsewhere, however, it was intensified. The Spaniards called home their fleet from Brest to support the siege of Gibraltar which had been begun in June 1779. By the end of the year, blockade by land and sea had brought the garrison close to starvation. At the same time the French were preparing a strong naval force to go to the West Indies where the valuable colony of Jamaica was the lure. With the summer this force could establish a naval superiority on the American coast and wrest from the British the one advantage they had in their struggle with the Colonies. With these widely separated commitments and the need to protect their own shores when the French decided to renew their invasion schemes—as it was certain they would do—the British Government was at its wits' end how to find sufficient force to stave off catastrophe.

Parliament had voted the huge sum of £21 millions for the Navy and authorised the recruitment of 85,000 seamen and marines; but much time was needed to see the results. Meanwhile, to save the Empire from dissolution, a man was needed whom the Government could trust to act with vigour and zeal in command in the main theatre across the Atlantic and make the best use of such force as was available.

Such a one was the fierce old gentleman eating his heart out with frustration in Cleveland Row. The prospect was too charged with dire possibilities for the Government to ignore him any longer. Sandwich submitted Sir George Rodney's name to the

King. To dispel any doubts the sovereign might have had, he added:

'I omitted to mention to your Majesty that, if Sir George Rodney should from his indigence have any temptation to take advantage of purchasing stores or anything else of that sort, he will have no means of doing it at present, as there will be a Commissioner on the spot thro' whose hands all that business must be transacted.'

In October 1779, Sir George Rodney, Admiral of the White and Rear-Admiral of England, was appointed Commander-in-Chief on the station he had so long coveted and pressed for—the Leeward Islands.

VIII

So in October 1779 George Rodney set off by coach down the Portsmouth Road on his way to hoist his flag in the *Sandwich*, a stately three-decker of ninety guns. The spare figure in the blue, white and gold of an admiral's uniform reclined uneasily in the corner, a bandaged foot on the seat opposite resting beside a gleaming new gold-laced cocked hat. The lined face with the sunken cheeks winced from time to time as the coach gave a heavy lurch. The man in a sober brown suit sitting beside the admiral shot an anxious, quizzical look at his patient. For this was Dr Gilbert Blane, Rodney's personal physician, whom he had persuaded to accompany him to sea and help to keep at bay the attacks of illness which so often prostrated him.

For the tide of fortune had turned very late. Rodney was now sixty-one. Not a great age for a man of normal health and experience; but the combination of long periods confined to the contaminated living space of overcrowded wooden ships of war, the damp, cold discomfort of winters at sea, the coarse, badly-cooked food, the heedless maltreatment of the system which made up an eighteenth-century gentleman's regular dissipations, and the mental stress of financial desperation, had taken its toll of his constitution. The physical signs were the gout in hands and feet, recurrent fevers—perhaps the residual effects of malaria picked up in the West Indies—and urinary difficulties. Temperamentally he had become more testy and intolerant.

Nevertheless his spirit was unimpaired, as the eagle look in his eyes proclaimed. Now that his chance had come at long last, he was brimming with determination to make his dreams come true; to lead a regenerated British fleet to victory and wipe out the shame of the past two years. He was eager to be away. Five ships of the line had been allocated for him to take as reinforcement for the Leeward Islands Station where he was confident the naval war must be lost or won. Under his protection was to go the season's trade convoy for the West Indies.

At the same time an expedition to relieve Gibraltar was preparing, and there was the trade convoy for the East Indies, awaiting escort clear of French or Spanish attack. It was decided to despatch the whole in one huge armada under the command of Rodney. Fifteen ships of the line from the Channel Fleet would join his flag. Having relieved Gibraltar and Minorca, Rodney would go on across the Atlantic, and the Channel Squadron under Vice-Admiral Digby would return home.

Going on board the *Sandwich*, where his white admiral's flag with the red St George's Cross was broken out at the mainmast head, Rodney was confronted with a gloomy report on the state of his command. Hardly a ship was ready for sea. Extensive repairs were needed to most of them. The materials and equipment necessary were lacking. The officials responsible were indolent. Rodney set about spurring them into activity. Messages of biting reproach, for all the stately eighteenth-century language in which they were couched, were addressed to those responsible.

Discipline in the ships of the Channel fleet he found had deplorably deteriorated under the slack hand of Sir Charles Hardy and his seventy-year-old successor, Geary. (Samuel Hood's view on the matter has been quoted earlier.) Hawke, too, had commented that Hardy had 'allowed the discipline of the fleet to come to nothing'. Similarly Barrington was to write to Sandwich 'what I have seen at Portsmouth during the short time I have been second-in-command of the fleet would have made me run mad had I been Commander-in-Chief.'

Rodney addressed himself to those most responsible, his captains; they felt the firm hand of authority on the wheel of affairs. They bestirred themselves; but they did not look with affection on their stern, uncompromising master.

Rodney himself was being driven also—by his ambition, his need to re-establish a reputation, by a sincere and fiery patriotism as well as by a Government desperate to save a situation rapidly becoming catastrophic. He strained every nerve to get his fleet ready, but when December came in, many of the ships were still short of stores and provisions. On the 8th, Sandwich appealed to him, 'For God's sake go to sea without delay. You cannot conceive of what importance it is to yourself, to me, and to the public, that you should not lose this fair wind; if you do, I shall not only hear of it in Parliament, but in places to which I pay more attention. . . . I must once more repeat to you, that any delay in your sailing will have the most disagreeable consequences.'

By the 11th Rodney was ready to go, even though many of his ships of the line were incompletely stored and his frigates would have to follow later. But now the wind was foul, back in its prevailing south-westerly quarter. To Lady Rodney he wrote from Spithead:

'I have now received my sailing orders and shall sail the moment the wind comes fair; when that will be, Heaven knows, for it blows hard at south-west. . . . Everything here is noise and hurry. The wind continuing westerly gives more time to the fleet to get ready. I wish I was once at sea. You know then an admiral has not a tenth part of the trouble and fatigue as when in port. Ministers and merchants are eager to have me gone, but I cannot command the seasons.'

Again, five days later, 'I wish to Heaven the wind would come fair that I might get to sea. You know I should then only have to discipline the fleet, and have done with writing, a thing I detest; yet every hour, day and night, I am sending or receiving expresses. Even now at five o'clock in the morning I can scarce catch a moment to know how you and the dear girls are.'

For another week, while Rodney fretted, the wind held steady and strong in the south-west. At last on the 23rd December—'It is now stark calm, and in all appearances it will soon produce an easterly wind. Should that be the case, to-morrow, early in the morning we shall leave the port and put to sea with a noble fleet and a convoy of three hundred merchant ships from the Downs.'

So the great armada on which rested the hopes of the King and his Government to stave off disaster, got ponderously under way. (In the flagship's gun-room was Mr Midshipman John Rodney, not yet fifteen, the admiral's eldest son by his second wife.) There remained much to be done to make an efficient force of the squadron of men-of-war. One of Rodney's last letters before sailing, addressed to Lord George Germain, Secretary for the Colonies, indicates the line of conduct he intended to pursue.

'The delays that have been at this port and the almost total loss of naval discipline is almost beyond comprehension. It shall be mine to restore it.'

By the first day of 1780 the fleet was clear of the Channel. By 4th January it was safe to send the trade for the West Indies on its way unescorted. Four days later the remainder rounded Cape Finisterre. That Rodney's luck had turned was made apparent at daybreak on 8th January. Against the dawn light to the north-eastward were silhouetted the masts and sails of twenty-two ships. They could only be French or Spanish. Without hesitation the admiral loosed his men-of-war in chase.

The strangers proved to be a Spanish convoy of deep-laden store-ships and victuallers out of San Sebastian on their way to supply the Spanish fleet lying at Cadiz. Taken by surprise, they and their escort—consisting of a 64-gun ship, the *Guipuscoano*, four frigates and two corvettes—surrendered almost without firing a shot as they were overhauled. The *Guipuscoano* proved to be a fine, well-armed and well-built ship. In honour of the Duke of Clarence, serving as a midshipman in the fleet, Rodney re-named her the *Prince William* and made her escort to the captured store-ships which were sent back to England. The victuallers he kept with him to swell the supplies for Gibraltar.

It was a splendid start to Rodney's enterprise. The captured cargoes were as urgently needed by the Spanish fleet as they were welcome in the dockyards of Portsmouth and Plymouth and the beleaguered fortress of Gibraltar. It was to be followed by an even greater success. As the huge array of ships sailed slowly down the Spanish coast, Rodney's frigates stopped and spoke with a number of neutral merchantmen bound northward. From them they learnt of the presence of a Spanish squadron of fourteen of the line patrolling off Cape St Vincent.

It seemed unlikely that the enemy would allow themselves to be engaged by so superior a force as Rodney commanded; but the Spaniards' reputation for a lack of preparedness and good order offered some hope. As Cape St Vincent loomed ahead, Rodney signalled for all ships to prepare for battle, so that all was in readiness when the Cape was rounded on the morning of the

[101

16th January and the fleet bore away south-eastwards for the Straits of Gibraltar. In the line-of-battle ships the cabin bulk-heads had been 'shaken' and stowed away, the guns had been stripped of their rough-weather lashings and rigged with their operating tackle; ammunition—round shot and canister, flannel wads and cartridges of gunpowder—filled the ready-use stowages round them; shot-plugs, oakum and tallow for the carpenters to stop any shot-holes were supplied and laid ready on each deck. On the stained mess-tables in the cockpits were laid out the forceps, saws and knives which comprised the simple equipment required for the rough surgery of the day. All that remained to be done to go into action was to beat to quarters and send each man and boy to his assigned station.

And at 1 p.m. came the signal that everyone was waiting for. A flutter of flags at the masthead of the *Bedford* (74), in the van, reported a fleet to the south-eastward. On board the flagship, the admiral was confined to his cabin, tortured by an agonising attack of gout. The news being brought to him by his flag-captain, Walter Young, Rodney ordered the signal for Line Abreast to be made. It was not to be imagined that if the enemy fleet was as weak as had been reported it would stay to fight. If, on the other hand, the main body of the Spanish fleet had come out from Cadiz to intercept him, it was necessary for Rodney to preserve his well-ordered line during the approach.

But against all expectations, as the enemy ships rose up over the horizon, not only were they seen to number only eleven of the line and two frigates, but, instead of losing no time in making good their escape, they were leisurely pausing to form line of battle from the disordered bunch in which they had been cruising. The Spanish admiral, Don Juan de Langara, had in fact allowed himself to be totally surprised. He had received intelligence of the British relief convoy but had convinced himself that it would be without a strong escort. No frigates had been thrown out to bring early warning. Now, on the wings of a rising westerly gale retribution was bearing down.

In the *Sandwich*, Rodney's flag-captain kept him informed of the situation. Not many hours of light were left of the short winter day in which to come up with the enemy. The weather bore all the signs of a coming gale. Young suggested signalling for a

102]

General Chase which would release the British ships from keeping station in line and allow the fastest to press on ahead. With the night and storm coming on, it meant taking a heavy risk to surrender control of the large fleet and let the ships plunge forward into a mêlée. And meanwhile the priceless convoy must be left unshepherded and defenceless.

Rodney pondered for a time, then boldly decided. Not only did he agree to the signal for the chase; he added that for engaging the enemy from to leeward. This would put his ships between the enemy and their line of retreat into port; but it also accepted the risk of a lee shore on to which in the stormy night disabled ships might be driven. Fortunately, however, there would be a full moon. And so the great ships thrust forward under every sail their straining masts could bear, while down below the drums beat the call to action stations.

It was soon clear that if the enemy were caught it would be a running fight with the British ships coming one by one into action; for some of the ships of the Channel fleet had copper-sheathing on their hulls, adopted primarily as a protection against the destructive teredo worm of tropical waters. It also prevented bottoms from getting foul with weed and barnacles. The coppered ships now forged ahead. By four o'clock the *Defence*, *Resolution* and *Edgar*, seventy-fours, were up with the enemy. Pouring broadsides into the rear ships of the Spanish line, they pressed on towards the van. That no doubt should exist as to what was expected of his captains during the night, Rodney, coming into action at dusk, hoisted the signal to engage the enemy closely.

In the fading daylight it had not been possible to make out the composition of the enemy force. Rodney wanted no mistake to be made as to his flagship's role in the battle. He sent for Mr Silas Hyscot, the sailing master of the *Sandwich*. 'Master,' he said, 'this ship is not to pay any attention to merchantmen or small ships of war. Lay me alongside of the biggest ship, the admiral if there be one.'

Already a Spanish 70-gun ship, the *San Domingo*, had blown up. At six o'clock another had struck. By the light of the moon which poured down on the wild scene of storm and battle, the tall ships surged on before the wind, their broadsides thundering.

Five other Spaniards, including the flagship, the 80-gun

Fenix, had struck their colours, before two in the morning when the *Sandwich* was laid alongside the leading ship, the *Monarca*. One terrible broadside from the much more powerful *Sandwich*, and the Spanish colours came fluttering down. By now a high sea was running. Somewhere near were the dangerous shallows along the Spanish coast. It was time to call a halt and secure the prizes. Already one, the *San Augustin*, had taken advantage of confusion and darkness to slip away. It was tricky and hazardous work to shift prisoners and send prize crews to get control of the shattered ships of the enemy. At daybreak the two junior flag-ships, the *Royal George* and *Prince George*, reported that soundings showed them to be in shoal water. It was with great difficulty that Rodney's ships and prizes could claw themselves to windward and safety. Two prizes, the *San Julian* and the *San Eugenio*, drifted helplessly to leeward, one driving ashore, the other being retaken by the Spaniards.

Nevertheless four ships and the person of the Spanish admiral remained in Rodney's hands. The *San Domingo* had been destroyed, leaving only one survivor. Only four of Langara's eleven ships of the line escaped, much damaged.

It was with justifiable satisfaction that Rodney dictated to his secretary William Pagett his report to the Admiralty to 'congratulate their Lordships on a signal victory obtained by his Majesty's ships under my command over the squadron commanded by Don Juan de Langara wherein the Spanish admiral and the greatest part of his squadron were either taken or destroyed.'

Once the decision had been taken to accept the risks of night action on a lee shore the battle was never in doubt, having in mind the odds against the Spaniards. Rodney acknowledged in his report 'the gallant behaviour of the admirals, captains, officers and men I had the honour to command,' and 'ventured to affirm, though the enemy made a gallant defence, that had the weather proved but even moderate, or had the action happened in the day, not one of their squadron had escaped'. Privately, however, he had a different tale to tell. Faction and back-biting evidently raised their heads again as soon as the guns fell silent, some of the accusations apparently being levelled at Rodney himself. Disloyalty to their Commander-in-Chief was certainly rife

104]

amongst his captains, many of whom had resented his reproofs. It was fed by the encouragement given to them to write private reports to friends at the Navy Board or the Admiralty. Thus the flag-Captain, Young, wrote to Middleton, the Controller, claiming that it was only because of his urging that the ailing admiral could be roused to give the signal for the chase and that Rodney 'on account of his ill state of health and natural irresolution' wished to 'have the ships called off from the chase'. Young did not hesitate to say the same to brother captains. The admiral, on the other hand, wrote in glowing terms of the conduct of his flag-captain in whom he continued to repose complete confidence until Young's death in the West Indies in the following year.

Rodney, unable to leave his cabin, had naturally to act upon accounts of the situation brought to him by Young. Equally naturally common courtesy would make him discuss possible courses of action with his flag-captain. Gilbert Blane, the physician, who was present, records just that—a discussion followed by a decision by Rodney. But the decisions could be no one's but Rodney's. The risks were to his reputation and to no one else's.

That such calumny was going the rounds did not escape Rodney. To his wife he wrote disdainfully, 'One thing I can say without dread of reproach—that I can defy envy, malice or even villainy to tax me with not having done my duty even to the utmost extent; but without a thorough change in naval affairs, the discipline of our navy will be lost. I could say much, but will not. You will hear it from themselves. I have done them all like honour, but it was because I would not have the world believe that there were officers slack in their duty.'

To Lord Sandwich he was more explicit. 'It is with concern that I must tell your Lordship that my brother officers still continue their absurd and illiberal custom of arraigning each other's conduct. My ears have been attempted to listen to the scandal; I have treated it with the contempt it deserved. In my opinion every officer did his duty to his King and Country. I have reported it so. . . . The unhappy difference between Mr Keppel and Sir Hugh Palliser has almost ruined the Navy. Discipline in a very great measure is lost . . . and officers presume to find fault *and think*, when their duty is implicit obedience. Faction and Party is so predominant in the Navy. . . . I see plainly the necessity of the old discipline's being revived, and where I have the honour to command, it shall.' In his reply the First Lord feared 'the picture you give of the faction in your fleet is too well drawn. It is very prevalent here, but not what it was a year ago. Time and moderation, in those that are high in the naval department, will, by degrees, get the better of this bane of our discipline, and of every thing that is valuable and comfortable in the service. . . . I most exceedingly applaud your resolution to shut your ears against the illiberal language of your officers, who are inclined to arraign each other's conduct. I have heard some whispers of the same kind, but have followed your example in giving no countenance to them knowing that they proceed from the private animosities that now distract the service'.

Meanwhile the news of the fleet's double success had been rapturously received in an England which had for so long been treated to nothing but sorry tales of incompetence or defeat. In a letter from his eldest daughter Jane, aged thirteen, he heard how,

'Everybody almost adores you; and every mouth is full of your praise. Both your letters are reckoned exceeding good ones. The Tower and the Park guns were fired last Monday; and that night and the next there were illuminations. . . . There are a great number of songs going about the streets, the choruses always, "Brave Rodney for ever". . . . I congratulate you upon the thanks of both Houses of Parliament. It is nothing new to you as you had them last war. I have loved Lord North ever since he spoke in the House about you. I hear the King is exceedingly pleased with you. He said at the drawing-room, that he knew when Rodney was out, everything would go well. Lord Oxford told it to mamma, at the Duchess of Chandos' last night.'

Lady Rodney wrote that 'it is not only a source of gratification to individuals, but to the nation in general; and the ministerial people feel it very sensibly. It is a lucky stroke for them at this juncture.' Sandwich indeed was profoundly relieved at the happy turn of events. 'I scarcely know,' he wrote, 'how to find words to congratulate you enough upon your late glorious successes, and upon the eminent service you have done your country.'

'The worst of my enemies now allow that I have pitched upon a man who knows his duty, and is a brave, honest and able officer. I will not tire you with panegyric, but am not the less eager in dealing out to all around me the praises due to your merit. I have obtained you the thanks of both Houses of Parliament. In the House of Lords I made the motion myself; and mentioned what, perhaps, you were not aware of, that you had taken more line-of-battle ships than had been captured in any one action in either of the two last preceding wars.'

The Spanish ships taken were indeed, in Rodney's words, 'as fine ships as ever swam. They are now completely refitted, manned and put in the line of battle, and, I will answer for them, will do their duty as English men-of-war, should the enemy give them an opportunity.' Their addition to the Navy List went some way towards reducing the superiority of the combined Franco-Spanish fleet over the British and reduced the haunting fear of a repetition of d'Orvilliers' mastery of the Channel. Rodney was disappointed therefore not to be given some ships additional to the original force allotted to him as reinforcement for the West Indies. Much was expected of him there. To achieve it he needed the best ships available. Copper-bottomed ships were what he cried out for.

The coppering of ships' hulls, at this time being extended to all ships of the Navy as fast as dockyard facilities would permit, was a development with important implications with regard to the relative sailing qualities of British and French ships, particularly abroad where, in the absence of dry-docks, it was difficult to keep ships' bottoms clean—free of barnacles and weed which multiplied rapidly in tropical waters—as well as to combat the destructive teredo worm. The British were greatly in advance of the French in the fitting of copper sheathing. The first British ship on which it was tried had been a frigate in 1761. By 1779 seventeen ships of the line had been coppered and in the next two years it was to be extended to all ships.

The French, on the other hand, only took to coppering in 1780, their fleet in the West Indies in 1782 still having a number still uncoppered. The better design of their ships from a sailing point of view was thus to a great extent nullified. Writing to Middleton from the West Indies of the advantages of copper Walter

[107

Young said, 'It is impossible for me to describe the advantages attending it and, indeed exceeds the expectation of everyone. The advantage from the helm alone is immense, as they feel them instantly and wear in one third of the distance they ever did; it keeps them tight and covers the neglects in your dockyards from bad caulking; increases their speed in every situation, more particularly in light winds tending to a calm, which is no small advantage in this and every fair weather country.'

These advantages had shown up during the Moonlight Battle when the coppered ships had quickly outstripped the remainder in chase of the enemy.

'I flattered myself,' Rodney wrote to the Admiralty, 'that the greater part of the copper-bottomed ships who sailed with me from England would have been ordered to have accompanied me to the West Indies. I must therefore humbly submit to Their Lordships' consideration whether, considering the state of His Majesty's ships at present in the West Indies, it will be in my power to force the enemy to Battle, without they are equally desirous of it as myself, unless their Lordships are pleased to order an additional number of copper-bottomed or clean ships from England in the lieu of such as they may please to order home.'

In the first flush of delight with Rodney's achievements, Sandwich assured him, 'You shall have copper enough, and you shall have everything that I can give towards proving the truth and regard with which I am your very sincere friend.'

In the meantime, however, Rodney had to be content with the *Sandwich* (90), *Ajax* (74), *Montagu* (74), and *Terrible* (74), when on 18th February 1780 having relieved Gibraltar and Minorca he parted company with the Channel fleet and convoy under Digby and bore away for Barbados. There he arrived on 17th March. Anchoring in Carlisle Bay, he was disgusted to find no message from Hyde Parker, the rear-admiral in command of the station, giving him a rendezvous at which to find him. Nor had any frigates been stationed to windward to intercept him with such information, as he considered should have been done.

Rodney was so ill that he had himself carried ashore. Hardly had he done so than intelligence reached him that Admiral de

Guichen with a French squadron of four ships of the line and a large convoy carrying troops was on passage from Brest and expected to arrive shortly at Martinique. The news had been brought from England in the frigate *Alert* which had touched at Barbados on the 15th before going on to Hyde Parker at Gros Islet Bay, St Lucia; but the captain had not thought to leave any message at Barbados against Rodney's arrival. Thus it was not until the *Alert*'s return on the 20th that Rodney had the vital information. Though he did all in his power, it was too late.

His four ships of the line and the *Alert* were put under the command of Captain Uvedale of the *Ajax* who was instructed to 'proceed without a moment's loss of time' to the northward to try to intercept the French convoy. If the convoy's escort was too powerful to attack, Uvedale was to try to draw the enemy towards Hyde Parker's squadron which was expected to be cruising to the windward of Martinique. Uvedale was soon back with the disheartening news that de Guichen had entered Fort Royal on the 22nd unmolested, with the convoy and *sixteen* ships of the line.

Hyde Parker's failure to take action in good time made a bad impression on Rodney and a poor start to the relations between the two admirals. They were in any case by nature poles apart and fated to get on badly. Parker, an unreflecting, hide-bound naval officer of limited outlook, possessed a bitter, choleric temper which had earned him the nickname of 'Old Vinegar'. It was unlikely to help him to get on good terms with the unbending, distant Rodney.

Parker had allowed inertia to defeat him during the six months he had been in command of the Leeward Islands Station since Byron had returned home in August 1779. On d'Estaing's departure in July, the British had been left in greatly superior strength to the French and had remained so even when reinforcements under de Grasse and La Motte-Picquet had arrived at the end of the hurricane season. Parker had been anxious to take advantage of the situation to recapture some of the islands lost to the French, but he had been unable to rouse either Mr Burt, Governor of the Leeward Islands, or General Prescott in command of the troops.

Then, in February 1780, General Vaughan had arrived. Plans

had been at once concerted for an attack on the island of St Vincent. Parker concentrated his squadron of seventeen of the line at St Lucia. By the third week in March 2,000 troops were embarked in three of the battleships and the frigates. Thus when news of de Guichen's approach reached Parker no squadron was at sea to intercept the French, who were consequently able to concentrate a superior fleet of twenty-two of the line at Fort Royal and themselves go over to the offensive.

Parker admitted his mistake and that he had given all his attention to the projected expedition, as otherwise the squadron 'would infallibly have fallen in with this French convoy and have engaged them before they had made a junction with their ships at Fort Royal'. His regrets did little to mollify his new Commander-in-Chief, however. Rodney was furious at the great opportunity missed. He was thus in a mood of fierce determination to whip the lethargic West India squadron into activity and to impose a taut discipline when he arrived with his four ships of the line at Gros Islet Bay on 27th March and took over the command.

IX

WITH the arrival of Rodney and de Guichen at their respective
bases of Gros Islet Bay in St Lucia, and Fort Royal, Martinique,
the two most skilful naval tacticians of the day faced one another
across forty-five miles of water. In numbers the two fleets were
roughly equal; twenty-one British sail of the line against twenty-
three French. A distinct advantage lay with the French, however.
Apart from the superior design of their ships which usually gave
them the better sailing qualities, de Guichen's were nearly all
fresh out from their home base, thoroughly refitted and with
clean bottoms. Rodney's, apart from the force he had brought
with him, had first suffered the furies of the hurricane season in
the West Indies and then lain idle, their timbers opening under
the heat of the tropical sun, while the ravages of dry-rot and
teredo worm had operated unchecked. Rodney's flag-captain,
Walter Young, was soon to be writing to Middleton, 'If you do
not get home the *Princess Royal*, *Albion*, *Suffolk*, *Magnificent*,
Vigilant, *Trident*, *Stirling Castle*, *Elizabeth* and *Grafton*, they
will in four months share the fate of the *Cornwall* and *Fame* who
are now totally lost. What Admiral Parker did respecting those
ships last hurricane months by keeping them in this country he is
to answer for.'

A further advantage held by the French was in their system of
signalling. British signals had remained virtually unaltered for a
century and were primitive in the extreme. In pursuit of sim-
plicity they were limited to the hoisting of a single flag with
perhaps a pendant below it, variations in the meaning being
achieved by hoisting it on different masts. A Union Jack at the
mizzen peak, for example, ordered the Line Ahead; the same
flag at the mizzen-top ordered the fleet to go about, beginning

with the rear ship. The number of signals possible was thus fairly small and they were used up indicating one or other of the Standing Fighting Instructions or the Additional Fighting Instructions issued by Commanders-in-Chief. No variations of these instructions could be signalled so as to take advantage of some unforeseen development during an engagement.

That the Instructions themselves were issued in a confused, methodless fighting code with no index and were couched in language which must have been difficult to understand even by those used to eighteenth-century syntax, made the situation no easier for a commander aiming at precise manœuvres other than the simplest. At this very time a new code of signals and a revised and enlarged set of Instructions were being devised by Richard Kempenfelt. Much of his inspiration came from studying the French system. They did not come into general use in the Navy until Rodney's day was over. Lack of them was to play a large part in events about to unfold in the West Indies.

The two commanders were well matched and in many ways of the same school. Both believed in the supreme importance of precise manœuvre by rigidly controlled formations. Subordinate admirals and captains were strictly bound by signalled instructions and departed from them at their peril. De Guichen was admired in his own service for the nicety with which he could handle a formation. D'Estaing, in particular, recorded his admiration for de Guichen's elegant and intricate manœuvres when he watched him anchor his squadron in formation. Rodney similarly considered de Guichen the most capable commander in the French Navy. He was eager to cross swords with an opponent so worthy of his steel. Had his opponent been of the same mind, there can be little doubt that the greatest sea battle of the era of sail must have ensued.

The Frenchman, however, was influenced not only by the basic doctrine of the French Navy, discussed previously, which eschewed the idea of a battle between equal forces being fought to a decision, but also by his instructions which bade him only 'to keep the sea, so far as the force maintained by the English in the Windward Islands would permit, *without too far compromising* the fleet entrusted to him'.

Rodney, on the other hand, was always inspired by a

112]

thoroughly offensive spirit, ready to give battle even to a superior force of the enemy, confident that his skill in manœuvre would nullify the enemy's advantage in numbers. But to achieve this he needed a fleet trained, disciplined and flexible. The West Indies squadron was far from any of these. The indiscipline of individual captains, against which every senior officer of the time inveighed, had to be rooted out before he could rely upon his tactical manœuvres being correctly performed; and the long idleness in an enervating climate had banished the seamanlike skill needed to keep good station with unwieldy ships of the line.

Rodney set about rectifying matters with an unbending severity which did nothing to earn him the affection of those upon whom the rod of correction fell. His methods have been un-favourably compared with those of Nelson in the following epoch; but Nelson's 'band of brothers' was never the contentious, back-biting, intriguing set of men, divided into warring political factions, with whom Rodney had to work. In Nelson's day, discipline in the Navy had been restored—by Rodney, amongst others. The way was thus open for encouragement of intelligent anticipation or interpretation of orders in accordance with the known wishes of the commander. Rodney had no time—nor could he rely upon a sufficient fund of goodwill—to woo his subordinates into a state of loyal affection on which he could rely. He felt—and made it known—that he had to have implicit obedience, even *unthinking* obedience. If he could not make the fleet into a happy one, he would at least make it disciplined and efficient.

Five days after his arrival at St Lucia the business of taking over command from Hyde Parker, establishing the new fleet organisation, wooding and watering the ships, was complete. On 2nd April the signal to weigh anchor was broken out at the mast-head of the *Sandwich*. Off Gros Islet Bay the fleet assembled and under a flood of orders, exhortations and reprimands from the Commander-in-Chief, formed up and bore away northwards for Fort Royal, Martinique. Rodney was throwing down the gauntlet to de Guichen.

The French admiral had been no less energetic. Within a day of his arrival he had put to sea again to attempt the recapture of St Lucia. He had found Hyde Parker's squadron at anchor and, like d'Estaing before him, had been frustrated by the fluky, contrary winds in the lee of the island. Disappointed, he had withdrawn to Fort Royal. There he set about preparing for an expedition, in concert with the Marquis de Bouillé, Governor of Martinique, to capture Barbados. The appearance of Rodney's fleet off his base, boldly closing the harbour mouth, 'near enough to count all their guns and at times within random shot of some of their forts', failed to draw de Guichen. Battle to decide in one decisive clash of arms the dominion of the sea in the West Indies and American waters was no part of the French strategy. Though victory would bring about the extinction of the British Empire in the West, the French persisted in a belief that the same results could be achieved with less risk by merely neutralising the British fleet so as to allow their own invading forces to reach their objective unmolested.

Two days of offering battle bringing no results, Rodney returned with his fleet to Gros Islet Bay, leaving fast-sailing frigates to watch Fort Royal and send warning of any move by the enemy. In the middle of the night of 15th April, the alarm came. By the morning of the 16th, Rodney's fleet was reaching northwards up the lee side of Martinique, past Fort Royal—which he could see was empty.

De Guichen had, in fact, got under way on the 13th. A convoy for San Domingo had sailed at the same time. To cover it before doubling back towards Barbados, which was his main objective, he had gone north-westward. His progress held down to that of the unwieldy convoy, he had not got far, and at noon on the 16th a multitude of sails on the horizon to leeward told Rodney that his moment had come. The 'General Chase' was hoisted. Under a cloud of sail the line-of-battle ships surged forward. By five o'clock the enemy were plainly in sight and were counted—twenty-three of the line and attendant frigates. Having sent his convoy away, de Guichen placed himself between it and the enemy and awaited the outcome. By dusk Rodney had closed the distance between the two fleets to a few miles. Against a fleet superior in numbers to his own and in good order, he had no wish for a mêlée in the dark such as that with Langara. Forming his ships into line ahead, and stationing two frigates between the fleets to keep him informed of the enemy's movements, he spent

114]

the night matching manœuvre for manœuvre with de Guichen to preserve his commanding windward position until daylight.

Dawn revealed the two fleets steering to the northwards on parallel courses. The steady trade wind was blowing from the east so both fleets were on the starboard tack. With the first light de Guichen made his first attempt to shake off the enemy. He ordered his fleet to reverse course by tacking, all ships simultaneously. The disarray of his line—not unnatural after a long night of manœuvring—was increased by this move until it extended to some ten miles. Rodney's ships had kept better formation. Spurred by repeated signals from the flagship at dawn, they had corrected the disorder of night. Closing to two cables' length apart—400 yards—their line covered some six miles.

It is perhaps a suitable moment here to remind ourselves of the leisurely pace of relative movement in the encounters between fleets in the age of sail—a slowness not easy for a modern mind to appreciate. A ship of the line was no slim clipper, built for speed or for sailing close to the wind. Her hull was broad in the beam, with a pronounced 'tumble-home'; that is to say, bulging outwards towards the water line; for the weight of her guns was carried high, and this, making for instability had to be counteracted by breadth of beam. With a fair wind, a press of sail, a calm sea and, above all, a clean bottom, she was capable of speeds up to ten knots. When sailing close—and this meant not less than about seventy degrees off the wind—she would be reduced to half that speed under good conditions. When in line of battle the flagship would not carry the maximum sail possible, first because she had to adjust her speed to that of the slowest in the fleet, and second, so as to give all ships something in hand for station-keeping.

The process of forming line out of a disordered array of ships was a long one, with such little variation of speed between the slowest and the fastest; so a commander had to act in good time. A fleet released from control by the signal to chase could not be quickly re-formed if the situation called for it. It was to avoid being caught with his line in disarray that emphasis on good station-keeping was placed by a competent admiral.

Two fleets coming in sight of one another on a clear day were usually several hours sailing apart even if both wished for an encounter—a rare occurrence. Even when on the field of battle and manœuvring for an advantage, there was often time for the Commander-in-Chief to call a frigate alongside for her captain to hoist out a boat to take him on board the flagship for orders. He might then have to pass them to each ship of the line as he sailed along it. An admiral could on occasion call a council of war of flag officers aboard his flagship while in sight of the enemy. An hour might pass between the hoisting of the signal to 'bear down and engage' and the first broadside. As the two fleets floated in stately majesty towards one another, there was plenty of time for captains and admirals to bring out their signal books or the Fighting Instructions and discuss the meaning of obscure passages, just as Byng and his secretary are recorded as doing at Minorca.

Apart from the slow speed of ships the time it took for manœuvres such as tacking or wearing must also be taken into account. Given a fresh breeze and not too rough a sea, a ship of the line could usually go about on to the other tack in about ten minutes. If it was very rough, tacking was probably not feasible, the ship losing all her way as she came up into the wind. She would then miss stays and fall back on to her original tack or get taken aback and gather stern way—neither of which would permit the preservation of any sort of line. Under such conditions it was necessary to wear ship to gain the other tack. In doing this much distance was inevitably lost to leeward. In very light winds it was also difficult to gain sufficient way to complete the manœuvre of tacking. Again, it would be necessary to wear instead, though there were instances of single ships hoisting out their boats to tow the bow round. This would extend the evolution over half an hour or more.

Thus for a fleet to tack or wear, all ships together, required at least fifteen minutes, and at the end of it the formation would probably have lost some of its compactness. To reverse course by tacking or wearing in succession, that is to say the van ship leading round and the remainder following, could take as much as two hours for a fleet of twenty ships, depending on the strength of the wind. Once committed to this manœuvre a commander could do nothing until it was completed without sacrificing all orderly formation.

116]

When considering fleet tactics of the age of sail, their slowness, the irrevocable nature of an evolution once begun, the limited signals available, the impenetrable clouds of smoke which enveloped everything once the guns began to roar, the virtual, immobility of ships as soon as their rigging became damaged— all these must be borne in mind if we are to appreciate the problems of admirals and captains.

But as the sun sprang up out of the blue tropic sea on the morning of 17th April 1781, it was at once clear to Rodney that an opportunity was offering itself to bring off a coup such as he had often dreamed of.

Here was an opponent 'misconducting his line'. If the British line could be kept in tight formation the whole of it could be brought against the rear of the enemy fleet in overwhelming force before the enemy's van could come back to its support. At 6.45 Rodney 'gave notice by public signal that my intention was to attack the enemy's rear with my whole force, which signal was answered by every ship in the fleet. At 7 a.m., perceiving the fleet too much extended, I made the signal for the line of battle at one cable's length asunder only.'

For the next ninety minutes, in the gentle breeze of early morning, the two long lines of stately ships passed on opposite courses. Across the intervening water the crews on either side stood gazing at the enemy with whom they would soon be exchanging devastating broadsides. On the gun-decks all was ready, powder and shot supplied and the cannon run out with their muzzles thrust through the open ports. In the tops, red-coated marines stood leaning on their muskets. Until the flagship made the signal to bear down on the enemy line there was no more to be done except an occasional haul on the braces to fill or back a topsail to keep station in the line. Old salts exchanged comments on details of the enemy's rigging or the cut of his sails. The raw 'landsmen' and 'waisters' thought more, and with a chill churning of their bellies, of the rows of black gun muzzles waiting to hurl death and destruction at them. The older hands hid their own qualms under rough mockery of those who had never been under fire, or by contemptuous references to the 'Mussoos'.

Then at 8.30 a flag broke out at the *Sandwich*'s masthead. It was repeated by the frigates stationed on the opposite side from the enemy for that purpose, and by every ship of the line. As it came fluttering down, all helms were put up and to the cry of 'Weather Braces' the yards were squared round, the ships now running, in line abreast, down wind towards the enemy. The drums beat to quarters. Guns' crews tumbled down the hatchways out of the sunlight to the dim spaces below. Gun captains blew the slow matches fixed to their linstocks till they glowed brightly and gave last-minute savage exhortations to the crews they had spent so much time training for just this moment. (*See page 190.*)

On the quarter-deck of the *Sandwich* Rodney stood with his flag-captain, Walter Young, gazing at the enemy line to see their reaction to his manœuvre. De Guichen could escape the trap Rodney had laid for him yet. He could turn and run away down wind, abandoning his projected expedition against Barbados; but this was unthinkable, opposed by a force inferior to his own. Though he wished to avoid a battle *a l'outrance*, honour demanded that he should fight rather than fail in the purpose for which he had come to sea. Alternatively, he could reverse the course of his fleet, all ships going about simultaneously. Rodney's thrust would then be at the French van and support could quickly be brought up to frustrate his intentions.

And sure enough, to Rodney's disappointment, he saw the enemy ships turn simultaneously, with admirable precision, first away, showing their sparkling stern windows, and then on, round, hauling their wind until they had completed the manœuvre of 'wearing' to reverse their course. The old fox de Guichen had 'discovered his intention', thought Rodney. He may have done; but it seems unlikely, from what was to follow later. In fact, de Guichen's signal to reverse course had been made before Rodney's manœuvre had been appreciated.

For the moment, however, Rodney was foiled. At 9 o'clock he signalled his fleet to haul their wind on the larboard tack. Once again the two fleets were passing on opposite courses. The French were still widely extended. Rodney's, exhorted by a stream of signals addressed to individual ships to keep better station, was admirably compact at 'two cables' length asunder'. For all his tactical ability de Guichen seems not to have realised his danger.

At ten minutes past ten Rodney saw opportunity again being

presented to him. Up went the signal for ships to wear together round on to the starboard tack, which would bring the two fleets once again on to similar courses. To avoid confusion and danger of collision this manœuvre had to be initiated always by the rear ship of the line, in this case the 74-gun ship *Stirling Castle*. She was commanded by a rugged old character, the oldest captain in the fleet, Robert Carkett. He had risen from the lower deck, and gained his promotion for conspicuous gallantry in the previous war when first lieutenant of the 64-gun ship *Monmouth*. The *Monmouth* had chased and fought to a standstill the much more powerful French ship *Foudroyant* of eighty guns. Carkett's captain had been killed early in the action and it was under the command of her first lieutenant that the *Monmouth*, herself hammered to a hulk, had forced the surrender of her opponent. When two other English ships came on the scene, it was to Carkett that the Frenchman had insisted on handing his sword.

Thus Carkett's courage could never be doubted. But he was painfully slow and he was solidly obtuse. The latter characteristic was to emerge tragically as the day wore on. At this stage it was the former which was in evidence. On several occasions the *Stirling Castle* had already been rebuked for tardy acknowledgement of signals. Now, nine minutes after the general signal to wear, she had made no move, holding up the whole manœuvre. It required a special signal under her distinguishing pendant to make Carkett understand what was required of him.

By 10.36, however, the whole fleet had wore round and was on the same tack as the enemy. It was organised in the customary three squadrons. The van squadron of six ships commanded by Rear-Admiral Parker in the 90-gun, three-decker *Princess Royal* was led by the *Stirling Castle*. Then came the centre, seven ships under Rodney himself, followed by the rear, six ships of the line under Rear-Admiral Joshua Rowley in the *Conqueror* (74) with a 50-gun ship *Centurion* 'to assist the Rear in case of need'. For a time Rodney watched to see if the enemy would once again reverse course. By 11 nothing had happened. Something of his danger had penetrated de Guichen's mind for he had signalled his ships to 'crowd sail, close up the line and prepare for battle'; but it had had little or no effect and the French line still straggled, ten miles long compared to Rodney's compact formation still covering about six. The British admiral, in case his men should think that the morning's manœuvres were intended for any other purpose but bringing on an action—many were probably contemptuous of what seemed the fussy evolutions of the elderly martinet newly put over them—also made the signal to prepare for battle. At the same time he altered the course of the fleet to close gradually the distance between the lines without too obviously betraying his intention to de Guichen. At 11.50 Rodney knew his moment had come. To his masthead sped the flag which ordered the Additional Fighting Instruction No. 21. Undoubtedly on every quarter-deck in the fleet the book containing the Fighting Instructions was produced and the leaves thumbed to discover what was required. For no captain can have memorised the whole of the confusing set of orders contained therein. What they found, read as follows:

'If the squadron should be sailing in a line-of-battle ahead to windward of the enemy and the Commander-in-Chief would have the course altered in order to lead down to them, he will hoist a Union Flag at the main top-gallant-masthead and fire a gun. Whereupon every ship in the squadron is to steer for the ship of the enemy, which, from the disposition of the two squadrons, it must be his lot to engage notwithstanding the signal for the Line Ahead will be kept flying; making or shortening sail in such proportion as to preserve the distance assigned by the signal for the line, in order that the whole squadron may, as near as possible, come into action at the same time.'

In Rodney's mind there could be no doubt as to what this order entailed, particularly in view of his earlier signal giving his intention to concentrate upon the enemy's rear. Furthermore his previous unsuccessful attempt to bring off his desired coup had been correctly carried out and therefore, presumably, understood.

Despite his life-long criticism of—and even contempt for—the general run of his brother officers, with their narrow, un-questioning attitude to tactics, their hide-bound enslavement by the letter of the Fighting Instructions, their unimaginative conception of how a battle must be fought, Rodney could not foresee that, in this case, they might pitch upon one sentence of the Instruction, misconstrue it, and ignore the remainder. But, alas, the shades of Mathews and Byng haunted the quarter-decks of British men-of-war. To the minds of many brave but simple naval officers they had been condemned because they failed to carry their fleets into action in such a way as to engage the whole enemy line simultaneously, leading ship against leading ship, van against van, centre against centre, rear against rear. To such men 'the ship which it must be their lot to engage' was never in doubt and now they acted accordingly. In the *Sandwich* the helm was put up. The great three-decker swung majestically round to the creak of yards being braced round square to the wind as it came astern. The rear squadron and the centre copied the *Sandwich*'s motions. Rodney could see others in the van similarly bearing away down wind. The great moment of his life had come. By patient, careful manœuvre he had caught the foremost naval tactician of the French Navy completely off balance. As the signal to engage, followed shortly by that for 'Engage the enemy closely' went to his masthead, he knew that decisive victory must be his. In the light wind prevailing there was no time for de Guichen to counter Rodney's manœuvre before action was joined. Too late the French admiral realised his position—that his rear faced annihilation.

But now for Rodney came bitter disillusionment. Away to starboard something odd was happening in the van squadron. The leading ship, the *Stirling Castle*, instead of bearing down directly for the enemy ship opposite her, was reaching forward towards the enemy van. Then, on signals from the *Princess Royal*, the remainder of the van squadron also, one by one, put their helms down, hauled their wind and followed the *Stirling Castle*'s example. The three rear ships of Hyde Parker's squadron, *Albion*, *Terrible* and *Trident*, in conformity with Rodney's intention and in obedience to the last clause of Instruction No. 21 which called for maintenance of the line in close order, at first continued correctly to keep station on the centre squadron. But Parker signalled them to follow him. Torn between the behests of two masters, they chose to obey Parker, though reluctantly. Unaccountably the *Grafton*, leading ship of the centre squadron, also slanted away to follow the van. *(See page 191.)*

Rodney's splendid plan was ruined. The degree of his own distress can be gauged by the fact that in the frigates, whence the whole action could be seen, tears of mortification ran down their captains' faces. On the quarter-deck of the French flagship, the *Couronne*, the commander of the French troops, who had seen de Guichen's dismay at the turn of events, now cried out, 'Courage, mon général! The English desert their commander.' And so it must have seemed to Rodney.

Nothing remained to him but to carry the centre and rear squadrons into the closest possible action. Something might thus be saved from the fiasco. But even here he was ill-served. The second ship of the centre squadron, the *Yarmouth*, was commanded by Nathaniel Bateman, another 'tarpaulin' like Carkett. Like Carkett, he had been raised from the lower deck as a reward for conspicuous gallantry—in his case during Mathews' ill-starred Battle of Toulon. Like Carkett, he had never forgotten Mathews' disgrace; and like Carkett he had already proved a thorn in Rodney's flesh owing to his mishandling of his ship and slowness in obeying signals. Seeing the *Grafton* next to him sheer away, Bateman could neither decide to do likewise and at least lay himself alongside an enemy, even if it was the wrong one, nor to bear down with the *Sandwich* and support his admiral. He hesitated, put his helm down to follow the *Grafton* but failing to brace round his yards was taken aback and came to a standstill at long gunshot from the enemy to windward.

What could be done by means of the inadequate signals available Rodney did. He signalled to the *Yarmouth* for closer action, to make more sail, for ships to windward to come into the admiral's wake, for the *Yarmouth* to do the same; but it was three hours later when the battle was about to come to an end before the bemused Bateman brought his ship within hail of the *Sandwich* when detailed instructions could be given him.

Meanwhile things were also going wrong in the rear. The *Montagu* of Rowley's squadron, receiving a devastating raking broadside from ahead as she was coming into action, went out of control and turned to port instead of to starboard, thus going into battle on the wrong (port) tack. When some of the French ships wore round also, Rodney ordered his squadron to follow them. Both sides, except for the *Montagu*, which was too shattered to manœuvre, soon turned back again, but Rowley's unauthorised behaviour had not escaped Rodney's eye and he would be called to account for it later.

But now the *Sandwich* had been carried into action. The frenzied fight she put up against heavy odds—poorly supported as she was—was in tune with the frustrated fury of the admiral whose flag she flew. The first enemy ship she ranged alongside was a comparatively small one, the *Actionnaire* of sixty-four guns —which was quickly forced out of the line to leeward. Then the *Intrépide* of seventy-four guns came up to take the *Actionnaire*'s place. She, too, was no match for the bigger *Sandwich*. She hauled away, heavily damaged.

By now the *Sandwich* had passed through the French line to leeward and was lying virtually cut off from support. Signals to the *Yarmouth* and *Cornwall* and other ships to windward to get into line astern of him had little effect. The French admiral at first feared that his line had been broken and his rear cut off. Then he suddenly realised that a chance to strike in superior numbers at the British flagship was being offered. He himself and his immediate neighbours were disengaged owing to the gap left by the misconduct of the British van. Wearing round with them, his own 80-gun ship and two seventy-four's, he came sailing down to overwhelm the *Sandwich*. For ninety shattering minutes Walter Young fought his ship against these odds. His foretopmast fell in a tangle of torn rigging. Eighty round shot tore through the *Sandwich*'s sides. In reply the French ships were beaten to a standstill. The *Couronne* was set on fire, and a number of her crew leapt overboard, and, swimming to the *Sandwich*, were taken prisoner. And at the end of it, it was de Guichen who withdrew, carrying his whole fleet away with him to leeward.

Too many of the British ships were crippled aloft for Rodney to attempt to follow. For the tactical mistakes made had not prevented a number of them from getting into close action. The French custom of firing high, at the rigging, had achieved its aim thereafter—as a comparison of the casualties on either side indicate. Against British figures of 120 killed and 354 wounded, the French lost 222 killed, with 537 wounded.

So ended the Battle of Martinique. Both sides claimed the victory; but the French claim cannot be conceded. De Guichen, abandoning his ulterior object of an attack on Barbados, retreated to his defended base at Basseterre in the island of Guadeloupe. Patching up his ships as best he could at sea, Rodney followed him there but found him unassailable under the shore batteries. De Guichen would have to make for Fort Royal eventually to refit, however, so Rodney placed himself to seaward of it and awaited a renewal of battle—a challenge which de Guichen declined. And while Walter Young and his men strugggled to make the battered *Sandwich* seaworthy again, Rodney, at his desk in the great cabin, composed his official report on the battle. The bitterness of his heart burst forth in the concluding paragraphs:

'It is with concern inexpressible, mixed with indignation, that the duty I owe my Sovereign and country obliges me to acquaint their Lordships that, during the action with the French fleet on the 17th instant, and his Majesty's, the British flag was not properly supported.

'I cannot conclude without acquainting their Lordships that the French Admiral, who appeared to me to be a brave and gallant officer, had the honour to be nobly supported during the whole action.'

Mindful of the appalling effect upon the discipline and reputation of the Navy of the Keppel and Palliser controversy. Lord Sandwich suppressed the first of these two paragraphs. The praise of the enemy without any corresponding approval of the conduct of his own subordinates told its own tale, however. The controversy which followed spread itself over several months, owing to the time necessary for letters and their replies to cross the Atlantic. It will be more convenient to deal with it completely and at once.

All England was soon buzzing with surmise; but meanwhile Sandwich replied, 'Every time we hear from you, we receive fresh cause to approve your conduct. If you go on in the same style, you will oblige me to study how to write panegyric, which, till of late, I have had but little occasion to practise.

'I hope you will not be fearful of pointing out the persons you think deserving of censure. In this you will have all the world on your side, as we shall not be satified unless those are brought to shame and punishment who have robbed you of the glory of destroying a considerable part of the naval force of France, though you gave them battle with an inferior fleet, and many of your ships scarce fit to keep the sea.'

Rodney could hardly have been blamed if he had ordered the

court martial of a number of his subordinates, including Hyde Parker, his second-in-command. By their failure to maintain the line of battle at the distance apart ordered they had exposed themselves to certain conviction. Believing as he did, and with justification, that the most brilliant victory in the annals of the Navy to that date had been snatched from him by their desertion or stupidity, it would have been understandable if the Commander-in-Chief had been fiercely vindictive. Such wholesale prosecution, however, would have had a disastrous effect on the morale of the service and of the West Indies fleet in particular. Indeed, as Rodney wrote to his wife, 'If all were to be tried who misbehaved on that day. I know not where judges could be found, and I do not choose delinquents should try delinquents.' Instead he set about disciplining and educating his subordinates so that no repetition of the disastrous events of the 17th April could ever happen. Meanwhile he confined himself to ordering the trial of Captain Bateman and of Lieutenant Appleby of the *Montagu*, who he thought had cravenly withdrawn his ship from battle after his captain had been killed. The latter, in fact, was honourably acquitted when it transpired that the *Montagu* had been so crippled as to be unable to manœuvre.

Replying to Sandwich three months after the battle, in the cool light of considered judgment, he named those of his captains whom he considered had fought well, leaving silence with regard to the remainder as his form of condemnation.

'It is with real pain and grief of heart that. . . . I find myself under the necessity of adverting to (a subject) so disagreeable as that contained in the second paragraph of your letter.

'That His Majesty's flag was not properly supported, is a melancholy truth which no man has, nor can have, more reason to lament than myself, but it is a truth which my duty to my Sovereign, and to my country, will not permit me to suppress, and I am sorry to add, my subsequent reflections upon the actions of that memorable day, and the consequences thereof, will not allow me now to palliate; at the same time I must freely confess, that the task of bringing to trial and punishment all those who appeared to be, through error of judgment, or otherwise, delinquents, on that occasion, is a task, not only painful to my feeling, but, abstracted even from the difficulties attending the

[125

same under the critical situation of naval affairs in this part of the world, would, in my poor judgment answer none of those salutary effects which might reasonably be expected at home therefrom.

'I have therefore, only selected Captain Bateman, who commanded his Majesty's ship the *Yarmouth*, and was one of my own division, and Lieutenant Appleby, first Lieutenant of the *Montagu* who succeeded to the command of that ship on his captain's being wounded, and rendered incapable of performing his duty, and whose misconduct appeared too manifest and notorious to be overlooked, having with my own eyes beheld their gross neglect of my orders, and inattention to my signals, to be tried at a court martial, whenever the situation of affairs will admit of court martials being held.

'I have only to add, what indeed I have already requested, the favour of you, Sir, to convey to their Lordships, that to this inattention of signals, both in the van and the rear divisions of the squadron under my command, is to be attributed the loss of that glorious opportunity (perhaps never to be recovered) of terminating the naval contest in these seas.

'I cannot conclude without taking notice of my having, in justice to the character of Captain Bowyer, of his Majesty's ship *Albion*, and Captain Douglas, of his Majesty's ship *Terrible*, which I heard had been unjustly and unworthily traduced in the public papers at home, certified, under my hand, my sincere belief that those gentlemen really meant well, and would have done their duty had they been permitted. The former of them has twice had an opportunity of proving himself a brave and gallant officer.

'On this subject I should be guilty of the greatest injustice, if I did not voluntarily, and unasked, give this public testimony to the character of Captain Young, of the *Sandwich*, whose gallant and intrepid behaviour, not only on the 17th of April, but on every subsequent occasion, has been such as to merit all that can be said in his praise.

'Equally unsolicited and free are the certificates I have given those brave officers, Captain Houlton of his Majesty's ship the *Montagu*, and Captain Molloy, of his Majesty's ship *Trident*, both of whom bore down to engage the enemy, agreeable to the signal I made for that purpose. The former having the misfortune of being dangerously wounded, his ship was withdrawn from the battle by the first lieutenant; the latter was commanded by the admiral, in whose division he was, to follow him.

'More certificates I have not given, nor shall any consideration in this life induce me so far to prostitute my honour and character as an officer, as to give, under my hand, what is not really dictated by my heart and conscience.'

One of the 'delinquents' was Commodore Thomas Collingwood whose broad pendant flew in the *Grafton* leading the centre division, which had followed the bad example of the van. It was a personal tragedy for him:

'The best and bravest officer under my command' (Rodney wrote) 'has taken his following Mr Parker's bad example so much to heart that it has destroyed him; I mean Commodore Collingwood. Nothing that I could say or do or write to him could restore his peace of mind, and with the deepest concern I must acquaint your Lordship that that gallant officer has lost his senses for many days, and yesterday was put on board the *Brilliant* frigate in order to go to Lisbon, but it is impossible for him to arrive at that place.'

That Rodney added many to his toll of personal enemies by his despatches is not surprising. The bitterest was probably Hyde Parker, who seems never to have understood what he had done wrong. Rodney told Sandwich that 'After the action he attempted to assail me with the grossest flattery, comparing me to the greatest officers that had ever existed in the naval line, and that it was with the greatest concern he saw I was not supported in the action. I treated his fulsome flattery with the contempt it deserved.'

It can be imagined that 'Old Vinegar' returned to his flagship choking with rage, a rage which was constantly fed by the indignities he suffered in the subsequent weeks when his rank did not exclude him from the flood of reproof and reprimand with which Rodney lashed the fleet into discipline. The indictment contained in Rodney's despatches, particularly that which contended that Parker had prevented the rear ships of his squadron from doing their duty, made irreconcilable enemies of the two men. When Rodney's wish to be rid of Parker was agreed to by the Admiralty, he wrote, 'It was with great pleasure I received the Admiralty's orders by the last packet to send home Rear

[127

Admiral Parker with the following convoy. He is a dangerous man with a very bad temper, hostile in the highest degree to the Administration.' On arrival in England, Parker addressed himself in fury to Sandwich who had some difficulty in persuading him not to publish his own account of the action, justifying his behaviour.

Rodney's passage with Joshua Rowley gives a clear and hardly attractive picture of the icy, uncompromising tone he adopted with subordinates who angered him. Rodney had called upon the rear-admiral to explain 'why he was so great a distance from the centre and did not obey signals', conduct which he considered had saved the whole French rear and centre from being taken. Rowley explained how he had followed the enemy's rear ships when they turned away as he 'had conceived from the signal you had made previous to the action that 'twas your intention to make the greatest impression on the rear'. Rodney's reply was that 'the painful task of thinking' was for the Commander-in-Chief; the rear-admiral had but to obey signals and orders.

Such a denial of initiative to subordinates displays to modern eyes a serious flaw in Rodney's system of command, though it is a phenomenon which has recurred at times in the Royal Navy, notably in the 1914–18 war, when it can be said to have been the principal cause of failure at Jutland. Rodney, however, saw the restoration of strict discipline as his primary task if victory was to be achieved.

Rodney had been loth to take direct action to punish Carkett of the *Stirling Castle*, the unwitting initiator of the whole unhappy turn of events on the 17th April. He had known him a long time and knew of his heroic past. He made allowances. He had, however, said in the unpublished portion of his despatch that 'had Captain Carkett, who led the van, properly obeyed my signal for attacking the enemy, and agreeable to the 21st Article of the Additional Fighting Instructions, bore down instantly to the ship at that time abreast of him, instead of leading as he did to the van ship, the action had commenced much sooner and the fleet engaged in a more compact manner'.

Carkett, when rumours of this filtered back to him from England, unwisely wrote to ask Rodney for confirmation. In justifiable indignation the admiral replied,

'I have received your letter of yesterday, acquainting me, that you are credibly informed, that in my public letter to the Admiralty, relative to the action with the French fleet, on the 17th April last, your name was mentioned.

'It certainly was; and that you mistook, and did not properly obey my signal for attacking the enemy, agreeable to the 21st Article of the Additional Fighting Instructions, by not bearing down instantly to the enemy's ship, then opposed to you, but led to the van ship, notwithstanding you had answered my signals, signifying that it was my intention to attack the enemy's rear, which signal I had never altered; and, of course, it behoved every officer to have paid the utmost attention to it.

'Your leading in the manner you did, induced others to follow so bad an example; and thereby forgetting that the signal for the line was only at two cables' length distance from each other, the van division was led by you to more than two leagues distance from the centre division, which was thereby exposed to the greatest strength of the enemy, and not properly supported.

'Could I have imagined your conduct and inattention to signals had proceeded from anything but error in judgment, I had certainly superseded you, but God forbid I should do so for error in judgment only. I only resolved Sir, not to put it in your power to mistake again upon so important an occasion as the leading a British fleet to regular battle.

'You must now, Sir, give me leave fairly to tell you, however painful the task, that during the time you have been under my command, you have given me more reason to find fault with your conduct as an officer, than any other in the fleet (Captain Bateman excepted), by your inattention to signals, and, Sir, by negligently performing your duty, and not exerting yourself as it behoved the oldest captain in the fleet, by setting an example of briskness, activity, and scrupulous attention to signals.

'Did you do so?—when, upon the first signal I made for a line of battle abreast, and then going down to provoke the enemy to come out to battle, you hauled your wind, instead of making all the sail you possibly could to get into your station, agreeable to the first Article of the Additional Fighting Instructions,—thereby setting a very bad example to all the young captains.

'Judge yourself what I must have felt, to observe, that the two

[129

oldest captains of the fleet I had the honour to command were the only persons I had just reason to reprimand by public signal, and let them know *they had not obeyed*. Your almost constantly keeping to windward of your station, in sailing afterwards; the repeated signals made for the ship you commanded to get into her station; your being at an amazing distance from the fleet the night before the battle; my being obliged to send a frigate to order you down; your being out of your station at day-break, notwithstanding the line of battle was out all night—all this conduct indicated an inattention which ought not to have been shown by an officer who had been bred in the good old discipline of the western squadron; and which nothing but the former service you had done your king and country, and my firm belief of your being a brave man, could have induced me, as commander of a great fleet, to over-look.

'You may judge what pain it has given me to write this letter to an officer I have known so long, and for whom I have always had a regard; but in great national concerns, and where the service of my king and country is intrusted to my care, it is imperative on me to do my duty, and to take care that those under my command do theirs. Both of which, without favour or partiality, I shall strictly adhere to.'

The controversy over the Battle of Martinique can perhaps be left on this indignant but scrupulously fair note. Carkett remained in command of the *Stirling Castle*—surely indicating that Rodney's bark was often worse than his bite—only to go down with his ship when she was lost with all hands during the devastating hurricane of October 1780. Bateman was convicted at his court martial and dismissed the Service.

Rodney always held the 17th of April 1789, to have been the great occasion of his life. Years later, Sir Gilbert Blane was to write that even when acclaimed for his great victory at the Saintes, Rodney insisted that he would have preferred to rest his reputation upon this action with de Guichen and 'looked upon that opportunity of beating, with an inferior fleet, such an officer, whom he considered the best in the French service, as one which, but for the disobedience of his captains, might have gained him an immortal renown'.

X

CONCENTRATING on the agitation and argument over the Battle of Martinique has carried us on two months during which much had happened. It is necessary now to retrace our steps.

At the close of the battle, it will be remembered de Guichen took his fleet, much shattered, to the anchorage of Basseterre in Guadeloupe. There Rodney followed him and stood back and forth in the offing challenging him to renew action. The French fleet remained snugly under the protection of their shore batteries.

Basseterre had few facilities for refitting ships, however. Knowing this, Rodney stationed himself off Fort Royal, confident that de Guichen would be forced to make an early bid to regain his base. In spite of the parlous condition of his own fleet— the *Sandwich* was only with difficulty kept afloat—the British admiral was ready to offer battle again. His hardihood was in vain, however. Stores and equipment for repairing the French fleet were supplied from the neutral Dutch island of St Eustatius, conveyed in two ships belonging to a traitorous English merchant living at St Kitts.

This trading with the enemy through St Eustatius had long been a thorn in the flesh of British commanders in the West Indies. It had begun before France entered the war, English merchants seeing no harm in trading with the American colonies whom they, like a great many people in England, refused to look upon as rebels. What these merchants considered as, at the worst, smuggling, became plain treason when France joined the rebels. This did not deter them, however. Lord Sandwich, writing in September 1779, commented that 'from conversing with Admiral Barrington . . . two-thirds of the provisions that we carry out under convoy from England and Ireland, is on its arrival in our islands, immediately shipped off for St Eustatius and from thence to Martinique, without which the French could not keep their fleet in a condition for sea . . . the rapacity of the merchants overbears all legal obstructions, and nothing but more forcible coercion can restrain them from anything in which they find their immediate interest'.

So long as Holland remained neutral little could be done; but the time was coming when retribution would fall. Meanwhile Rodney's patched and leaking ships could not remain long off Fort Royal. Repairs were urgently needed. The wounded had to be put ashore. Jury-rigged as many of the ships were after battle damage, it was difficult to maintain station between de Guichen and his base against the trade wind, and the strong westerly currents which ran between the islands. Walter Young was writing at this time to Middleton, 'The Fleet is in a shattered condition. For God's sake and our country's send out copper-bottomed ships to relieve the foul and crippled ones with masts and stores of all kinds. With those, everything will be done: if you do not, but misery and disaster must ensue.'

The Admiralty was in fact doing its best to reinforce Rodney. A squadron of five ships of the line under Commodore Walsingham had been assembled, but for weeks it lay windbound, unable to get out of the Channel, and it was to be the middle of July before it arrived. A further reinforcement of five ships had been ordered to be sent from the North American Station. The kind of stupid inefficiency against which Rodney so often inveighed stepped in to prevent it. The sloop *Bonetta*, carrying the despatches with the order for Admiral Arbuthnot, commanding in North America, was dismasted in a gale while on passage across the Atlantic. She lay refitting at Providence in the Bahamas for several months during which time her captain took no steps to forward the urgent letter. It is impossible not to feel with Rodney that 'had their Lordships' order been obeyed it would have been attended with the most glorious success to his Majesty's arms and in all probability fatal to the naval power of his enemies'.

Meanwhile the odds remained in de Guichen's favour. Leaving frigates on patrol to watch for the enemy, Rodney retired to St Lucia. On the 6th May came the expected news of the French fleet to windward of Martinique. At once Rodney stood out to sea again, ready, in spite of the crazy condition of many of his ships, to offer battle once more. For four days the British beat painfully against wind and current in the strait between Martinique and St Lucia. They were still to the south of Point Salines, the southern tip of Martinique, by some fifteen miles, when the enemy fleet was sighted.

Enjoying the windward position, it was in de Guichen's power to bring on an action when he chose. Rodney could only hold his position between the enemy and his object and await the outcome. De Guichen's intention on putting to sea had been to attempt an attack on St Lucia; but whether he wished to persist in this aim or to regain his base at Fort Royal, he had first to brush Rodney aside. A period of complicated manœuvring now set in, therefore, with Rodney trying to force a decisive battle while de Guichen sought to avoid totally committing himself. 'Nothing could induce them to risque a general action,' wrote Rodney to Sandwich, 'tho' it was in their power daily: they made at different times motions which indicated a desire of engaging but their resolution fail'd them when they drew near and as they sail'd far better than his Majesty's Fleet, they with ease could gain what distance they pleased to windward.'

The French, in fact, each afternoon when the wind became fresh and steady, ran down towards the British line as though to engage; but on each occasion, before coming into gun range, they hauled their wind and kept away. Each admiral strove to outmanœuvre the other. De Guichen, profiting by the lessons he had learnt on 17th April, had drilled his fleet and attained a degree of perfection in manœuvre which brought reluctant applause from his opponent. Rodney, still raging at his subordinates' incompetence on that occasion, worked ceaselessly to the same purpose. Soon after the Battle of Martinique he had announced his 'intention of hoisting my flag in time of action on board the centre frigate appointed to repeat signals, having the other frigates attending to carry orders to particular ships to enforce the signals I may find it necessary to make'.

On 12th May he did this, shifting his flag to the frigate *Venus*. The methods he employed to bring discipline and efficiency into the fleet emerge from the report to Lord Sandwich in which he tells of this unorthodox move.

'It is impossible for your Lordship to conceive the infinite utility of this resolution. . . . It is inconceivable in what awe it kept them. No regard was paid to rank. When either admiral or captain were out of their station a signal was instantly made, and a frigate dispatched with orders, which had so good an effect that frequently when they saw the frigate approach they got into their station, and I always recalled them when they do.'

Walter Young, who, for all Rodney's praise of his courage and good seamanship, was a carping critic behind his chief's back, did not see things the same way. He told Middleton that 'When the French fleet came down on us the first time he left me in a confused state and, in short, I did not know he was out of the ship,' a statement it is hard to credit. Young went on to say that 'His being in a frigate was of no service as he always kept to leeward of the line. The enemy being to windward he could never be a judge of it: but at last I got him persuaded to keep between us, which he attended to in the last rencounter'.

The disloyalty of a flag-captain writing in such a way to a member of the Navy Board is a good example of the intrigue, so rife in the Navy, against which Rodney set his face. Middleton was a great administrator of the Navy but he never flew his flag at sea and had no qualifications to be the critic he was of Rodney's capabilities. Young was Middleton's protégé, and probably owed his appointment to him. Rodney was undoubtedly a difficult master. Both Young, and Hood later, stigmatised him as 'unsteady' and 'irresolute', criticisms easily made by subordinate officers on whom the responsibility does not lie. Rodney's painful illness was enough to make him irritable. The burden of campaigning with a fleet of crazy, shattered ships, against heavy odds, must have made decisions infinitely difficult to take. Thus Young's censures, usually coupled with self-glorification, were probably in the main factually correct but unsweetened by any sympathy for his chief's handicaps.

By the 15th Rodney was ready to try a ruse on his opponent. When the French bore down in line abreast to make their customary feint, he waited until they were fully committed and then signalled to his fleet to crowd on sail. His object was to surge ahead—to windward—while the French were running down wind. Then, by going about on to the other tack in succession (the leading ship turning and the remainder following in her wake) he might with luck gain at last the windward position. He hoped that de Guichen, deceived into thinking he was running away, would fall into the trap. Whether his ruse would have worked cannot be known. Rodney commented that de Guichen 'had the vanity to think that we were retiring; and with a press of sail approach us much nearer than usual. I suffered them to enjoy the deception, and their van ship to approach abreast my centre'. But then came a sudden development as the wind veered from its usual easterly quarter to south-east. The British who were sailing close-hauled on the port tack on a southerly course, were forced to turn to starboard on to south-west to keep their sails full.

The change of wind, however, played into Rodney's hand. His planned alteration of course on to the starboard tack must now ensure him the windward gage. The signal sped to the *Sandwich*'s masthead. The *Albion* (Captain Bowyer) leading the line obeyed with gratifying promptitude and was followed by the ships of Admiral Rowley's van squadron.

De Guichen at once saw the danger he was in. His fleet wore round, all ships together, and, as Rodney claimed, 'fled with a crowd of sail'. Nevertheless, with the windward gage, Rodney would be in a position to force an action unless the French ships' sailing quality was vastly superior to that of his own. For the next half an hour Rodney could see the ships in the van tacking, one after the other, on to the new course. Once the whole line had 'turned the corner', the situation would be in his hands. Frustration and gout forgotten, he paced the weather side of the quarter-deck, halting now and then to assess the relative position of the two fleets. But Fortune's smile proved only momentary. Only about half of the line had come round on to the new tack when the wind backed to its original quarter as suddenly as it had previously veered. De Guichen, swinging his ships round on to the port tack—a southerly course—was once again to windward. The British fleet, turning to port to keep sails filled on the starboard tack, could steer north-eastwards for the enemy, but as de Guichen continued under a press of sail, could not cross ahead of his line. The *Albion* in fact struck the enemy line at about its centre. Approaching head on, she and the other ships of the van had to submit to a punishing raking fire before they could bring their own broadsides to bear. As she ran down the French line, the *Albion* sustained the fire of fifteen enemy ships. As Rodney reported it:

'The van, led by that good and gallant officer, Captain Bowyer, about seven in the evening, reached their centre, engaged it to their rear, and was followed by Rear-Admiral Rowley's squadron (who then led the van), the centre and rear of his Majesty's fleet following in order. As the enemy were under a press of sail, none but the van of his Majesty's fleet could come in for any part of the action, without wasting his Majesty's powder and shot, the enemy wantonly expending a deal of theirs at such a distance as to have no effect.'

De Guichen's narrow escape was evidently taken to heart by him, for 'the enemy kept an aweful distance till the 19th'. Both fleets had been ceaselessly manoeuvring for the windward gage— de Guichen to retain it yet not quit the field, Rodney to gain it. An unexpected shift of wind on the 19th again offered Rodney a hope of weathering the enemy line. But hug the wind as he would, he 'had the mortification to be disappointed in those hopes'. A similar encounter to that of the 15th resulted. Once again the van suffered the most.

Both fleets, indeed, were now at the end of their endurance. The French were running short of provisions. Both sides had ships so damaged that only with difficulty could they be kept afloat. Rodney had been daily receiving messages from his captains that their ships were in danger of foundering, but grimly he had made them stick it out. Now, however, the time had come to make for shelter and repair. On the 21st the two fleets, as if by mutual consent, abandoned their long duel, de Guichen heading northwards and rounding Martinique to enter Fort Royal, Rodney going to Barbados. Three of the British ships, the *Conqueror*, *Boyne* and *Cornwall* were too knocked about to sail on a wind and were forced to run for St Lucia. The *Cornwall* in fact, and the *Fame*, another seventy-four which had not been fit to join the fleet, were eventually to sink in Gros Islet Bay.

Thus the contest of wits between the two most skilful tacticians of the day came to an end. At the end of it, de Guichen, sixty-eight years of age, was quite worn out. In one of the engagements he had lost a son. Now he asked to be recalled,

136]

pleading that 'The command of so large a fleet is infinitely beyond my capacity in all respects. My health cannot endure such continual fatigue and anxiety'. Yet the following year he was to be found commanding a much larger force in home waters. It is not unfair to conclude, therefore, that it was Rodney's dogged persistence and determined offensive spirit which he no longer cared to face.

Rodney, six years de Guichen's junior, did not minimise the strain imposed by the long duel. To Sandwich he wrote:

'I dare say your Lordship, who knows what a poor constitution I have always had, will be surprised how I could bear the infinite fatigue that must have attended me as a commanding officer on this occasion. The greatness of the object enabled my mind to support what my strength of body was scarce equal to, and though I did not go to bed for fourteen days and nights, yet at times, when the fleet was in perfect order, I stole now and then an hour's sleep upon the cabin floor, which refreshed me more than a whole night's sleep would have done in England. . . .

'It had this good effect that the many and different manœuvres made by both fleets learnt my admirals and captains to be what none of them were before, officers; and has been a school as I hope will give England a number of excellent officers in future times.'

To his wife, he admitted that 'Nothing but the goodness of the weather and climate could have enabled us to endure so continual a fatigue. Had it been in Europe half the people must have sunk under it. For my part it did me good'.

It had been a remarkable effort on the part of every man in the fleet, indeed. To his son George, the admiral wrote with justifiable pride about his flagship—the worst but by no means the only heavily damaged ship during the action of 17th April:

'Had the Action lasted half an hour longer, the *Sandwich* must have sunk; it was doubtful for twenty-four hours after whether she could be saved. Perseverance and the Active Behaviour of my men, who deserve everything a grateful Country can bestow, saved her, stopped her Leaks, refitted her and for three successive Days enabled her with the Fleet to pursue the Enemy who flew before us and most carefully avoided another Action.'

Something of the little-known social life of the lower deck of the times is revealed by an incident connected with the battle. A woman—doubtless not the only one—'wife' of one of the sailors, was on board the *Sandwich*. Her presence came to the knowledge of the admiral through her taking the place of her wounded man in the crew of a twenty-four-pounder gun. After the battle Rodney had her brought before him and, having terrified her with a thundering reproof for the breach of regulations her presence on board represented, rewarded her with ten guineas for her valour.

That women remained on board with their men, contrary to regulations, when a ship sailed for a foreign station was by no means uncommon. Cases have been unearthed, through study of ships' books, of their actually being entered on the ledger and paid the wages of their late husbands who had been killed in action. No contemporary accounts have come under the author's eye, however, of how married life was carried on at sea in the total lack of privacy of the crowded lower deck.

The period of training under Rodney's stern and critical eye which the long encounter had provided evidently wrought a transformation in the discipline and efficiency of the fleet, for he was now able to report 'that since the action of the 17th April, and during the pursuit of the enemy's fleet, and in the two rencounters with them, every officer of every rank and denomination, was obedient and attentive to orders and signals, and I am convinced, if the enemy had given them an opportunity, they would have done their duty to their King and Country'.

There was little rest to be had for the fleet at anchor in Carlisle Bay, Barbados. From dawn to dusk, the boats were out plying to and from the shore, towing water-casks to be replenished, fetching wood for the galley fires. Under the carpenters' directions, damaged masts and yards were repaired or new spars fitted. Boatswain's parties rove fresh rigging. Leaking planks and ships' side timbers were caulked. Fresh provisions were embarked. The sick—there were many—and the wounded were sent ashore to the hospital. There was a multitude of tasks to put the fleet into condition for battle. The work went on night and day.

There was no time to be lost. A few days after the fleet's

arrival, the frigate *Cerberus* sailed into the harbour bringing momentous news. Captain Mann told Rodney that when on patrol off Cadiz at the end of April he had discovered a large Spanish force—twenty sail of the line, he estimated, and upwards of one hundred transports and merchant ships in convoy. He proceeded to shadow them and by 4th May had established that they were making for the West Indies. Crowding on sail he had shaped course for Barbados to bring warning to the Commander-in-Chief. A few days later the frigate *Brilliant* and the cutter *Rattlesnake* ran in with confirmation of the news.

Rodney was pleased by the initiative shown by their commanding officers. 'I shall order them all back to their station,' he told the Admiralty, 'but cannot forbear expressing to their Lordships my approbation of the merits of these officers, who thought it their duty to leave their station, and convey to me with speed, intelligence of such importance.'

The nerve-racking slowness with which events unfolded during manœuvres of two fleets in sight of one another and moving into battle has been commented on earlier. Strategic pace, geared as it was to the speed of sailing ships, was similarly of a nature to try the nervous fortitude of a commander to the utmost. News from Europe often took five weeks or more on passage by fast 'packet'. It ran the risk of capture or shipwreck or it might be long delayed by foul weather.

All movements locally, amongst the islands, were dominated by the constant easterly winds and the strong west-running currents set up by them between the islands. The poor weatherly qualities of ships of the line often made it almost impossible to get to windward of the chain. Frigates and schooners bearing vital news might be delayed from the same cause. Once a decision was arrived at—perhaps on scanty, out-dated intelligence—days or even weeks of painfully slow progress might have to be borne before it could become known whether that move had been the proper one.

Always there was the danger inherent in any move to leeward, involving the slow and laborious beat back to windward if it proved wrong. A force once divided could only be concentrated again by despatching a frigate with orders for a rendezvous. Meanwhile the enemy might have passed in the night, or just

over the horizon by day, on his way to attack some point left un-
defended. The nervous strain on an admiral must have been a
long-drawn mental agony at times, as he endlessly paced his
quarter-deck asking himself if he was doing right.

Straining every nerve to get ready, it was not until 7th June
that the fleet could put to sea. It was still working its way out of
harbour when frigates which Rodney had spread to windward to
reconnoitre brought the news that the Spanish fleet had been
sighted 150 miles to windward of Martinique. With all possible
speed Rodney took the fleet northwards, and next morning was
off Martinique. Three ships were sighted; they crowded sail and
fled northwards. Two were captured and proved to be a merchantman and a transport out of the Spanish convoy. From them
Rodney learnt the true strength and composition of the force—
twelve ships of the line, five frigates and eighty-three transports
carrying 11,400 troops, the whole under the command of Admiral
Josef Solano. It became clear, too, that after being sighted by the
British frigates Don Solano had altered course to the northwards
for the passage between Guadeloupe and Antigua.

The situation confronting Rodney was on the face of it a
desperate one. If a junction was made by the French and Spanish
fleets, his seventeen ships would be opposed by thirty-six.
Though, as he wrote to the Admiralty, 'without a reinforcement
from England, nothing of great consequence can be undertaken,
or expected,' he determined to take a bold line by placing himself
off Fort Royal. He called first at the Carenage, St Lucia, hoping
to find some of his cripples in a condition to join him and reduce
the odds; but of the four ships of the line there, two were in a
sinking condition, another fit only to be sent home, and the
fourth—Rowley's flagship the *Conqueror*—still lacking her
masts.

Arriving off Fort Royal with seventeen of the line and two
50-gun ships, Rodney found that of de Guichen's twenty-three
ships, seventeen had sailed two days before. Frigates located
them lying in the lee of Dominica. Rodney was in something of
a dilemma. Though his instinct was to go after de Guichen and
attack him before he could make junction with the Spaniards, he
realised that 'To have gone to leeward after the enemy's fleet
could have answered no end whatever, as they had it always in

their power to draw me farther to leeward without risking a battle; by which means, the six ships of the line, with the troops from Martinique, under that enterprising general, the Marquis de Bouillé, might have attacked either St Lucia or Barbados without a probability of my arriving in time to their assistance'.

The danger inherent in dropping away to leeward and being unable to beat back was a constant factor in the calculations of an admiral in the West Indies and has to be borne in mind when considering the moves made. In this case Rodney allowed himself to hope that the Spaniards had carried on to their own port of Havana in Cuba, and he decided to keep 'the port of Fort Royal Bay and the road of St Pierre, as closely blockaded as it was possible to be done with ships under sail; and at no small expense of the enemy's powder, shot and shells—without any effect'. Nevertheless, when his cruisers brought the news that de Guichen's fleet 'was increased to twenty-four, by several large ships with Spanish colours joining them from under Dominica', he was forced to go over to the defensive. He was expecting the early arrival of the reinforcements under Commodore Walsingham, not knowing that they had been wind-bound in the Channel for three months. Meanwhile he retired to St Lucia where his 'presence might be of the greatest utility in assisting the commanding officer of his Majesty's troops in St Lucia in putting that island in such a state of defence as to secure it, should his Majesty's service require the departure of the fleet to attack the enemy or to defend any other of our islands attacked by them'. At the same time he stopped the sailing of the homeward-bound trade convoy 'till it was in my power to secure it from insult in these seas'. On 17th June he was joined by the *Russell* (74) from North America with the infuriating news of the miscarriage of the Admiralty orders to Arbuthnot to send five of the line to the Leeward Islands. Arbuthnot had finally received the orders on 17th March. Though reinforcements sent then would have been too late to turn the scale in the Battle of Martinique, five of the line even now would have been invaluable help to Rodney, and it is not clear why only one ship was sent to him.

The month of June dragged by with Rodney standing watchfully on the defensive. Warnings had been sent to all the British islands to put themselves in a state of defence. By July the campaigning season would be almost over with the approach of the hurricane months. As the sailors' doggerel had it:

> July — Stand By
> August — Go you must
> September — Remember
> October — All over.

Yet the enemy made no move. The Spanish convoy had been sent on to Havana and on the 19th June the combined fleet had entered Fort Royal. There they had remained, with Rodney's frigates watching them—twenty-seven ships of the line to Rodney's eighteen—until the night of 5th July when the combined fleet, showing no lights, slid silently out of harbour. They could not give the slip to Rodney's frigates, however, and they were shadowed as they made their way north to Guadeloupe and then westward. The frigate *Alert* followed them as far as Santa Cruz; then assured that they were abandoning the Lesser Antilles, she sped back to give the Commander-in-Chief the news.

Rodney at once set things moving. Walsingham had at last arrived, on 12th July, with his five of the line and a troop convoy. As soon as they had watered, he sent Rowley and Walsingham with a squadron of ten of the line to Jamaica—all ships urgently needing refit at home—to defend the island and, when the danger had passed, to escort the important Jamaica convoy with the season's trade for England. Then, leaving Commodore Hotham with six of the line for the protection of the windward islands of St Lucia, Barbados and Tobago, he sailed with the remainder to accompany the West Indies convoy as far as St Kitts.

There Rodney solved the mystery of the enemy's inactivity. 'On my arrival here, I received secret intelligence (and which has never deceived me) of the violent disagreements between the Spanish and French admirals; that the Spaniards absolutely refused to co-operate with them in any enterprise whatever, openly declaring their court had been deceived, and that they were made to believe, before they left Spain, that they would find, on their arrival in the West Indies, the French in possession of all the Caribbee Islands. The rancour between the two nations, by all accounts, and by many intercepted letters, was fatal to several officers; and the sickness and mortality in both fleets, had reduced them very much.'

The removal of the threat to the West Indies for the time being lifted a load of anxiety from Rodney's mind. It gave him time to consider what his next move ought to be. It also gave him comparative leisure in which to enjoy the flood of good and flattering news which came from home in the long-delayed letters brought by Walsingham. He found he had become a national hero. A country conditioned by an almost continuous tale of setbacks and defeats since the beginning of the war, was very ready to hail the unequal battle against Langara and the botched action of 17th April as resounding victories. He now heard of the Vote of Thanks passed by both Houses of Parliament for the former and of the pension granted to him as a reward— £2,000 to him for life, and life pensions for his widow and children after his death. He was offered the choice of a pension or of appointment as Lieutenant-General of Marines, a highly-paid sinecure. On Sandwich's advice he accepted the former as the latter 'will carry no future consequences with it, and will be liable to the same accident as other offices held during pleasure'.

For the first time for many years his mind was at ease, at least so far as his personal affairs were concerned. On 30th July 1780 he was writing to Lady Rodney: 'All I want is, to pay off my debts as soon as possible; I shall not be easy till this is done. . . . Let me be clear of all demands, and our income will be more than sufficient to live as we ought, and to save money. . . . Many prizes have been taken since my command here, but none very valuable. I hope Fortune may soon smile upon me, for all your sakes. As yet, all has been war and battle.'

Ambition still rode him, however, for at the same time he was writing to Sandwich of the 'present happy situation in my affairs which are now not only sufficient to discharge my debts, but likewise sufficient to spare a sum of money, if necessary, to bring me into Parliament.'

From Lady Rodney came flattering titbits of London gossip. Referring to the delays in sending him reinforcements she wrote:

'Shamefully remiss indeed have they been at home, to suffer you to remain all this time without proper reinforcements. Everyone cries out Shame; yet though every one knows your inferiority, he expects wonders from you, and has not been disappointed. I have frequently remarked to such as indulge in such expectations, that they ought not to raise them so high, but consider how inferior you were to the enemy; but the answer has always been, "We know that, but we know Rodney, and can hope everything from his skill and bravery." . . . The nation appears to place its whole dependence upon you. . . .'

Lady Rodney wrote from the house in Portman Street which she had taken. She sent a vivid description of the Gordon riots during which Rodney's eldest son, George, now an officer in the Guards, had been with the troops called out to deal with them:

'You will hardly credit the situation this country has been in for this fortnight past, by the conduct of one very wrong-headed and deluded young man. Lord George Gordon (who is of no religion) has stood forth as a champion of the protestants. The public prints will explain it all to you; but there is no describing the horror and confusion that reigned in this city. Seven great fires raging at once, which seemed to threaten the total destruction of the metropolis—every jail thrown open, mobs in thousands parading the streets, going from door to door demanding money, and threatening on refusal to burn the house down. At last, the King, as chief magistrate (as he termed himself) put himself at the head of the military, without waiting for the civil power. The troops were ordered to fire on the people that assembled, and many were destroyed, but certainly deserved their fate. No parliament sat—no courts of justice—no business went on for some days. The Horse Guards scour the streets night and day. . . . During the whole of one of the nights of this confusion I sat up, and the dear girls with me, ready to go off. Every person that had a place to go to, went out of town. Mr Lascelles, Lord Townsend and Mr Stapylton, the first in this street, quitted their houses, which were threatened to be burned, as were the Horse Guards stables, which were directly opposite to me; and as the wind set directly on this house, I concluded we should be compelled to leave it, so I sat up, prepared for the worst, with my poor brats, though where to have gone I had not determined, it being difficult to make a choice in the three evils which presented themselves—the mob, the fires, and the troops, who fired indiscriminately. Mr Rodney was on duty in the city, and, thank Heaven, escaped any accident.'

In reply to Lady Rodney's anxious inquiries as to his health, Rodney wrote, 'The fatigue of body and mind that I have undergone for these six months past has been such, that I am much surprised, now it is in a manner over, how I could possibly get over it. I hope to have a little rest for a month or two, but greatly fear I shall be laid up with the gout, as I feel myself much out of order, and far from well. The agitation of my mind, and my anxiety at Walsingham not joining me sooner, have been such as not to be easily conceived. Had he joined me but one month sooner, both the French and Spanish squadrons had, in all probability, been destroyed.'

Sending news of their eldest son, John, the admiral said:

'John is very well, and has been kept constantly at sea, to make him master of his profession. He is now second lieutenant of the *Sandwich*, having risen to it by rotation; but still I send him in frigates: he has seen enough of great battles. All he wants is seamanship, which he must learn. When he is a seaman, he shall be a captain, but not till then.'

Young John, indeed, was enjoying a meteoric career. He was not yet sixteen. He had gone to sea first in 1778 with Admiral Byron. Promotion in time of war for those with interest was often rapid, vacancies from death or illness or through the natural process of expansion of the fleet being frequent. Regulations as to the necessary qualifications were winked at. Nelson had been made a post-captain on the Jamaica station the previous year at the age of twenty-one. Rodney, at the request of Lord Sandwich, had promoted Lord Robert Manners 'another young man of fashion, now in your squadron, concerning whom I am tormented to death ... if you could contrive by some means or other to give him rank, you will infinitely oblige me.' Lord Robert at the time was twenty-one. Three years later as captain of the *Resolution*, ship of the line, he was to be mortally wounded at the Battle of the Saintes.

Nevertheless Rodney jibbed at promoting unsuitable candidates, however well recommended. 'A poor wretch Lord —— and another have been sent me,' he wrote to his wife. 'He looks like a girl, and has not the least appearance of an officer. I have made them as good a present, and have sent him back captain of sloop. More I will not make him. Such officers as these I never desire to see. He may be a very good young man, but he has not fire enough in him for me. No consideration whatever shall induce me to promote indifferent officers over the heads of good ones. Merit has little chance of preferment in peace. Where I command, it shall have the preference in war, let who will recommend.' Constantly pressed thus by influential patrons to promote their protégés, it is not to be wondered at that Rodney nursed his own son's career. He did nothing by halves, however. At the Moonlight Battle with Langara, 'John had the honour to command a gun, and he will be a Lieutenant as soon as I leave (Gibraltar), a vacancy being kept for him.' By July, as we have seen, he was second lieutenant of the flagship.

To be sure, Rodney saw to it that he learnt his profession. In May, he was writing, 'John is perfectly well, and has had an opportunity of seeing more service in the short time he has been from England, than has fallen to the lot of the oldest captain in the navy. It will be of infinite service to him. He is now gone on a cruise, in one of my frigates, to look out for a Spanish fleet of twenty sail of the line.'

It was, nevertheless, gross nepotism when John was given command in the following year of a frigate. Even in the eighteenth-century Navy, a post-captain of sixteen was probably unique. On the other hand, that Rodney saw in youthfulness no bar to preferment is shown by the career of Sydney Smith, later famous for his defeat of Napoleon at Acre. Smith was also a midshipman of the *Sandwich* when Rodney hoisted his flag in her. Soon after the Battle of Martinique he was promoted lieutenant and two years later Rodney made him a post-captain at the age of eighteen.

The lull brought about by the departure of de Guichen to lee-ward and the imminence of the hurricane season allowed Rodney to send the West Indies trade on its way home. With the convoy went those ships of the line most urgently in need of refit and repair at a home dockyard. Sandwich had been exhorting him 'For God's sake contrive to send home your bad ships. We cannot bear to lose any of the line; our present list is too small, and we shall be open to much censure if we suffer any further diminution'. The Admiralty was indeed in desperate straits for ships in home waters. Threatened by a possible combination of the French and Spanish fleets as in 1779, they could raise a fleet of only twenty-two of the line against a total of nearly double that number of the enemy.

Rodney therefore cut his fleet to the bone, assuming that reinforcements would be sent to him as soon as the hurricane season was past. He could not be at ease, however, until he knew what de Guichen planned to do with his fleet during that time. Letters taken from a captured French ship indicated that twelve of his ships of the line were to go to North America. Such a force would establish a great superiority over Arbuthnot and have a disastrous effect on the war with the colonies. In the absence of confirmation of this intelligence Rodney hesitated to commit himself.

'I am really at a loss how to act at this present moment,' he told Sandwich. 'Every intercepted letter going to France mentions the infinite importance of St Lucia and their determined resolution to attack it at all events when opportunity offers. At the same time I think America may want my assistance.'

In the meantime Rodney set about, with some gusto, the chastisement of his *bête noire*, St Eustatius, so far as the restrictions imposed by Dutch neutrality would permit him. His despatch on the subject is dated 12th August, 1780, from the *Sandwich* at sea.

'Having received undoubted intelligence that the American Rebels carried on a most pernicious commerce at the island of St Eustatius, which was likewise an asylum for their Cruizers, from whence they received every Succour, and were thereby enabled greatly to annoy the trade of his Majesty's loyal subjects, I thought it absolutely necessary to station a squadron of frigates, in such a manner as, I was in hopes, would intercept and destroy the Ships and Vessels belonging to his Majesty's Rebellious Subjects bound to the island.

'Some of the frigates employed on that service, pursued five Sail of his Majesty's pyrattical Rebellious Subjects, armed for war, on the 6th of August. They took shelter in the road of St Martin, a small island, part belonging to his Majesty and part to the States General.

'The Pyrattical Rebels had the insolence, after they were at anchor in the road, to insult his Majesty's flag in the grossest manner, by daring to hoist their rebellious colours, with a broad pendant, bringing a spring upon their cables, and pointing all their guns into his Majesty's sloop, the *Rover*. The Dutch Governor took no notice of this insult, but permitted the Americans to wear their pyrattical Colours.

'Notice of this insult being immediately given me at St Christopher's, where I then was, with his Majesty's fleet, I instantly despatched Captain Robinson, with a squadron of frigates, and his Majesty's ship *Intrepid* to St Martin's, to seize or destroy the American pyrattical vessels and to acquaint the Dutch Governor that every Attention and Respect should be paid to the Dutch flag while they kept within the rules of neutrality; but that his suffering so gross an Insult to the British Flag, and his permitting the Americans to wear their rebellious and pyrattical Colours in his road, so directly contrary to treaty, was a convincing proof to me that he either could not, or would not prevent it. I had therefore sent a squadron of the King, my master's ships, to chastise the Insult. They seized all the American vessels; and I have the pleasure to acquaint their Lordships, that it has had so good an effect, and has brought the Dutch Governors so much to their Senses, that they now pay some attention to Ancient Treaties, and acknowledge that they know no American colours, nor suffer any to be hoisted in their ports in the West Indies.'

Rodney had suffered much from the aid given by the Dutch under the guise of neutrality to the French fleet. His enjoyment at the opportunity to revenge himself in some measure is plain to see. The time was to come when old scores would be wiped out in one devastating sweep.

By the end of August Rodney was still in the dark with regard to de Guichen's movements. He knew that he had taken his fleet to Cap François (now Cap Haitien) the French base in Haiti, in July. Frigates had been stationed to watch the enemy; but to bring tidings from so far to leeward was a long haul. He knew also that a very large convoy for France would need escorting by at least a portion of the French fleet. On the other hand he believed that twelve of de Guichen's ships were under orders for America. His judgment told him that this was the proper move for the enemy to make; and in fact Lafayette and the French Minister to the United States had written imploring the French admiral to come north. But de Guichen had had enough. His orders were to go home and he would not take the responsibility of going against them. On 16th of August he sailed with the trade convoy for Europe, leaving ten of the line at Cap François.

Rodney knew nothing of this; but at sea with his remaining ten ships to the northward of the Leeward Islands where he might have sea room in the probable event of a hurricane he captured an American ship from which he got momentous news. A French squadron of seven of the line under the Chevalier de Ternay, with a number of troop transports, had arrived at Narragansett Bay and occupied Rhode Island. Rodney at once shaped course for New York.

'As it plainly appeared to me,' he reported on his arrival there on 14th of September, 'that his Majesty's territories, fleet and army in America were in imminent danger of being overpower'd by the superior force of the public enemy . . . without a moment's hesitation. . . . I flew, with all the despatch possible, to prevent the enemy's making any impression upon the continent before my arrival there.'

XI

RODNEY's entry upon the American scene was the cause of chagrin in more than one direction. George Washington is on record as being brought near to despair when, instead of de Guichen on whom he had been counting to rid him of the weight of British sea power, Rodney dropped anchor off Sandy Hook. Nevertheless, Rodney's influence upon the course of the war in America was to prove only a negative one, resulting—in combination with de Guichen's absence—in disrupting Washington's plans but not greatly assisting the British Army commander, General Clinton.

The move to North America was strategically correct. Before learning of it, Sandwich had already written giving it his approval:

'I am very glad,' he wrote to Rodney, 'that you tell me you shall hold yourself in readiness to assist in America, or wherever the enemy may endeavour to make their impression, for that is the only measure that can give us security. It is impossible for us to have a superior fleet in every port; and unless our Commanders-in-Chief will take the great line, as you do, and consider the King's whole dominions as under their care, our enemies must find us unprepared somewhere, and carry their point against us. I own I think that they are now gone to America. . . .'

That de Guichen would lack the enterprise and intuition to bring aid to his American allies at this critical time could not be foreseen. As it was, however, the naval force already on the North American Station was sufficient to blockade de Ternay at Rhode Island and to engage him on equal terms should he attempt to escape. The only enterprise which might have been made possible by the access of strength represented by Rodney's force was an attack on de Ternay's squadron in harbour, an operation which Rodney considered should have been undertaken much sooner. The general convinced him, however, that it was now too late, the enemy having strongly fortified the place.

The naval Commander-in-Chief, Vice-Admiral Marriot Arbuthnot, could see no reason, therefore, for the incursion into his station of an officer senior to himself. When he received Rodney's official notification:

'You are hereby required and directed to put yourself under my command, and follow such orders as you may from time to time receive from me for his Majesty's Service, for which this shall be my order.'

he felt a deep and implacable resentment.

Rodney, as senior officer on the station, had at once assumed control of operations, adjusting the disposition of some of Arbuthnot's line-of-battle ships and sending some of his frigates on patrol along the American coast to deal with the enemy privateers which were ranging unopposed and doing considerable damage. At the same time he had busied himself in concert with General Clinton putting his squadron at the disposal of the Army for operations the general had planned. In communicating these arrangements to Arbuthnot, Rodney had been the soul of courtesy; his letters, so far as they concerned action by Arbuthnot, offering suggestions and alternatives rather than giving orders:

'I therefore, Sir, leave it to your consideration and Choice, either to remain with the Squadron employed in watching Monsieur Ternay, or return to New York, for the reasons I have suggested, and leave the blockade to Rear-Admiral Graves.

'As I am convinced no Man has his Majesty's Service more at heart than Yourself, I am sure you will do that which in your Judgement shall appear best, and favour me with the Resolution you may take.

'Being a total Stranger to the Navigation in the neighbourhood of Rhode Island, I must leave it to you, whether (now the Equinoctial Gales are passed, and the Moon increasing) the Squadron under your command should not put to sea, and cruize, if it can be done, without imminent danger, off Rhode Island. . . .'

(Arbuthnot customarily blockaded Rhode Island from his anchorage in Gardiner's Bay, some twenty-five miles away).

Arbuthnot's reply was couched in such insubordinate terms that conflict between the two men was inevitable.

'As one part of your letter points at my Inducement for remaining occasionally in Gardiner's Bay, I judge it necessary to explain myself on that Head.

'It has, Sir, been my constant Endeavour, by that means, to keep the Ships constantly wooded, victualled, and watered, that, should the enemy's Squadron unfortunately give me the Slip, not a moment ought to be lost in the Pursuit. How far, Sir, your Conduct (similarly circumstanced as you are) is praiseworthy and proper, Consequences must determine.' (This was a jibe at Rodney, the ships he had sent to cruise having suffered in a gale).

'Your partial Interference in the Conduct of the American War is certainly unaccountable upon principles of Reason and precedents of Service. The Frigates attendant upon a Cruizing Squadron you have taken upon you to Counter Order, a due representation of which, I shall certainly make where it will have every possible Effect.'

From this moment nothing but bitter hostility between the two admirals could be hoped for. Yet Rodney, stigmatised by many as so difficult to get on with replied in courteous and conciliatory terms to Arbuthnot, several grades of rank junior to him as an Admiral of the White, though some six years older.

'I am honoured with your letter of the 16th Instant and am sorry that my Conduct has given you Offence, none was intended on my part. Every Respect due to you as an Officer and a Gentleman my Inclination as well as my Duty led me to pay you in the strictest sense. If any designing men, by their insinuations, have induced you to deviate from that good Sense and Politeness which Mr Arbuthnot was always known to have, I am sorry for it; and am convinced, in your cooler moments, when you reflect upon some of the Paragraphs in your Letter, you will wish they had been couched in more friendly terms.

'It was not Inclination or Choice that brought me to America. It was the Duty I owed my King and Country. I had flattered myself it would have met with your Approbation. I am sorry it has not; but I own I have the Vanity to think it will meet with *his*

Approbation whose it is the greatest Honour a Subject can receive.

'Your anger at my partial Interference (as you term it) with the American war, not a little surprises me. I came to interfere in the American war, to command by sea in it, and do my best Endeavours to put an end thereto.

'I knew the Dignity of my own Rank, and the Power invested in me by the Commission I bear entitled me to take the Supreme Command, which I shall ever do on every Station where his Majesty's and the public Service may make it necessary for me to go, unless I meet a superior officer, in which case it will be my duty to obey his Orders.

'On my arrival off the Hook, I instantly despatched four Ships to join you, which made your Squadron thirteen of the line—a force fully sufficient to attack Monsieur Ternay's squadron of eight sail of the line, which I am convinced would have been the Consequence, if he had given you an Opportunity. I left it entirely to you, Sir, how to dispose of that Squadron as to answer so desirable an End.

'Your having detached the *Raisonnable* to England, without my knowledge, after you had received orders to put yourself under my Command, is, I believe, unprecedented in the Annals of the British Navy. My duty will oblige me to report it to the Lords Commissioners of the Admiralty.

'Your having detached the *America* and *Prudent* on a three weeks' Cruize, between the north end of St George's Bank and Cape Anne, convinces me that you thought the remaining part of your squadron fully sufficient to defeat any designs of Monsieur Ternay; but I own, as you have given me no reasons for so doing I cannot approve of the separation of the Squadron while Monsieur Ternay lies with his whole force at Rhode Island.

'You must excuse me, Sir, if I think myself in a great measure responsible for the Disposition of his Majesty's ships on the coast during my continuance thereon; and as Superior Officer of his Majesty's ships on this station, have taken upon me to dispose of them in such a Manner as appeared to me most conducive to his Majesty's and the public Interest——'

In spite of this reasoned and, considering the provocation of the junior officer's insubordinate letter, remarkably conciliatory reply, Arbuthnot appealed in furious terms to the Admiralty against Rodney's assumption of the command. Sandwich stood by Rodney and told Arbuthnot:

'You must be sensible, Sir, that according to the use of the Navy, a Senior Officer has always a right to take an inferior one under his Command whenever the good of his Majesty's Service makes it necessary . . . you will have less reason to be surprised at Sir George Rodney's coming to North America when you recollect that you yourself pressed for his personal Assistance in your Letter of the 20th of April last. . . .'

At the same time the Admiralty told Rodney that 'their Lordships . . . entirely approve of your Conduct in going in person to North America. Their Lordships no less approve of the Dispositions you have made of his Majesty's ships since your arrival on the coast of America the Wisdom of which is evident from the Success with which it has been attended, by the Capture of no less than thirteen of the Rebels' Privateers.'

Nothing would appease Arbuthnot who continued to rail at Rodney's conduct. It soon emerged, however, that it was the loss of the perquisites of command, rather than of the power or prestige that irked him. Shortly after Rodney's arrival on the station one of the frigates he had taken over from Arbuthnot's command made a rich prize. Rodney at once claimed and secured his legal share—in this case one half of an eighth, the other half being divided by the two junior flag-officers on the station, Arbuthnot and Graves. Arbuthnot exploded in rage.

Prize money, however, though certainly the principal, was not the only bone of contention. Arbuthnot had organised his station as a personal and extremely profitable property with corruption rife to a degree shocking even by eighteenth-century standards. Perhaps the most disgraceful was the profit made by manipulation of funds allocated for the care of the sick and wounded which Gilbert Blane, now appointed physician to the fleet, uncovered.

Walter Young summed up the position, writing one of his regular letters to Middleton:

'I am exceedingly sorry to inform you that Mr Arbuthnot does not draw well with either his superior or any other officer. The loaves and fish, in both departments, have occasioned much disappointment, and I am afraid this said prize money is, and will

154]

be, the bane of all public service. You will be astonished to hear of the conduct of some of our supposed great men—and of a Secretary; in short, Sir, Mr Arbuthnot is so led by Mr Green, that he is either directly or indirectly in possession of every place, under the Navy—victualling, sick and hurt, and every other branch where the public money can be got at. . . . . The abuses of the hospital are beyond description; this Mr Green has had the physician discharged (turned out) and every other person who has impeded his rapacity.'

The exposure of these disreputable proceedings increased Arbuthnot's resentment to fever pitch. He missed no opportunity to attack Rodney in his letters home. Rodney was inured to such things, however. Writing to George Jackson, Second Secretary of the Admiralty, he commented loftily.

'I find myself, my dear Sir, a Butt for Envy and Malice. I had rather have Envy than Pity. I will go on and endeavour by exerting myself in the service of my King and Country to deserve more Envy and more Malice. It cannot hurt me for I am resolved to do my Duty, and no Rank whatever shall screen any officer under me who does not do his Duty. The Good, the Worthy, the truly Brave officer will love and Honour me, others are unworthy my notice. All shall be treated like Gentlemen and none under my Command shall ever have reason to tax me with Disrespect to them; but I will be the Admiral.'

An insufferably pompous letter to modern ears perhaps, but, though we have it from Walter Young that Rodney was indeed pompous in his manner, eighteenth-century style lent itself to such phraseology. It was against officers of Arbuthnot's stamp that Rodney was thundering.

Urging more vigorous methods of conducting the American war, in a letter to Lord George Germain, he claimed that it would have been 'brought to a speedy conclusion . . . and with honour to Great Britain, had those persons who were entrusted with the command of her fleets and her armies preferred their own, their King's and Country's honour to lucrative and factious motives by which means they have, according to my conception of things, betrayed the whole, and ought to be held forth, and undergo the just punishment and resentment of an injured nation.' Princely fortunes, he said, were being made by 'a long train of leeches who

F

suck the blood of the State and whose interest prompts them to promote the continuance of the war'.

Rodney always took his fair share, by the standards of the day, of any perquisites of office. To keep the record straight it should be noted that it was at this time that John Rodney, aged sixteen, was given post rank as captain of the frigate *Triton*; furthermore Rodney stepped over the bounds of seemliness—though not of legality—in promoting his own followers to vacancies which occurred in Arbuthnot's ships. Rejecting Arbuthnot's protest, Sandwich told Rodney—'I acknowledge your right; but you will allow me to say that I wish you had not exercised that right, as it will distress many individuals, occasion great division and uneasiness in the Service'. Nevertheless the pursuit of personal ends was never consciously allowed to detract from the good of the Service—a point which must be re-considered later in examining the most notorious incident of his career in the following year—the capture of St Eustatius. But Rodney had a blind spot which prevented him from perceiving the antagonisms he raised by his arrogance and ruthlessness.

Arbuthnot was an example of the poor material from which the Admiralty had to select their flag-officers owing to the refusal, for party political reasons, of so many admirals to serve under a Tory Government. At this time he was sixty-eight years of age. His peculations and his notoriously bad terms with General Clinton were not deemed grounds for relieving him of his command. Early the following year, applying to come home, he told Sandwich.

'I have lost almost totally the sight of one eye, and the other is but a very feeble helpmate, constantly almost obliging me to call in assistance to its aid in discovering particular objects. Besides this I have been seized with very odd fits, resembling apoplexy, because almost instantly I faint, remain senseless and speechless sometimes four hours and sometimes longer, and when I recover am ignorant of the past. . . .'

He lived, nevertheless, to the ripe old age of eighty-three, and indeed, soon after writing this letter, was leading his squadron of eight sail of the line into action with a similar French force off Chesapeake Bay. It is not surprising that he failed to distinguish himself.

With the coming of autumn, Rodney began to fret to be back in the West Indies where, as always, he felt sure that the main struggle at sea must be fought out. On 16th November 1780 he set out with eight ships of the line for Barbados. No inkling of what he was to find there had come to him. From a vessel which came in to New York shortly before his departure, 'which left St Christopher's (St Kitts) on the 11th of October (having been blown out of the road in a sort of hurricane) I learn that everything was quiet in the Caribee Islands'. Quiet, indeed, it was; but it was the quiet of total desolation. On the 10th October a hurricane of unprecedented ferocity had swept through the islands leaving a trail of destruction.

Rodney was shocked at what he found at Barbados. 'The most beautiful island in the world has the appearance of a country laid waste by fire and sword,' he wrote to Sandwich. To his wife he said:

'You may easily conceive my surprise, concern and astonishment, when I saw the dreadful situation of that island, and the destructive effects of the hurricane. The strongest buildings, and the whole of the houses, most of which were of stone and remarkable for their solidity, gave way to the fury of the wind, and were torn up from their very foundations; all the forts destroyed, and many of the heavy cannon carried upwards of a hundred feet from the forts. Had I not been an eye-witness, nothing could have induced me to have believed it. More than six thousand persons perished. . . . The hurricane proved fatal to six ships of my squadron . . . and the remainder of my squadron, which I left with Commodore Hotham, are useless, having lost all their masts, and no stores here to replace them.'

The French islands had, of course, also suffered. Friend and foe had indeed drawn together under the blows of the common enemy. The Marquis de Bouillé had returned, under a flag of truce, a number of survivors from ships wrecked on Martinique, saying that he could not look upon such unfortunates as enemies.

The full extent of the disaster was not yet known to Rodney and he was writing to Sir Peter Parker, commanding at Jamaica, calling for assistance with stores, not realising that that island had also been devastated. He was also urging the return to him of the *Thunderer* (74), Commodore Walsingham's

[157

flagship, and the *Berwick* (74), not knowing yet that the former had been lost with all hands, the latter dismasted and forced to bear away to England. The one piece of good news to blunt the edge of disaster was that Antigua, where the only British dockyard in the Lesser Antilles lay, had been spared. Repairs to a few ships could be undertaken there—but there was a general shortage of stores.

Relief was on its way, however, in the shape of eight ships of the line, including a 90-gun three-decker, the *Barfleur*, flying the flag of Rear-Admiral Sir Samuel Hood. The ships had long been promised as replacements for the uncoppered and defective ones sent back at the end of the previous season. The choice of Hood as second-in-command was a happy stroke on the part of Sandwich. To find suitable flag-officers willing to serve under Rodney had not been easy. There were those who were not prepared to subordinate themselves to one so strict in his conception of discipline. He had indeed few friends in the Navy by this time. He had done nothing to cultivate any. Then there were those whose party political loyalties would not let them serve the Tory administration. Others, perhaps genuinely, pleaded ill-health in excuse for refusal. To solve the problem, a special promotion to the flag-list was made, the list including Hood and Francis Samuel Drake who was already serving under Rodney with the rank of commodore. As Sandwich wrote to Rodney:

'It has been difficult to find out proper flag officers to serve under you; some are rendered unfit from their factious connections, others from infirmity or insufficiency; and we have at last been obliged to make a promotion in order to do the thing properly. Sir Samuel Hood is to have his flag, and to bring out the next convoy to you . . . he will remain second in command to you; and with him and Admiral (Samuel) Drake, I hope everything will go on to your satisfaction.'

Rodney was pleased. To Hood he wrote:

'It gives me the highest satisfaction that the Admiralty have appointed you to serve with me, as I know no-one whatsoever that I should have wished in preference to my old friend, Sir Samuel Hood.'

Hood had been serving as Admiralty Commissioner at Portsmouth and had been made a baronet on the occasion of a royal

158]

visit to the dockyard. He and Rodney had seen much of each other during the time that the fleet for the relief of Gibraltar had been preparing. It was the renewal of an old friendship dating back to the days when Rodney had been a young post-captain and Hood a midshipman in the *Ludlow Castle*. In the last war, too, it will be remembered, Rodney had flown his flag in Hood's frigate the *Vestal* at the bombardment of Havre.

Hood's naval career had been seemingly near an undistinguished end. The son of a country parson, he had had to make his way up the ladder of promotion without much help from 'interest'. Still a captain at the age of fifty-six, the dockyard appointment would normally have been his last. His friendship with Rodney now sent him back into active service and was to give him the opportunity to prove himself one of the outstanding men of English naval history, a brilliant tactician, a great commander and leader. He was to become the patron and hero of Nelson who judged him 'the greatest sea officer I ever knew . . . equally great in all situations which an admiral can be placed in'.

Rodney was indeed fortunate to have Samuel Hood to serve under him in the critical time approaching. Had he possessed the wisdom to make full use of the splendid weapon placed in his hand, his fame and glory would have been without the flaws which were to develop.

Rodney was impatient for his old friend to arrive, for he had 'only nine sail of the line capable of going to sea, not one of which has spare rigging or sails'. But in the general hush of desolation which had descended on the islands Rodney saw an opportunity to strike a blow at the King's enemies. Information had reached him from St Vincent that, as at Barbados, the hurricane had damaged and weakened the defences and that the garrison was small and many of the troops sickly. In concert with General Vaughan, he decided to try to recapture the island. Making first for St Lucia to embark the few troops available, who with the marines of the fleet were to make the assault, the expedition was ready to sail by the 10th December. Then the admiral hesitated and for a time abandoned the operation. In the Windward Islands, where the inhabitants were to a great extent hostile to Britain or were indifferent enough to be suborned, nothing could ever be kept secret. News of the expedition soon reached de

Bouillé in Martinique. He acted briskly, sending replenishments of ammunition and food to St Vincent; so that when the British troops landed on the 16th they found themselves in insufficient strength to assault the citadel which, contrary to Rodney's intelligence, was in a good state of repair. The project had therefore to be abandoned.

Rodney, ever contemptuous of the West India colonists who, he insisted, would never stir a finger in their own defence, laid the blame on them for having let themselves be captured without resistance in the first place and then failing to come to General Vaughan's aid when he landed. Walter Young, however, so often critical of his chief, told Middleton that the whole affair had been thoroughly mismanaged.

Indeed, if Young is to be believed, Rodney was becoming increasingly unpredictable and 'unsteady'. He put it down to a sort of megalomania brought on by the exaggerated acclaim awarded him as a result of his defeat of Langara and what was also adjudged his victory at Martinique. To Middleton, Young reported:

'I have many matters to relate to you of inconsistencies, etc etc., but I shall suppress it on purpose to avoid giving uneasiness. I assure you I exert myself to the utmost of my power to keep our matters in order; at times they will get a little *outré*, but in this I am obliged to you great men at home for, who have so poisoned my admiral that he really and *ipso facto* thinks and believes himself to be the very man you have represented him. God help us, how much mistaken you and he are!'

There can be little doubt that the sudden change in his fortunes had gone somewhat to Rodney's head. After years of acute money troubles amounting to virtual bankruptcy, he was suddenly at sixty-three a rich man again. After years in total eclipse, this fiercely ambitious man was suddenly a popular hero as well as the professional head of his service. He had been made a Knight of the Order of the Bath. He heard in this month also of his election to Parliament as Member for Westminster.

'You will perceive,' wrote Sandwich who had arranged the matter on his behalf, 'that you are become a Senator in the most honourable and distinguished manner, without expense, and with almost the unanimous concurrence of the most opulent city in the

160]

world. . . .' This was very different from going, purse in hand, to the worthy shoe-makers of Northampton.

From St Vincent the squadron returned to St Lucia. Nothing could be attempted until the reinforcements from England arrived. Early in January 1781 they appeared, a vast cloud of sails to seaward of the Carenage. Soon they were working their way in to drop anchor, eight ships of the line and four frigates, all coppered, and more than a hundred merchantmen and store ships. A feverish activity reigned as, with the new materials and stores available, the veteran ships of the West Indies fleet fitted themselves for sea and for battle. Empty provision rooms were replenished with 'bread'—barrels of hard ships' biscuits—and meat—salt pork and beef in casks. For almost nothing was available locally following the devastation of the hurricane. Boatswains' parties were able to replace patched sails and much-spliced rigging. Carpenters got to work shaping spars to replace damaged yards and sprung masts; the 'booms', hitherto empty spaces over the waists, were once again the stowage for spare masts and yards. Gunners' parties sweated in the tropic sunshine striking down powder and shot into the magazines.

By the end of the month the fleet could boast twenty-one ships of the line ready for sea. On the 27th the sloop *Childers* arrived from England. She carried instruction for an immediate attack to be made upon the Dutch West Indies islands of St Eustatius and St Martin's. No orders could have been more welcome to Rodney who, as has been seen, had for long fumed against the partiality shown by the Dutch for England's enemies and the traitorous proceedings of British merchants who used the facilities of the Dutch islands to trade with the enemy.

Rodney and Vaughan lost no time in preparing to carry them out. The fast passage made by the *Childers* ensured that the news of hostilities with Holland could be known only to the British commanders, and by taking immediate action they prevented any leakage to the French. Three days after the sloop's arrival, Rodney, with his whole fleet, appeared off Fort Royal, 'to prevent the French penetrating our design' and at dusk, leaving six ships under Rear-Admiral Drake, the remainder slipped away. At day-break on 3rd February the flabbergasted Dutch of St Eustatius watched as the British fleet sailed into the bay and anchored

[161

with their guns covering the batteries and the frigate *Mars*, the only Dutch warship present.

A summons to the Governor to surrender brought immediate compliance. St Eustatius had fallen without a shot being fired—or almost so. The one incident took place when the *Prince William* (once the Spanish *Guipuscoano*) let fly a broadside at random after the island had submitted. Her commanding officer, Captain Stair Douglas, pleaded that the firing had been on the orders of some irresponsible junior officer—an indication of the indiscipline which could still exist. It evoked a remarkably mild reproof from the admiral:

'I must desire you will detect and punish the Delinquents, and read a Lecture to your Officers and Ship's Company of Silence and their paying implicit obedience to your Orders; two essential Articles almost forgot by the Inferior Officers and Men. It must be restored or the British Navy will be without discipline.'

Hearing that a Dutch convoy loaded with island produce had sailed thirty-six hours earlier for Europe, Rodney sent the *Monarch* (74), *Panther* (60) and the frigate *Sybil* in chase. They soon came up with the convoy and after a brief engagement with the 60-gun ship of the escort, in which the Dutch admiral was killed, the whole was captured and brought back to St Eustatius.

Gleefully as Rodney had descended on this 'nest of vipers', he had had no idea as to the vast accumulation of wealth he was to find on this little rocky islet, six miles by three.

'The riches of St Eustatius are beyond all comprehension,' he wrote to Lady Rodney. 'One hundred and thirty sail of ships in the road, with one Dutch man-of-war of thirty-eight guns, and five other ships of war, from fourteen to twenty-six guns, belonging to the Americans, and more than one thousand American prisoners.'

The waterfront of the town consisted of a continuous line of warehouses which were let out to French, Spanish, American and British merchants at a rental of over a million pounds a year. They were packed with merchandise estimated to be worth £3 millions and including great quantities of naval stores. Even the beach was covered with sugar and hogsheads of tobacco. In an age when prize money was the respectable and legitimate hope of every officer and man, when the admiral's share at the capture of Havana nineteen years before was recalled, it was inevitable that prospects of vast wealth must have sprung to Rodney's mind as he surveyed it all. He hastened to deny such ambitions.

'It is a vast capture,' he wrote. 'The whole I have seized for the King and the State and I hope will go to the public revenue of my Country. I do not look upon myself entitled to one sixpence, nor do I desire it; my happiness is having been the instrument of my country in bringing this nest of villains to condign punishment. They deserve scourging, and they shall be scourged.'

Rodney's righteous wrath was directed primarily at the traitorous British merchants, great quantities of whose goods were found in the storehouses, destined for the most part for the enemy, American or French. It was found that twelve of the ships lying in the road had belonged to the convoy brought out by Hood and which had slipped away to St Eustatius on approaching St Lucia. All naval stores were confiscated and ordered to be sent to the naval base at Antigua. Everything else which could be sold on the spot was put into a huge auction, at which the late owners were not allowed to bid, and were sold for a fraction of their real value. The rest was loaded for despatch to England in a large convoy.

In spite of Rodney's disclaimer, it was fairly certain that the King would do as he did very soon—surrender all his claims in favour of the naval and military forces. It was imperative therefore that the legality of any seizures and confiscations should be established beyond doubt. The King's gift had expressly exempted any goods forming part of a legitimate trade with the neutral Dutch. Examination of the merchants' books produced evidence which satisfied Rodney and Vaughan that any such trade was a cloak for trading with the enemy. The two British subjects most involved were arrested and sent home as prisoners for trial. With them, addressed to the office of Lord George Germain, the War Minister, went the books and papers containing the evidence of their guilt and of that of other merchants.

(They) 'had basely and with treasonable Views dishonoured themselves and their Country', he told his son, George. 'I have seized all their Effects most of which were calculated to enable the Public Enemy to continue the Ruinous War. In vain they have attempted to solicit me; I give not the least Ear to their Requests but tell them they are Public Enemies to the State and shall never receive from me the least favour. I love my King and Country and from my soul abhor a Traytor'.

Rodney's hasty condemnations and sweeping confiscations were based on evidence which seemed irrefutable to a mind unversed in the subtleties of the law. It should have given him pause, however, when the Attorney-General of St Kitts addressed a remonstrance to him on behalf of the merchants of that island who were deeply involved. They claimed that their goods which had been seized were part of their legitimate trade with the Dutch as permitted by Act of Parliament. They also gave notice that as the insurance they had taken out for them to cover transhipment to England was now invalid, Rodney and Vaughan would be held responsible for their safety. Rodney's longstanding indignation with the West India merchants for their traitorous and rapacious conduct robbed him of all caution. The Attorney-General was brushed aside and the protests of the merchants dismissed.

It was foolishly rash behaviour on the part of a man who had been notoriously desperate for money to discharge his debts. He was soon sending home bills for large amounts to George, his son, with which he was entrusted to pay off all debts and to buy a London house. George himself was assured of a handsome patrimony on the strength of which he borrowed money to 'purchase his Company' in the Foot Guards. His father also encouraged him now to marry, the suggested bride being a daughter of Thomas Harley, brother of the Earl of Oxford.

'When you see Mr Harley,' wrote the admiral, 'who is a very old Acquaintance, remember me to him and, my dear George, if your Heart is touched by either of his Daughters, indulge the Flame; she is of a great and noble family.'

George took the advice and in April 1781 married Anne Harley. It is impossible not to exult with Rodney at the joyous turn in his fortunes. After the years of embarrassing shifts and stratagems, affluence and peace of mind were suddenly his. That he was unwisely hasty in laying his hands on what he had no doubt was rightfully acquired is understandable. He was to live to regret it, alas, and the merchants were to have their revenge in the long run. They would attack his pocket through suits in the Admiralty Court and his reputation through the medium of the Opposition in Parliament where not only his probity but his competence as commander-in-chief were to be assailed. In both he provided his detractors with a certain amount of ammunition. For the splendour of the booty not only blinded him to the legal risks he was taking but dimmed his strategic vision in the weeks that followed the capture of St Eustatius.

The first indictment of Rodney's behaviour at this time has been that, seduced from his duty by the Aladdin's Cave of St Eustatius, he failed to follow up his bloodless success there by striking promptly at the other Dutch colonies in the Caribbean, Curaçao and Surinam, while they, too, were unprepared to defend themselves. The criticism, based on letters of Samuel Hood, is not valid. Before the evidence is examined, the relations which had developed between the two admirals must be considered; for throughout the time that Hood was serving as second-in-command, he carried on a voluminous correspondence, behind Rodney's back, with Jackson, the Second Secretary of the Admiralty, and with Middleton. It contained a number of scathing criticisms of his chief, which must be considered in their proper place. Many of the criticisms were fully justified; but the way in which they were conveyed paints a picture of underhand intrigue, typical of the times, but nevertheless portraying a side of Hood's character which shows him, for all his greatness in command, a thoroughly disloyal subordinate.

Hood owed the sudden and unexpected renaissance of his fortunes to his supposed friendship for Rodney. Yet within a few months of his arrival in the West Indies he was taking every opportunity to blacken his character in private, while professing friendship to Rodney's face, as shown by an informality of address in his letters to his commander-in-chief highly unusual in that stiffly formal age. His letters began, 'My dear Sir George' and often concluded 'Your very affectionate and faithful humble Servant', further than which even a husband and wife rarely went at that time. That something occurred between the two men to turn Hood's friendship to hatred is very possible. Rodney, as we have seen, treated his subordinates with an icy, withdrawn superiority, demanding unquestioning obedience, which did nothing to win their friendship. Hood, endowed with self-esteem fully as much as his imperious chief, no doubt resented such an attitude. Had his sense of loyalty been greater, it is hard to believe that he could not have broken through the barrier of Rodney's hauteur to the lonely man behind it, troubled in mind by his financial entanglements and painfully infirm of body. Had he been able to do so, the resultant partnership must have been fruitful of successes as great as any in naval annals.

Hood could have supplied the mental activity which his ageing, ailing and tired chief had begun to lose and which, owing to his own extreme juniority of rank, he could otherwise only exercise in frustrated criticism.

Alas, Hood had no charm of manner. In years to come, his military colleagues during the capture of Toulon and the reduction of Corsica in the Napoleonic Wars were to complain of his unpleasant brusqueness. The courtly Rodney may have felt the same. Hood was by disposition a censorious man, intolerant and critical of others' weaknesses. Colleague after colleague is castigated in his letters for incompetence and folly. For all his surface friendliness, he may have been unable to disguise from Rodney his envy and contempt. The portrait of Hood painted by Sir Joshua Reynolds at about this time is not that of a man of tolerant or sympathetic nature. The heavy jaw, the rat-trap mouth, the suggestion almost of a sneer, must have been a handicap when tactful persuasion of a senior was called for.

The abandonment of the projected expedition against Curaçao was the first subject for Hood's criticisms. He blamed it equally on Rodney and Vaughan who, he said, became too engrossed with gathering in the booty at St Eustatius to do their duty. From his own account, written for Jackson's private ear, this indictment only holds good for the general:

'Upon my going on board the *Sandwich* when we dropped anchor in St Eustatius Road,' he wrote, 'General Vaughan took me aside and pressed me very strongly to speak to Sir George Rodney about going to Curaçao. I replied. . . . I would sound him upon the subject; I accordingly did and was listened to with attention. The next day Sir George asked me if I wished to go to Curaçao. I answered most readily. "Well," says he, "you shall have five sail of the line and some frigates." I replied the force was in my opinion full sufficient and trusted I should make a good report to him.

'I immediately wrote a note to the General to say I had succeeded with Sir George respecting Curaçao. . . . I received no answer from him, and, when I next saw him, repeated the subject of my note, to which he shortly answered he had no men. "This is very surprising, General," said I, "for when you urged me so pressingly to speak to Sir George upon this business, you did not know but you might meet resistance here and have your force diminished; but now you have got possession without the loss of a man you fly from your own proposition, which is what I wouldn't have expected from General Vaughan." '

Thus Rodney, at least, was favourable to the project, though he must always have had doubts of its wisdom for reasons which became more cogent when tidings reached him of a French squadron on its way to the West Indies from Europe. As he put it in a letter to his son, 'Sir Samuel Hood was under orders to attack Curaçao when I received an Express which obliged me to lay that Expedition aside as it is far to Leeward and is under the Station of the Admiral who commands at Jamaica.'

The news was to prove false, a frigate captain jumping too quickly to the conclusion that the squadron he had seen steering west was headed for Martinique. Nevertheless it stressed the danger of Rodney sending any of his ships of the line so far to leeward whence it might take a month or more for them to return should an emergency arise. The fact that it was outside his station was also a valid objection unless the operation was of grand strategical importance and could not be taken care of by the admiral in whose jurisdiction it lay. Sir Peter Parker at Jamaica would have been justified in thinking it a flagrant piece of prize-money poaching. Rodney sent a message to him instead, urging him to capture Curaçao. Hood, nevertheless, was disappointed and sour at being held back. Instead, on receipt of the alarm, he was given eleven of the line and ordered to pick up Drake's six blockading Fort Royal after which he was to cruise to windward of Martinique to intercept the approaching French squadron. Rodney in the *Sandwich* remained at St Eustatius to superintend the organisation and despatch of the convoy taking the immense booty to England. Once this was taken care of, he intended to get away to join Hood and resume the tactical command.

The business dragged on, however, and, once involved in the details of it, Rodney found himself unable to delegate it to other hands. On 8th April he was still telling Hood that he would be leaving it 'in a very few days to the care of General Vaughan and its garrison'. Two weeks later he was telling Lady Rodney, 'I cannot express the fatigue I have suffered at this island. Had I not stayed here, every villainy would have been practised, and by persons who call themselves English. I hope when the Convoy sails for England, which will be on the 30th of this month, Vaughan and myself will leave it.'

In the same letter he hopes that he will have permission to return to England with the trade convoy sailing on the 15th June. He also gives news of John. 'John is cruizing. He is now changed into a new ship, the *Sybil* of twenty-eight guns. . . . He is grown, I believe, to near six feet, and manly.' The notion of a still-growing stripling as a frigate captain is intriguing.

Rodney's departure continued to be put off from day to day. He had been for some time deprived of the support of Captain Walter Young, who had been stricken down with fever. On 2nd May, Young died. The *Sandwich* was still riding at anchor in the bay of St Eustatius when on 4th May look-outs reported a line-of-battle ship, crippled and low in the water, limping towards the anchorage. She proved to be the *Russell* (74). Her captain brought the first news that Hood had been in action with a French fleet. At last Rodney was spurred into activity. The *Russell* was hastily repaired and despatched to St Kitts to replenish her exhausted water supply. The assembled convoys for England, Jamaica and North America were bustled to sea and sent on their way, and Rodney, with the *Sandwich* and *Triumph*, sailed to join the fleet.

XII

WHEN Hood sailed from St Eustatius on 12th February 1781 with orders to cruise to the windward of Martinique to intercept the French squadron under M. de Tréeville, reported to be approaching, he expected to be joined soon by his commander-in-chief. In fact this was not to occur until 11th May. In the interval Rodney had remained at St Eustatius: feathering his nest, his enemies claimed, but 'attending to the very great and important concerns which absolutely require the attention of General Vaughan and myself', according to his own account. And while he lingered over affairs which should undoubtedly have been entrusted to subordinates, a great opportunity was to be missed and much mischief result.

So much is incontrovertible and, taken at its face value, makes a stinging indictment of Rodney's conduct. There is a reverse side to the coin, however. It is easy to forget that a commander-in-chief at this time had no operational staff whatsoever. Every detail of the organisation and maintenance of the fleet, its victualling, repair and discipline, went through the hands of one man with what assistance the flag-captain could give when not occupied with the business of managing his own ship. Rodney evidently relied much on Walter Young; but at this time Young was ill and soon to die.

In addition, Rodney himself was breaking down under the effects of the strenuous year of campaigning in the face of continuous adversity. Early in March his gout was so bad that he could barely write, and he was telling Sandwich that:

'The continual mental and bodily fatigue that I have experienced for this year past preys upon me so much that unless I am permitted to leave this climate during the rainy season, I am convinced it will disable me from doing my Duty to his Majesty and the State in the active manner I could wish and have been used to. . . . I must therefore entreat your Lordship to lay me with all humility at his Majesty's feet, and to beg his Royal Permission, that in case my health should be such, at the end of this campaign, as to require a northern climate to restore it, he will be graciously pleased to permit my return to Great Britain during the three rainy months. The very passage will, in all probability brace me sufficiently to enable me to return hither in October, should his Majesty deem my presence here, during the season for acting, necessary. . . . I have a *complaint*, owing to too much activity and exertion, which, I am told by my physician, will absolutely require my leaving the torrid zone, as by relaxation it will daily increase.'

The complaint, indeed, was the painful and hampering one of stricture. With such an ailment, as well as his long-standing and increasing gout, it is not to be wondered at that Rodney's powers were failing. Today, such an invalid would not be left to carry the burden of a command. Hood was perfectly capable of shouldering it; but he was one of the most junior rear-admirals on the list, and it would have created an uproar if such an important command had been given to him. On the other hand those admirals of sufficient rank and seniority for the command had not got the confidence of the Admiralty or of the general public, who trusted 'Brave Rodney', and no other, to bring victory in the disastrous war. And indeed they were justified by his record. After the capture of St Eustatius Sandwich wrote:

'Upon every despatch we receive from you a new panegyric is necessary, as you give us no opportunity of writing but to convey applause. I own that my talents upon this subject are almost exhausted, and I really believe that the next conquest you make I shall have nothing to say, but barely to repeat my acknowledgements for the great services you have done your country.'

This is, of course, an exaggerated paean of praise for an unopposed conquest; but for the Government in danger of defeat by the Whig Opposition eager to make terms for peace, the news of St Eustatius had been a life-restorer. Rodney had been made a Knight of the Bath in November of the previous year. Now there was talk of a peerage. Sandwich begged Rodney not to give up.

'The whole government, and the public in general, are satisfied while you retain your command. What can you wish for the public service, or for your own honour and advantage, by leaving it for a single hour? The war cannot last much longer; why had you rather that the scene in the West Indies, where you have reaped so many laurels, should close under any other management than your own?'

Rodney can hardly be blamed if he stayed on; but it was not surprising that his judgment was impaired during this time. The unfortunate results must now be recounted.

Hood, with the greater part of the fleet, seventeen sail of the line, cruised to windward of Martinique from 12th February to 17th March. By this time it had become clear that the news of French reinforcements on their way had been false. Calculating that there was little likelihood of any French force arriving in the West Indies before the middle of April, Hood began to press Rodney to allow the fleet to return to harbour to refit and refresh themselves so as to be in good order when the time came. Fresh provisions had long been exhausted and scurvy had made its dreaded appearance in a number of Hood's ships. His disgust was great, therefore, when, instead, he was ordered to take his ships to leeward and blockade Fort Royal.

On 15th March, Rodney wrote to him from St Eustatius:

'I sincerely feel the Disappointment you have had in not meeting Mons. Tréeville. I think it impossible but he must be gone to Leeward. However, the blockading of Martinique becomes now highly Necessary, and I am convinced by your Cruizing off Fort Royal it will be impossible for him to escape an Action should he come. . . . 'Tis impossible for me to express the Fatigue and Plague I have undergone but had I not remained here everything had been confusion and imposition. . . . I am so tired that I can only say that I have desired Leave to go Home with the Convoy. Adieu, my Dear Old Friend. . . .'

Rodney, with the fabulously rich convoy loaded with the St Eustatius' booty ready to sail at last, had also become anxious lest the four French ships of the line at Fort Royal should slip away either to carry an expedition to retake the Dutch island or to intercept the convoy.

Hood went as far as a subordinate could go in protesting against the move. On 1st April he wrote to his chief:

'I begin to be extremely impatient for the honour of seeing and acting immediately under your flag, as I do not feel myself at all pleasant in being to leeward; for should an enemy's fleet attempt to get into Martinique, and the commander of it inclines to avoid battle, nothing but a *skirmish* will probably happen, which in its *consequences* may operate as a defeat to the British squadron, though not a ship is lost and the enemy suffer most. If, therefore, your apprehensions are over with respect to an attempt upon St Eustatius by a *coup-de-main* and think the Dutch convoy safe from the ships in Fort Royal, I most humbly beg leave to suggest, with all due submission to your better and more enlightened judgement, whether it would not be more advisable, when the whole of the very respectable force you have done me the honour to commit to my charge are watered, stored, victualled and collected together, that it be stationed to windward, with a proper number of frigates to look out. The chance would be abundantly more in my favour for effectually crushing any squadron of the enemy coming to Martinique, than by cruizing before Fort Royal. . . .'

Hood's prophecy was to prove correct, but it did not move Rodney, absorbed with the business of St Eustatius. Replying, he produced an additional reason for keeping the fleet off Fort Royal.

' 'Tis with concern that I cannot possibly concur with you relative to the Fleet under your Command cruizing to the windward of Martinique at this critical moment. I am well acquainted with the distressed condition of the Inhabitants of that Island and of the infinite importance it is to the State that their distresses should be multiplied by a close Blockade, which I must by all means desire that you will persist in, and station your Squadron of line-of-battle ships and frigates in such a manner as you may think most proper to answer so desirable an End. I cannot by any Means approve of leaving the Bay of Fort Royal and the Ships therein, even for a Day unblockaded.'

Hood's hands were thus effectively tied and there was little more he could do but hold his position off Fort Royal, beating back and forth against wind and current, and await the outcome, while the scurvy made appalling inroads into the manpower of his ships. He and Rodney could reasonably expect to be given

172]

ample warning of any French squadron arriving from Europe. A letter from Sandwich written on 21st March was in fact en route telling Rodney that a fleet of twenty-five sail of the line was lying ready at Brest, which he suggested were intended 'to check your conquests'. This airy announcement by the First Lord, with no compensating promise of reinforcements or that any attempt to blockade Brest would be made, might appear to be totally irresponsible. But there was, in fact, little that could be done to contain the enemy at this stage of the war when the Government's past neglect of naval construction was coming home to roost. The whole British naval force in Home Waters was absorbed in another expedition to relieve the still beleaguered fortress of Gibraltar. While it was thus occupied in March and April, not only did the French squadron for the West Indies sail unhindered, but the convoy carrying the St Eustatius loot was intercepted by a squadron under La Motte-Picquet and the greater part of it captured.

Not even frigates had been stationed off Brest to carry the warning quickly to Rodney and Hood. Thus it was that Hood's first intimation of an enemy force approaching was the sight of one of his own frigates bearing down towards him under a press of sail, the signal for an enemy fleet in sight flying from her masthead, at first light on 28th April. It was the Comte de Grasse with twenty of the line, his flag flying in the huge *Ville de Paris* of 110 guns, and a convoy of 150 sail.

With Hood held down to the westward of Martinique by the trade wind and the west-running currents, de Grasse was in no hurry. He hove-to to windward of Point Salines and sent ashore to announce his arrival and to arrange for concerted action the following day when he would appear off Fort Royal. Early the following morning he was in motion advancing through the channel between Martinique and St Lucia, his line of battle forming a screen for his merchantmen who hugged the coast. By 10.35 he had rounded the Diamond Rock and was steering northwards across the wide entrance of Fort Royal Bay in line ahead. Hood was to leeward, running south, and he now tacked his ships together to range up alongside the enemy on the same course, offering battle with his seventeen ships to de Grasse's twenty.

Hood's ships were all coppered, so that his squadron was probably faster than that of de Grasse who had only twelve ships copper-sheathed. The French ships were fresh out of dockyard, on the other hand, and the uncoppered ships would not yet have acquired much marine growth, so the difference was not very great. Furthermore, French ships as a rule were superior to the British when beating to windward. Thus Hood could not force an action from the leeward position. He could only wait and hope that de Grasse, using the capability to do so conferred by the windward gage, would take up the challenge. Following the usual French strategy, de Grasse was interested at first only in seeing his convoy safely into harbour. He held off therefore, firing at long range, so ineffectually that Hood disdained to reply.

By 11.20 both fleets were approaching the north shore of Fort Royal Bay and both now reversed course, Hood by tacking, de Grasse by wearing. Thus they turned inwards, towards each other, so reducing the distance between them. On the run south broadsides were exchanged but still at an indecisive range. Unable to get at his enemy, Hood brought to under topsails and 'invited the enemy's fleet to come to me'. It was to no avail and as the French sailed on, keeping away at long range, although their superiority had now been increased by the addition of the four ships of the line from Fort Royal, Hood again filled his sails and kept abreast of them, exchanging ineffectual broadsides. 'I believe never was more powder and shot thrown away in one day before,' Hood told Rodney, 'but it was with M. de Grasse that the option of distance lay and he preferred that of long shot.'

The van of the two fleets now began to run out of the lee of the land as they once again approached the channel between Martinique and St Lucia. An example of the importance of the maintenance of the line in close order was now to appear. The four leading ships of Hood's line—shorter, of course, than his opponents—caught the freshening breeze and drew away from the remainder. They found themselves opposed by double their own number of the enemy who quickly took advantage of the situation. Though they gave a good account of themselves, the *Russell*, *Intrepid*, *Torbay* and *Centaur* were heavily damaged before support could be brought to them to ease the pressure.

The rest of the day was spent in wary manœuvring by both

174]

sides. From the *Russell* came urgent messages to Hood that she 'was in great distress, having received several shot between Wind and Water, that the Water was over the Platform of the magazine, and gaining upon the Pumps, and three of their Guns were dismounted'. At dusk he ordered her away to St Eustatius where, as has been recounted, she brought Rodney the first news of the action. The next day, 30th January, the two fleets continued to face each other in line of battle. Though de Grasse's primary objective had been achieved and he had no longer to concern himself with his convoy, he still refused action. Finally Hood: 'Having been informed that the *Intrepid* made so much water that they could scarce keep her free, and that the *Centaur* was in the same state, owing to the number of shot between wind and water, and that her lower masts were very badly wounded, which, added to the loss of the *Russell* from the line, and from the knowledge I had of the state of the ships in general, having upwards of 1,500 men sick and short of complement, I judged it improper to dare the enemy to battle any longer, not having the least prospect of beating a fleet of twenty four sail of the line capital ships, and knowing the consequence of my being beaten would probably be the loss of all his Majesty's possessions in this country, I thought it my indispensable duty to bear up, and made the signal for it at 8 o'clock.'

Thus Hood's prophecy of the outcome of being stationed to leeward of Martinique was fulfilled. At the cost of several ships badly damaged he had been able to achieve nothing. And now the British naval superiority in the Antilles had been exchanged for an inferiority in numbers, with crews dying so fast from scurvy that Hood had been 1,500 men short of complement during action.

On the arrival of the crippled and sickly *Russell* at St Eustatius, Rodney at once put to sea with the *Sandwich* and *Triumph*, and shaped a course southwards for St Lucia where he expected Hood to be; but when passing St Kitts he fell in with three of Hood's badly damaged ships, the *Centaur*, *Intrepid* and *Torbay*, suffering from underwater damage and in danger of sinking. They were brought safely into Basseterre Road, however, and patched up in time to sail again with Rodney for a rendezvous with Hood to windward.

On 11th May junction was made off Antigua. The new

situation posed a serious threat to the remaining British islands in the Windward group—St Lucia, Tobago and Barbados. St Lucia had been left reasonably well fortified and the main fleet anchorage at Gros Islet Bay covered by batteries which Rodney had erected on Pigeon Island. Tobago had also been recently strengthened by the despatch of troops and cannon, and was by nature easily defensible. Barbados, however, the oldest British colony in the area and vital to preserve from the point of view of prestige alone, had never fully recovered from the effects of the great hurricane. It was thus relatively defenceless. Furthermore at Barbados, Rodney could send to hospital the hundreds of men sick of the scurvy and could expect to obtain the vegetables and fresh food to restore their health. As soon as Hood's ships had taken in a minimum supply of water at Antigua, therefore, the fleet steered directly for Barbados.

When the frigate *Pegasus* joined the fleet the same day with news that St Lucia was invested by the whole of de Grasse's fleet and that troops under de Bouillé had been landed, Rodney did not deflect from his course. 'As Captain Stanhope informed me that the *Santa Monica*, *Thetis*, *Sybil* and *Scourge* sloop, were arrived in the Carenage,' he wrote, 'I was in no pain relative to the fate of St Lucia, as I was convinced, from the strength of Morne Fortuné, the Vigie and Pigeon Island, the enemy could make no great impression.'

The arrival of the frigates—one of which was John Rodney's *Sybil*—was the saving of the situation. Though the *Thetis* was wrecked by an over-eager master as she was entering the Carenage, sailors and marines from all the ships were sent to strengthen the defences of Morne Fortuné. De Bouillé, receiving a defiant message from the garrison commander when he called upon him to surrender, decided that the British positions were too strong to be assaulted. When de Grasse confidently anchored in Gros Islet Bay, he found himself under a heavy fire from Pigeon Island and had to cut his cables and escape to sea. The French troops were re-embarked and the expedition abandoned.

Rodney arrived at Barbados on 18th May. Anchoring in Carlisle Bay, he set about 'to land the sick and water the fleet, who were in great distress for vegetables also, the scurvy raging to an uncommon degree among the sailors and marines.'

Writing to Jackson, Hood places the blame for this squarely upon Rodney in terms that are difficult to refute:

'I dreaded what we now experience, early in March, and when I found the squadron and convoy reported by Captain Linzee could not be coming to these islands, I pressed Sir George Rodney to let the ships go into port to refit and be put in good order, and to give the poor fellows what refreshment we could. . . . But doubtless there never was a squadron so unmeaningly stationed as the one under my command, and what Sir George Rodney's motive for it could be I cannot conceive, unless it was to cover him at St Eustatius. . . .

'As far as decency and any degree of propriety would permit me with an old friend and acquaintance, I gave my reasons against it. . . . I urged him upon the same score in several subsequent letters, and in my *private* ones was still stronger, for we are I believe on very good terms.'

The long lists of the sick and dying from scurvy make painful reading. Gilbert Blane, appointed Physician to the Fleet by Rodney, had already determined the best and easiest-to-procure anti-scorbutic, the juice of the lemon. To get captains and pursers to appreciate the fact and act on it and contractors to supply it was another matter. The widespread devastation of the hurricane of the previous October had made all sorts of fresh victuals scarce and expensive. The Navy Board had to be cajoled into approval of extra expenses. Contractors and pursers expected to make large profits out of all transactions. Nevertheless the more responsible captains, thoughtful for their people's welfare, would take trouble in the matter. 'The *Princessa* is so sickly and her Men dying so fast,' Hood wrote on the 23rd April, 'I was obliged to order her to Gros Islet on the 21st to put the worst of her Scorbutic Men on Shore. . . . I thank God the *Barfleur* continues pretty healthy. I have got Lemons and Limes for my Poor Fellows from every place I could which has prevented the Scurvy from taking that Root I am sorry to say it has in other Ships.'

It was not until the issue of lemon juice became regular practice in later years, largely as a result of Gilbert Blane's recommendations, that scurvy was finally eliminated. At the same time he campaigned against the other causes of sickness in ships—the neglect of cleanliness, ventilation and dryness, the widespread drunkenness encouraged by the issue of quantities of spirits, the want of proper bedding and lack of soap—and the absence of proper arrangements for the care of the sick and of medicines. His efforts took a long time to bear full fruit, but in the following year, when he returned to the West Indies with Rodney, a remarkable improvement in the health of the fleet there would be seen.

Meanwhile the fleet which Rodney brought to anchor in Carlisle Bay, Barbados in May 1781 was in sorry shape, physically and materially. It was to have little time to recuperate. On the 27th came news that Tobago was under attack. De Grasse and de Bouillé had taken advantage of their naval superiority to send a small expedition, consisting of two ships of the line and four frigates with 1,300 troops to Tobago while the attention of the British was taken up with the attack on St Lucia. On the 23rd the troops had been landed under cover of fire from the warships.

Rodney at once sent Rear-Admiral Drake and six of the line with troops embarked to the island's rescue. He was to put the troops ashore and try to bring the French squadron to action, but to return at once if he met a superior force. He had been gone but a day when Rodney's frigates brought the startling news that de Grasse with the whole of his fleet had been sighted to the windward of St Lucia standing to the southwards. Rodney was at once in a dilemma. If he put to sea to join Drake he would leave Barbados at the enemy's mercy. If he remained at anchor, Drake might be surprised and overwhelmed. Trusting to good fortune and good seamanship to save Drake, he gave orders for the fleet to be ready instantly to weigh anchor when his detachment should be sighted. Great was his relief, therefore, when daylight on the 21st May showed Drake's ships in the offing. Drake had fortunately been to windward when he sighted de Grasse and so had been able to make good his escape. The fleet was soon at sea and steering south for Tobago. The next afternoon it was in sight and Rodney sent away two small schooners to gather intelligence while he took the fleet towards the anchorage in Man-of-War Bay to land the reinforcement of troops under General Vaughan.

He was too late. An officer of marines, landed to reconnoitre, brought back the news that the island had capitulated the previous

178]

day. Rodney was furious and poured scorn on the Governor and the inhabitants for 'so precipitate a capitulation, when the country appeared to him so very defensible'. There is no doubt that the fort could have withstood a considerable siege, even against the additional force landed by de Grasse on 31st May; but the enemy's threats made it clear that defence would have been at the cost of devastation of the whole island, the flames from one of the plantations lending point to their demands. The local inhabitants, offered terms which would leave them in possession of their property, cannot be blamed if they saw little to recommend heroism.

Fearful now for Barbados, Rodney turned north to re-trace his steps. On the afternoon of the 5th June he overtook de Grasse, sighting him hull-down to leeward between Grenada and the Grenadines. By sundown he had closed the French fleet sufficiently to be able to make out its composition as twenty-four of the line and five frigates, as against his own twenty of the line. For once the British held the windward gage. Rodney could have forced a night action. Hood, ever captious, thought he should have done.

'The British fleet tacked and edged down towards the enemy, who I think was not more than twenty-two of the line, with one 50 and four frigates. . . . There be some who say that we never shall have such another opportunity of attacking them.'

Rodney had good reasons for not doing so. To leeward was the danger-studded area of the Grenadines. Battle would set both fleets drifting down into it in the darkness. Shipwreck for many could result and only luck would decide which side would come off best. Furthermore he feared the swift currents setting westwards. Once in their grip his ships might be swept to leeward into the Caribbean while de Grasse slipped away in the dark to the French-occupied island of Grenada and there 'rejoice at the sight of the British fleet being caught in their deception and driving far to leeward, which would certainly have been attended with the capture of Barbados.'

It is tempting to compare Rodney's caution unfavourably with what Hawke, the victor of Quiberon Bay might have done, or with his own verve in the Moonlight Battle. But, apart from the numerical odds against him, which he was prepared to accept, the

[179

situation was very different. Britain had her back to the wall, facing tremendous odds with the navies of Spain, France and Holland combined against her. At this very time in Home Waters the British fleet of twenty-four ships of the line was facing a Franco-Spanish fleet of forty-nine in the Channel. Rodney could expect no replacements for any ships lost, and meanwhile the safety of the British Empire in the west depended upon the continuance of his fleet in being. The wider implications of any local reverse were clearer to Rodney than to his less experienced and, at this time, less knowledgeable subordinate. No doubt there were many fire-eaters in the fleet burning to see the signal for battle at the flagship's masthead. But this was no time for quixotic risks—as he had earlier told Lord Sandwich. In this case he could only hope that de Grasse, with his superior numbers, would stand to fight the following day.

'I was in hopes to draw them by the next morning to the wind-ward of St Vincent, where we should have had sea room to have attacked them. With this in view, I gave orders that all the lights of the fleet should be particularly conspicuous to the enemy, that in case they chose an action, they might be sure their wishes should be complied with the next day.' Dawn, however, shewed a bare horizon. There was nothing for Rodney to do but to beat his way back to Barbados after sending away a part of Vaughan's troops to strengthen the garrison of St Lucia.

The season for campaigning in the islands had not much longer to run. Both fleets remained watchfully idle, the French at Fort Royal, the British at Barbados. It was no time of ease or repose for Rodney. His health continued to deteriorate. On the one hand Gilbert Blane was urging him to go home for treatment; on the other, came messages from home deploring his proposal to do so. Though he obviously had great confidence in Hood, he knew also that his own continuance in command played a major part in maintenance of public confidence in the conduct of the naval war, at least so long as he commanded success. His position in this respect was by no means as secure as it had been. Since the dramatic capture of St Eustatius and its wealth, things had gone badly. The record showed only an indecisive encounter between the fleets, the loss of Tobago and what could be represented to be a refusal on Rodney's part to fight. Nevertheless he felt it was his duty to stay so long as it was physically supportable. At the end of June he wrote to his wife :

'Judge then of my exhaustion of mind and body, and what I undergo; but it is my duty, and if I can please the King, to whom I owe everything, I must be contented to bear it. I have his leave to return to England during the rainy months, but how can I do it with honour, when his enemies have a superior fleet in these seas, and threaten all his dominions ?'

At times, however, his sufferings were such that he felt he could bear it no longer. On such occasions he would send for Hood and say that he must go and leave the command to him, only to reverse his decision when an easement occurred. Hood's character takes on an unpleasant hue from his correspondence with Jackson at this time. He had no sympathy for his ailing chief.

'It is quite impossible,' he wrote, 'from the unsteadiness of the Commander-in-Chief to know what he means three days together; one hour he says his complaints are of such a nature that he cannot possibly remain in the country and is determined to leave the command to me; the next he says he has not thought of going home.'

At the same time he was passing on ugly rumours at second-hand of barefaced peculation in the matter of the St Eustatius money.

'With respect to the concerns of St Eustatius, I am totally ignorant, not having seen any one account, or had a syllable said to me upon the subject. The irregularity and confusion is beyond conception; a quantity of money was brought from the island in the *Sandwich* but not a single soul acknowledges to know what the sum is, and a most Flemish account will, I am sure, be produced. The Admiral and General have a great deal to answer for, which I told them long ago; and they begin now to be in a squeeze, as many of their actions will not bear daylight.'

Rodney indeed was 'beginning now to be in a squeeze' and no doubt his anxieties bore heavily on his mind. It had been borne in on him at last that some of the 'traytors' he had 'scourged' were legally, if not morally, innocent. He and Vaughan had been forced to lodge £100,000 with Drummonds Bank to be held against any successful actions brought against them. To his agents at St Kitts and Antigua he had ruefully to send instructions 'that

[181

attention should be shown to those merchants or factors who have legally imported their goods directly from Great Britain to St Eustatius, and that you, as my agents, consent to their being restored'. Unfortunately most of such goods had been sold off at knock-down prices and the merchants were demanding their full value. The loss of so much of the plunder when the St Eustatius convoy was captured in April turned a difficult situation for Rodney into a catastrophe. The merchants' claims were to multiply until they became a flood that was once again to submerge him in debt.

Nevertheless he was still writing in buoyant tones at this time to his family about settling his original commitments. A house in London was still being sought, as is shown by a comment in a letter to his wife surprising to a twentieth-century ear, used more to praises of Georgian architecture.

'I am glad the house near Hyde Park was not bought. I dislike any new house: they are not built to last.'

The lull came to a sudden end early in July. The frigate *Nymphe* arrived from her station off Fort Royal with news that de Grasse and his whole fleet had sailed in company with a convoy of nearly two hundred merchant ships carrying the West India trade for France, and had gone to leeward. All was at once in a great bustle. Fast sailing sloops were sent to Jamaica and New York to carry warning to Sir Peter Parker and Thomas Graves. It had always been Rodney's fixed intention to carry the West Indies squadron to North America for the summer months, convinced as he was that the French must have plans to do the same. His only doubt now was whether he could go with it himself or send Hood to put himself under the flag of Graves. Ill-health defeated him and he decided for the latter.

Hood sailed with the fleet on 1st August with orders to escort the trade for Jamaica and then to go on to North America to join Graves. Rodney left the next day with the season's trade convoy for England. He had hoped to go home in the *Sandwich* which had served him so well and which was urgently in need of refit. As long ago as April he had told the First Lord that 'The poor *Sandwich* has almost done all her duty. I am loth to leave her, but it is necessary she should return to England in the summer months'. Alas, even that was too much for the gallant old ship. Before she could face the Atlantic she would have to be 'hove down'—careened and repaired—at Jamaica. Rodney shifted his flag therefore to the *Gibraltar*, once the *Fenix*, flagship of de Langara. Even now he hoped a cooler climate might restore him sufficiently, and he took with him the frigate *Pegasus* intending to shift to her and go to New York if that happened. His hopes were not fulfilled, however. In company with the convoy he crossed the Atlantic and arrived in England on 19th of September, 1781.

XIII

RODNEY's return to England in September 1781 was something less than a triumphant homecoming. To be sure, his son-in-law biographer, General Mundy, says that he set off from Plymouth 'amid the acclamation of a large concourse of British tars' and that 'Lord Powis' house in Albermale Street had been taken for his residence, where he arrived amidst the greetings of thousands of his countrymen, the women strewing his path, as he descended from his carriage, with flowers and garlands'. Nevertheless the lack of success against de Grasse, the loss of Tobago and the cloud of scandal in respect of St Eustatius which was gathering round his head had done much to wither his laurels.

By the King he was received with warmth and flattery and expressions of continued confidence in him. George III made it clear that he considered Rodney's return home a temporary affair and that as soon as his health was restored he would again take up his command in the West Indies. The Ministers, to whom Rodney's popularity in the country had been his greatest asset, were noticeably cooler in face of the attacks being mounted against his reputation inside and outside Parliament. A flood of actions in the High Court was being prepared by the West India merchants and traders. In Parliament their case was taken up by the Whig Opposition. There was no more talk on the proposal to confer a peerage, which had been mooted in the summer and considered so seriously that the Duke of Chandos had offered to sell him Rodney Stoke so that he could base his title on the family estate.

Rodney fought back against the aspersions being made on his reputation. From Bath, where he repaired with his family to seek a cure at the hands of Sir Caesar Hawkins, the eminent surgeon,

184]

he published a selection of his letters justifying his conduct at St Eustatius. Their evidence went a long way to clear him of all but an injudicious excess of zeal in his 'scourging of traytors' and of a lordly disdain for legal niceties. Unfortunately, however, the person who was entrusted with the publication included Samuel Hood's letter urging that he be allowed to cruise to the windward of Martinique to intercept de Grasse. This exposed Rodney to attack on other grounds. The letter gave his enemies a weapon with which to impugn his reputation as a commander as well as his financial probity.

Nevertheless the King, one of whose virtues it was not to desert a faithful servant in adversity, stood by him. In October, on the death of Lord Hawke, he raised him to the dignity of Vice-Admiral of Great Britain, placing him firmly at the head of his profession. The Government followed their master's lead. When on 4th December Burke, for the Opposition, let loose his oratory in denunciation, Rodney was in his seat in the Commons to answer. His statement was dignified but unconvincing, and though he was given the full support of the party in power and Burke's motion was heavily defeated, his reputation was all to make again when he finally sailed to resume his command.

Rodney's appearance at this late period of his life can be seen in a portrait by Sir Joshua Reynolds. The slight, spare figure he painted more than twenty years before remains, with little eighteenth-century portliness to mar it. The brown hair has gone, a white wig taking its place. The rounded, smooth features have sunk to leave the cheekbones prominent. The curving, sensual mouth has assumed a thin, tight line, at least partly on account of the loss of teeth. The easy, arrogant look has been replaced by a hawk-like expression, ardent and severe. The face clearly bears the mark of suffering undergone.

Today it seems astonishing that Britain's most important fleet should have been entrusted to an elderly, ailing admiral of whom it had been credibly suggested that, whether from ill-health or neglect of duty, he had failed at a critical moment. At the time, however, the Government, fighting for survival against the attacks of the powerful Whig Opposition, evidently felt that the country's faith in Rodney left them no choice. George Jackson wrote to Hood on the subject:

'I cannot reconcile myself to the Idea that has led Administration to the Resolution of letting him return. One only prevails with me, which is that as he *was* popular, should affairs go otherwise than well under any other Commander, they would not so easily answer the question, Why was not Rodney sent?'

Let it be remembered, however, that this was the same Jackson who, two years earlier, had written fulsomely to Rodney:

'I feel a Satisfaction in knowing your Welfare to be so inseparable from that of the Public, that in wishing for one I include Both. Your endeavours . . . will I am sure equal my zealous wishes for success and, I may add, which is more, they will be exerted to produce those Honours and Advantages our Country, at this time, so much stands in need of.'

It is equally remarkable that Rodney, suffering as he was from multiple ills, should have been willing to undertake the task. That ambition was a powerful spur is no doubt true; but there must have been a very real patriotism driving him also. From Bath on 4th November 1781 he wrote to Sandwich:

'I have the most flattering hope that a few days will restore my health in such a manner as to enable me to do my duty. May your Lordship never experience the pain and torture I have undergone since my coming to Bath, but Sir Caesar Hawkins assures me that in a short time my health will be perfectly restored . . . a few days, I am told, will remove my disorder, which is a violent stricture which prevents my making water, and which has been very bad indeed. . . .'

'P.S. Pardon this writing, my pain being very troublesome.'

On what reserves of fortitude did the suffering man of nearly sixty-four draw to enable him to embark in the *Arrogant* (74) at Spithead a month later, there to set about infusing something of his ardent spirit into the indolent officers leisurely preparing the ships he was to lead to the West Indies? There are many actions in Rodney's life which fall short of the standards expected of a hero of fiction; but few will deny him the quality of courageous endurance. The much-maligned Lord Sandwich paid his tribute in timely words of encouragement.

'The *fate of this Empire is in your Hands*, and I have no reason to wish that it should be in any other.'

Sandwich was speaking the bare truth. The four months since

Rodney's departure from the West Indies had seen the war take a disastrous turn. The British fleet in North American waters under Admiral Graves had missed a glorious opportunity to defeat the French under de Grasse; had suffered in consequence a strategic reverse which in turn had led to the surrender at York-town of the British army under Lord Cornwallis. The war with the colonies had been decided in favour of the Americans. The remainder of the Empire lay open to attack. The only force which could save it was the West Indies squadron, greatly out-numbered until Rodney could join it with the twelve ships of the line allocated to him.

Rodney's strategic prescience had enabled him to forecast with remarkable accuracy the turn of events in American waters. As soon as he heard that de Grasse had gone with his whole fleet to leeward on the 5th July, he had ordered away the fast sailing sloop *Swallow* carrying a warning to Admiral Graves at New York. Though he had believed that de Grasse would only take twelve or fourteen or the line north in response to Washington's appeals for help, he had sent Graves a further despatch by the *Pegasus* on the 1st August urging him to come south to meet Hood so that his fleet might be concentrated ready to meet de Grasse when he should arrive. With unerring accuracy he had named the Capes of Virginia, at the mouth of Chesapeake Bay, as the station he should take up.

Unfortunately this later despatch did not reach Graves until too late. Lacking Rodney's strategic sense, he had no certainty that de Grasse would come, or if he did, that it was against the isolated British army in Virginia that the enemy forces would concentrate. Both he and Clinton believed, until too late, that the Franco-American objective was New York. Thus while de Grasse was sailing north from Cap François with twenty-eight ships of the line, Graves lingered at Sandy Hook where he was discussing with General Clinton the possibility of an attack on Rhode Island. There Hood joined him on 16th August, 1781, with his fourteen of the line, bringing the force ready for sea up to nineteen capital ships.

Hood, disturbed at his senior's inactivity at such a critical time, anchored his ships outside the bar. He then set off by boat to pay his respects and to urge Graves to move his ships across the bar, a

G   [187 manœuvre only possible at high water, so as to be ready to sail at once should it be necessary. Graves agreed and by the 31st had completed his concentration. The previous day, unknown to either of the British commanders, de Grasse had arrived and anchored in Chesapeake Bay. Three thousand troops with artillery had been landed to join the Franco-American force investing Cornwallis' army at Yorktown.

Hardly had Graves joined Hood than intelligence reached him that the small French squadron of eight of the line under de Barras which had been at Rhode Island had put to sea on the 25th and gone south. Graves was soon following. He correctly guessed de Barras' destination to be the Chesapeake; but not yet did he realise that his move was part of a grand concentration of all their forces by the enemy. Not until his arrival off the mouth of the bay on 5th September was something of the new strategic situation borne in on him by the sight of 'a number of great ships at anchor which seemed to be extended across the extreme of the Chesapeake from Cape Henry to the Middle Ground'.

Expecting to find only de Barras' squadron—which in fact had not yet joined de Grasse—Graves had reason to be dismayed. He could hardly have expected to be immediately presented as he was with an opportunity to strike a crippling blow such as every sea commander sighed vainly for. At mid-day he saw the French sails breaking out and their ships begin to move out of harbour. With the wind at N.N.E. they had to tack to and fro before they could weather Cape Henry and gain the open sea. Thus it was in a straggling, formless line that they emerged. Their van squadron was clear while the remainder of the fleet were still beating their way out. Graves, in the commanding windward position, might at this stage have run down with his whole force and overwhelmed the enemy's van long before support could have reached it. He hesitated. No doubt a similarity to the opening stage of Byron's disastrous engagement off Grenada occurred to him. He wanted time to study the situation before committing himself. *(see page 192)*

Forming line of battle parallel to the enemy's course, he held off. Soon after two o'clock the French fleet, twenty-four of the line, was clear of the harbour; but their line was by no means formed. Their van was separated from the remainder and was

188]

considerably to windward. Thus the opportunity for Graves still presented itself of bringing the whole of his force against a part of the enemy's. Inhibiting him, however, was the unquestioning belief in the need not only to preserve the rigid line-of-battle, but to bring it into action van to van, centre to centre, rear to rear, each ship opposing that holding the same station in the enemy line. Such was the interpretation of the Fighting Instructions that was generally accepted. It assumed, however, that the enemy's line was similarly formed.

Faced by an enemy who was, in Jervis's words, 'misconducting his line', Graves was out of his depth. Finding that his line over-lapped that of the enemy, he first hove-to until van was abreast of van. When this had been achieved he at last decided to attack; but not by all ships bearing down together, roughly in line abreast; instead he ordered the leading ship to lead more to starboard, so that for more than an hour his line was slowly closing the enemy at an angle. At 3.46 the leading ships were within gunshot. The signal was hoisted to bear down and engage the enemy. The leaders were at once in close action, but with the signal for 'line of battle ahead' still flying, an order which was categorical in its implications—the remainder felt they could do nothing but maintain their station on a line joining the van ship to the flagship in the centre. *(see page 193)*

Thus most of the centre division came into action only at long shot, while the rear, under Hood, hardly fired a shot. De Grasse, unable to work to windward with his centre and rear to support his van, soon signalled for the latter to bear away to leeward. The action was thus broken off. With sunset all firing had ceased and the Battle of the Chesapeake had ended in an indecisive skirmish. The wretched Graves was to some extent the victim of the inadequate signal system in force. The day after the battle he sent a memorandum round the fleet which read:

'When the signal for the line of battle ahead is out at the same time with the signal for battle, it is not to be understood that the latter signal shall be rendered ineffectual by a too strict adherence to the former.' Hood's comments on this show that this was to him a sort of naval sacrilege. 'It is the first time I ever heard it suggested that too strict an adherence could be paid to the line of battle. . . . According to Mr Graves' Memo., any

1. *Martinique. 1781 April 17th, 8.30 a.m.* Rodney, by keeping his fleet at close stations, is able to threaten a portion of De Guichen's extended line. The latter (in foreground) avoids the threat by wearing his ships together.

2. *Martinique. 1781 April 17th, 12.30 p.m.* Rodney, having repeated his tactical success of threatening the extended French rearguard, loses his initiative because his captains, misunderstanding his instructions, haul out of close station to reach their opposite numbers in the French fleet.

3. *1781 September 5th, 2.20 p.m.* Graves, having worked his fleet round to head seawards, heaves to, while the French fleet (foreground) beats slowly out of the Chesapeake. A great opportunity missed by Graves to demolish the French fleet.

4. *September 5th, 3.45 p.m.* British van attacks the French van, but
   due to faulty interpretation of signals, the remainder of the fleet
   keeps to windward, out of range of the main French fleet (coming
   into foreground).

captain may break the line with impunity when he pleases.'

Hood, of course, had to justify the failure of his rear squadron to get into action. His solution of Graves's problem was the right one, nevertheless. 'Had the centre gone to the support of the van, and the signal for the line being hauled down, or the commander-in-chief had set the example for close action, even with the signal for the line flying, the van of the enemy must have been cut to pieces, and the rear division of the British fleet would have been opposed to those ships the centre division fired at and at the proper distance for engaging, or the Rear-Admiral who commanded it would have a great deal to answer for.'

Rodney's plan at Martinique has several points of similarity. Hood, for all his criticisms of Rodney, was to write after the Chesapeake, 'Had that Admiral (Rodney) have now led his Majesty's squadron from the West Indies to this coast, I will venture to pronounce that the 5th of this month would have proved a most glorious day for England.'

In truth the situation had been altogether too much for the limited ability of Graves. To Sandwich he confessed, 'the signal was not understood. I do not mean to blame anyone, my Lord. I hope we all did our best. . . . For my own particular, my Lord, I know not how to do more. If I err, it is from want of knowledge, not disinclination.'

The battle over, Graves's opportunity to attack the stronger enemy on reasonable terms had gone. Five of his ships, including his flagship the *London*, had received heavy damage. During the next three days the two fleets remained in sight of each other licking their wounds, de Grasse being to windward but showing no desire to renew the action. The strategical problem was as much beyond Graves as the tactical one had been. Called into conference on the day after the battle, Hood had given his opinion that the British fleet should make at once for the Chesapeake either to rob de Grasse of his anchorage or force him to fight to regain it. Graves did not agree. Even when de Grasse, on 9th September quitted the scene under a press of canvas, the British fleet remained hove-to. Hood again urged his commander-in-chief to make for the Chesapeake, and at last on the 11th Graves did so, only to find de Grasse securely in harbour, his numbers increased to thirty-six of the line by the arrival of de Barras.

Asked his opinion as to what should be done, Hood told Graves that 'he really knows not what to say in the truly lamentable state we have brought ourselves'.

Indeed, with an enemy nearly double his strength and in an impregnable position, with a quarter of his ships crippled and no base in the vicinity, there was nothing to be done. Graves turned northwards for Sandy Hook and the fate of Cornwallis's army was sealed. A month later it was forced to capitulate and the last chance of a successful outcome of the war with the colonies had gone.

The news of Yorktown reached London on 25th November. That the war with America had been lost was clear to everyone. It was equally clear that, with their hands freed of the necessity to support their American allies, the French would concentrate on ejecting the British from their remaining possessions in the West Indies. The Empire was indeed in mortal peril. That only Rodney could save it was the opinion of the King and the nation. His return to resume the command as soon as the squadron he was to take with him was ready, was settled. He professed himself sufficiently recovered to comply.

Early in December, in the intervals of replying to Burke's attacks, he was in London making final preparations when a summons to the Palace came. In the ensuing audience, the King told him that it had been learnt that de Grasse had sailed with his whole fleet back to the Windward Islands. Rodney must leave as soon as possible with whatever ships were ready. The morrow would find him afloat, the faithful servant assured his master.

He was as good as his word. A message came to Gilbert Blane. 'I must pass Hyde Park Corner this afternoon with daylight. There are my son and my secretary besides myself in the coach, and a place for you if you choose.' Blane, his appointment as Physician of the Fleet by now confirmed by the Admiralty, was not to be left behind. When the coach was announced, 'after an early dinner, a little before four o'clock', he climbed aboard. At the last moment a mutual friend, Sir Walter Farquhar the physician, came to take his leave. 'God bless you,' growled the old admiral. 'I will send you the Count de Grasse as a present.'

Once again the story of dockyard delays and negligence of officials has to be told. Rodney's new flagship the *Formidable*, a splendid three-decker of ninety guns, being at Plymouth, he hoisted his flag in the *Arrogant* (74). To the Admiralty he reported that 'although the squadron under my command are not complete, and neither of the frigates ready to attend me, I propose getting under sail at daybreak tomorrow. . . . I have sent another express to Plymouth to order the ships of my squadron to join me the moment I appear off the Sound. . . .' Against contrary winds the *Arrogant* beat laboriously down Channel. Plymouth Sound was reached on 17th December when the rising gale forced him to anchor in Cawsand Bay. 'Had I continued at sea this night,' he told Sandwich, 'I must have lost ground, as the wind blew very fresh, and a whole tide of flood coming on. . . . At present the wind blows very fresh at south-west, and the weather looks very dirty . . .' To his disgust he found only three of his squadron ready. The *Formidable* was one of those still being fitted out.

For the next three weeks he was storm-bound, a circumstance which enabled him to bring his drive to bear upon the indolent dockyard officers and captains. The port admiral—Milbank— came off worst in a battle of wills in the matter of transferring men from ships under refit to complete the complements of Rodney's squadron. To the First Lord, Rodney fumed: 'Your Lordship may easily judge my anxiety of mind occasioned by my long detention at this port; but I may venture to affirm that not a single ship would have been now near ready, had not my arrival obliged them to exert themselves in a manner unusual at this port. Indeed, my Lord, the Admiralty are cruelly treated, their orders have arrived in time and have been fully explicit, but there is such a slackness in carrying the orders into execution as gives me the utmost disgust.'

At this very moment Middleton, no admirer of Rodney, was echoing his words. 'Unless the fleet is managed otherways than it has been and the Admiralty office restored to its original institution and maintains a proper authority over its officers, no human means can save the country. The game is almost over and we have not a moment to lose.'

On 1st January 1782 Rodney wrote to his wife, 'It is impossible for you to conceive my chagrin at being detained in this horrid port, where I have experienced nothing but storms of wind, neglect, unwillingness, and disobedience to orders they have received from the Admiralty. Faction and party have descended so low as to enter the minds of even dockyard officers, and induce them to do their duty negligently, for which they deserve to be turned out . . . and sorry I am to say, that the sea-officers are more to blame than the dock-officers, and that my own captain is among the slow ones. I have given him notice that he will not remain my captain. I am convinced that if I had not arrived in this port, the *Formidable* would not have been ready these two months. She is now complete, and waits only for a wind to come out of the Hamoaze, but the masters, attendants and pilots are such dogs that they make difficulties of carrying her to the Sound.'

The flag-captain, John Symonds, had come home with Rodney as captain of the *Gibraltar*, and in the normal course of events had been transferred to the *Formidable*. Rodney's warning that he would have to go was no idle threat, but for the moment there was no successor at hand, nor was there a vacancy elsewhere to which he could be transferred.

An important appointment which Rodney made at this time was that of Captain Sir Charles Douglas, late of the *Duke*, another three-decker, to be 'First Captain'—equivalent to Captain of the Fleet today. Douglas was an enthusiastic gunnery expert, responsible for the introduction of a number of technical improvements which he had installed in the *Duke* and was now to do so in the *Formidable* also. Details of these improvements are given in Appendix A to this book.

Much has been made of Douglas's contribution to the campaign of 1782, on the assumption that all Rodney's ships had been given his gunnery improvements. The fact, however, is that only the *Duke* was completely modified, and the *Formidable* partly so, at the Battle of the Saintes.

One notable gunnery innovation there was in the ships which Rodney carried to the West Indies on this occasion. This was the installation of carronades as the upper deck armament. These were short-barrelled cannon and therefore light for their calibre, enabling 32-pounders to be mounted on the quarter-deck, poop and forecastle. For the same reason they were only short-range weapons; but at close quarters they possessed a tremendous smashing power—in fact they were originally called 'smashers'—

and at such ranges gave ships carrying them a considerable advantage over those not so fitted; and the French had not yet adopted them.

Skilful a technical expert as Douglas was, there is evidence to show that he was far from brilliant as a staff officer. Rodney at this time was desperately in need of a really competent chief of staff to take the burden of organisational detail off his shoulders. Hood was to record his contempt for Douglas's capabilities in this direction and to become voluble in his criticisms of the resultant muddle and confusion in the flagship.

'Sir Charles Douglas,' he was to write, 'is no more fit for the station he fills than I am to be an Archbishop. . . . I have been witness of his receiving orders that have appeared to my mind to be big with absurdity, and he has gone upon deck to direct their being executed, upon which I have more than once said, "I believe, Sir George, you are unacquainted with some circumstances respecting the orders you have just given to Sir Charles Douglas," which I have related and he has immediately acknowledged it, sent for Sir Charles, and asked him why he had not made known what he had just heard from me, which makes the orders he has received highly improper, and they have been put a stop to. Now, what I did was most certainly the *bounden* duty of a *first* captain. But all is confusion on board the *Formidable*, and not the least attention to a regularity of system and order.'

Making due allowance for Sir Samuel's liver, and for the probability that some of these shortcomings must have been the fault of the unsatisfactory Symonds, it is evident and unfortunate that Rodney did not have the support of a talented staff officer to take from his shoulders the burden of administration of a great fleet on a foreign station. That such was sorely needed, Hood had no doubt. 'Sir George Rodney requires a monitor constantly at his elbow, as much as a froward child,' he lamented.

The storms which held Rodney in that 'horrid port' at least enabled him to sail finally with the twelve of the line promised him and with his flag in the *Formidable*. They had also upset French plans to send reinforcements to de Grasse. On 10th December these had sailed from Brest—five ships of the line—as part of a force of nineteen under de Guichen, escorting a convoy laden with important naval and military stores for the West

198]

Indies. Two days later, when they were some 150 miles south-west of Ushant, in thick and squally weather, the smother had suddenly cleared to windward to disclose a British squadron of twelve ships of the line and one 50-gun ship under Kempenfelt.

Kempenfelt had been severely critical of the order which sent him to sea with a force so inferior to the one known to be under de Guichen's flag; but he had loyally obeyed it. Luck had now rewarded him; for he saw that the Frenchman had been caught with his warships away to leeward. Kempenfelt swooped on the convoy. The merchantmen scattered like a flock of frightened birds, but not all could escape. By nightfall fifteen had been secured under the eyes of the helpless de Guichen trying fruit-lessly to beat his way to windward and their defence. Had he had enough frigates, Kempenfelt considered, de Guichen would have suffered 'a most ridiculous disgrace—that of having all his convoy taken from him.' However, a few days later Kempenfelt's work was completed for him by the same gale that had forced Rodney into Cawsand Bay. The remnant of de Guichen's armada was scattered and crippled. Two ships of the line only were able to carry on across the Atlantic. The remainder put back into Brest for repairs.

Thus when the *Formidable* and her eleven consorts in wild weather at last succeeded in rounding Ushant on 17th January, 1782, Rodney had stolen a march on de Grasse's reinforcements. This was of the utmost importance. Once joined to Hood's twenty-two of the line Rodney would have sufficient strength to hold de Grasse in check and still spare a squadron to intercept his reinforcements when they should come.

He arrived at Barbados on 19th February 1782, five weeks out from Plymouth, a fast passage which Rodney found 'scarcely credible' in face of the 'storms and tempests, and contrary winds' experienced.

'None but an English squadron and copper bottoms,' he wrote to Lady Rodney, 'could have forced their way to the West Indies as we have done. Ushant we weathered in a storm but two leagues, the seas mountains high, which made a fair breach over the *Formidable* and the *Namur*. . . . "Persist and Conquer" is a maxim that I hold good in war, even against the elements, and it has answered, for till I got the length of Madeira, nothing but violent storms prevailed, which you are *sea-woman* enough to know were directly contrary. This being the first letter I have been able to write since my violent fit of the gout in both hands and feet, I am so tired that I must stop, and go on tomorrow.'

He was nevertheless too late to prevent the French from winning the first victory of the campaign. After the disaster at Yorktown in the previous October, Hood had been ordered back to the West Indies. He arrived at Barbados on 5th December with eighteen sail of the line. With the ships already on station his total force amounted to twenty-two.

Until the arrival of reinforcements under Rodney, expected soon, Hood's situation was parlous in the extreme. De Grasse was at Fort Royal with more than thirty of the line. The British squadron was worn out with continuous sea-time. Already, at the Chesapeake, Graves had commented that 'Several of the West Indies squadron were the shadow of ships more than the substance'. Hood's letters and despatches disclose their deplorable condition in more ways than one; from Barbados he wrote:

'We have several vessels here that are not of much use; for if their bottoms are not kept clean they will be liable to be taken and whenever they go to Antigua their crews desert and before they can be remanned become foul again.' In another letter he bewailed that 'all our ships go to ruin for want of caulking'. This is borne out by an appeal from Captain Thompson of the *Alcide* (74) at about this time which gives a good idea of the conditions under which the crews lived and the crazy state of the ships in which they sailed forth to do battle.

'The condition of the *Alcide* for want of caulking is very bad. We cannot wash the Lower Deck the seams are so open over the Bread Room, Sail Room and Store Rooms. While we wash the Main Deck the people cannot lay in their Hammocks, the sides and every other part in the same condition. Under the counter when at sea it runs in streams into the Bread Room. If you should think proper to suffer the ship to remain at Barbadoes, I imagine Caulkers and Rigging for the Fore Topmast may be procured, which is everything we shall want to put the ship in a condition for sea, except a Fore Yard, and I should imagine in the present state of affairs she may be sooner refitted at Barbadoes than at any place.'

In acknowledgement of this sad tale, poor Thompson was told to be ready to sail that very afternoon. In addition to the lamentable state of the ships themselves, Hood found himself so short of fresh victuals, even bread, that he was unable to cruise to intercept the French reinforcements expected. 'If I can only get a month's bread I will certainly sail and use my best endeavours to intercept the armament from Brest before it reaches Martinique . . . but if no bread can be got at Antigua or St Kitts I shall from necessity be compelled to remain in this bay or go no further than St Lucia till a convoy arrives from England.'

But at news that de Grasse was out, Hood took his fleet at once to sea on 14th December to meet him. Off St Lucia he heard that the French fleet, accompanied by a large number of transports, had manœuvred for a week in the channel between that island and Martinique, trying to beat to windward, but 'having carried away many topmasts and yards in struggling against very squally weather', had returned to Fort Royal Bay. As Hood guessed, the objective of de Grasse and de Bouillé had been Barbados. A week later they tried again, only to fail as before.

Defeated by the winds and currents, de Grasse now decided upon a fresh plan. On 2nd January he sailed from Fort Royal and vanished in a northerly direction. Hood sent frigates to search, and himself returned to Barbados which he still believed to be the enemy's objective. There he remained with no news of the enemy until the 14th, when a letter arrived from Governor Shirley of St Kitts. A large fleet of men-of-war and transports had been seen from the heights of the neighbouring island of Nevis. It must be wondered whether the captious Hood in his strategic dilemma discovered any funds of sympathy for Rodney's difficulties in similar circumstances the previous summer.

With twenty-two of the line he hurried north to his base at Antigua. The frigate *Lizard* joined him on passage, bringing the tardy news that St Kitts was invested; but before he could go to its assistance he had first to go to Antigua 'to get what flower I could as a succedaneum for bread' and to pick up troops under General Prescott. By 23rd January he was ready and put to sea determined to 'give battle to the Count de Grasse be his numbers as they may'. He had set a precedent while at Antigua of sending for his subordinate flag-officers, Rear-Admiral Drake and

Commodore Affleck, to explain his intentions to them. They in turn were to pass the information on to their captains. Such a thing was unheard of in the rank-conscious navy of that day. Its result was electrical. Though in fact the plan he set before them—of attacking the French fleet at anchor—was to be frustrated through an accident, every captain felt he had been put on his mettle to think of the admiral's design when a manœuvre was ordered rather than to obey blindly and unintelligently. It was to result in one of the most masterly tactical displays of naval history.

Owing to the accident, a collision between the *Alfred* (74) and the frigate *Nymphe* during the night, Hood's squadron was still rounding the southern point of Nevis at daybreak on 24th January. If Hood had not waited for repairs to be made in the *Alfred* he might as planned have fallen by surprise upon the French fleet to great advantage at dawn; for de Grasse had anchored his ships in Frigate Bay in no sort of order, so that the four or five ships to windward might have been overwhelmed before others could have worked their way into action in support. As it was, de Grasse, warned of Hood's approach, realised his danger and put to sea during the afternoon.

De Grasse had twenty-five of the line and two fifty's against Hood's twenty-two. During the night of the 24th the French kept a few miles to leeward of the British. At dawn Hood held the commanding windward gage and could have attacked. The odds were great—Hood thought the enemy had twenty-nine of the line—but not much worse than at the Chesapeake. Second thoughts had come to him, however. The relief of St Kitts was his immediate objective. 'Would the event of a battle have determined the fate of the island,' he was to write, 'I would, without hesitation, have attacked the enemy. . . .' There was perhaps another way of achieving this than a pitched battle against odds. Perhaps, too, ambition to show what might have been done at the Chesapeake had he been in command influenced him.

With de Grasse away to leeward he had a good chance to beat him to his anchorage and seize it for himself. The risks were great if de Grasse penetrated his design in time, for the British ships would then have to anchor while under fire. The manœuvre would call for an intelligent appreciation of his plan by his captains; but he knew them well by now and had confidence in them; trained as they had been under Rodney's stern eye and welded into a willing team by his own more sympathetic methods.

He formed his fleet into close lines of battle, ships one cable apart on the starboard tack, on a northerly course up the west coast of Nevis. De Grasse, some miles to leeward, was running south, confidently awaiting an attack by Hood's inferior force. Hood, under easy sail, waited until the French fleet was abreast of his own. Then a signal broke out at the masthead of the *Barfleur* and was repeated down the line. The sightseers crowding the hills of Nevis saw a press of sail blossom on the British ships which, with the wind on their quarters, began to surge forward towards Frigate Bay some twelve miles ahead.

Now de Grasse realised what was happening. He ordered his fleet to go about together on to the starboard tack and with the wind abeam his ships bore down in quarter-line (in *échelon*) to the attack. It was two hours before he could come into action, however, and all the time the British fleet was drawing across his bows and nearing the anchorage. At 2 p.m. Hood signalled for the fleet to anchor in succession in the order of sailing. Now came the critical moment. At 2.20 p.m. the enemy were in gunshot, the French van coming up against the British centre. The four rearmost British ships had dropped back, delayed by the poor sailing qualities of the *Prudent*, fourth from the rear. A gap opened in the line. The huge *Ville de Paris* pushed for it. It seemed as though the laggards must be cut off.

But Hood's faith in his captains was justified. The three ship's ahead of the gap, *Canada*, *Resolution* and *Bedford*, commanded by 'Billy Blue' Cornwallis, Lord Robert Manners and Commodore Edmund Affleck, saw the danger, reduced sail and dropped back. As Hood described it: 'The enemy gave a preference for Commodore Affleck but he kept up so noble a fire and was so supported by his seconds, Captain Cornwallis and Lord Robert Manners, that the loss and damage in these ships was very trifling and they very much preserved the ships in the rear.' Confident that the rear would hold off the enemy long enough for his purpose, Hood ordered the van and centre to press on to the anchorage. Already the leading ship was rounding up into the wind to drop anchor close in to the shallows of Basseterre Roads. One after the other the ships astern of her followed suit to anchor in an east-west line. Having swung to their cables, they were able to bring their starboard broadsides to bear in support of the hard-pressed rear. Baffled, de Grasse sailed past and withdrew to consider his next move.

Nevertheless the rear squadron and some of the centre had had to perform this manœuvre under heavy fire. Had the French fought with as much spirit as their opponents, Hood's rear must have been overwhelmed. Splendid seamanship and good gunnery had won the day. Young Lord Robet Manners wrote blithely home:

'The taking of this Road was well judged, well conducted, and well executed though indeed the French had an opportunity, which they missed, of bringing our rear to a very severe account . . . the most masterly manœuvre I ever saw.'

During the following day de Grasse twice led his fleet in to the attack with gallantry and spirit; but Hood had so adjusted the line of anchored ships that, with the aid of springs on their cables to swing them as desired, each French ship in turn was received by the fire of several of their enemy simultaneously. By the end of the day the French had had enough and they withdrew to a watchful station to leeward. De Grasse had, indeed, been outmanœuvred, and made a laughing stock. The effect of Hood's ingenuity on the morale of both sides was undoubtedly great; but it could not save St Kitts. The garrison, greatly outnumbered, had retreated on 9th January to the fort on Brimstone Hill. There they held out for more than a month. But on 12th February, when de Bouillé was able to bring into action against them a number of heavy guns, they were forced to capitulate.

De Grasse's fleet had meanwhile been increased to thirty-three of the line. Hood's wish was now only to 'carry the squadron to Sir George Rodney in as perfect a state as possible', and Rodney was expected daily. Once again Hood planned to outwit de Grasse, waiting to seaward hopeful of bringing the now greatly inferior British squadron to action. On the evening of 13th February, he called all captains to the *Barfleur* for orders. Synchronising all their watches, they were, at exactly 11 p.m. and without signal, to cut their cables and set sail, leaving a boat

204]

with a lantern in it to deceive the enemy. No other lights were to be shown and absolute silence maintained. Dawn breaking over the hills of St Kitts revealed to the duped de Grasse an empty anchorage and not a sail in sight.

Hood's squadron arrived at Antigua on 19th February. On the same day Rodney dropped anchor at Barbados. On the 25th junction between the two admirals was made off Antigua. With the two fleets again at roughly equal strength, the stage was set for the decisive encounter to decide the fate of the British Empire in the west.

XIV

THE news which greeted Rodney on his arrival was uniformly gloomy. As long ago as the previous November, as soon as Hood had set sail for North America, that enterprising old warrior de Bouillé had organised a surprise attack on St Eustatius, which fell to him without a shot. Rodney was justifiably furious when he heard the details.

'A garrison of eight hundred veteran troops, in an island impregnable if attacked by an army of ten thousand men,' he wrote. 'Yet Colonel Cockburne, with his eyes open, and after he had but the day before sent a letter to General Christie at Barbadoes, acquainting him that he had completed all the batteries, and made the island impregnable to everything but a surprise . . . the next day withdrew the guard from the battery where the enemy landed, displaced the man from the signal house and put a person in his place that could not see. . . . The Marquis de Bouillé and the three hundred soldiers that landed, expected nothing but being prisoners of war. All their boats were stove in ten thousand pieces, all their ammuntion wet, and not one firelock capable of going off. On firing the morning gun, the enemy concluded it was an alarm, and were ready to lay down their arms upon the first demand. They took courage upon their not being attacked, marched up to the fort, and rushed in with their bayonets. Cockburne was taken, the first man, on horseback; all the officers in their quarters, and the soldiers in their barracks.'

Poor Rodney. '£250,000 were seized by the enemy,' he complained, which he had 'insisted should be sent to New York with Sir Samuel Hood for the use of the army, whereby good bills might have been obtained, and the money long since lodged in the Bank'.

At the same time his fury with the disloyal West Indian merchants, self-righteously suing him in the courts and being ennobled by the eloquence of Edmund Burke, received fresh impetus. 'The fleet I found here in want of everything,' he wrote to Lady Rodney. 'There is no villainy some of the merchants of these islands are not guilty of, and they take every opportunity of carrying on a traitorous correspondence with the enemy. . . . The inhabitants of Basseterre, St Christopher's (St Kitts) suffered the enemy to land without firing a single gun, though they had three very good batteries. . . . The merchants of Basseterre put into their capitulation, that the ships coming from England should have leave to land their cargoes unmolested at that island; they forgot that another person's leave was necessary, when they chose to be French subjects. Not one barrel of provisions will I suffer to pass to the island. They are French, and as French I will treat them. The French, in want of everything, were glad to catch at that article, in hopes by that means to supply themselves with the provisions destined for St Christopher's. It is indifferent to the merchants who are the purchasers, provided that they get their price. I hear they intend to petition me. I shall treat them as they deserve, if they do, for I hate traitors.'

Besides St Eustatius, the French had taken the opportunity to surprise and recapture the Dutch colony of Demerara, six British frigates surrendering without resistance to three of the enemy. It is not to be wondered at that Rodney felt that many naval officers of his day needed a strong hand and a stern eye to compel them to do their duty.

Now, hastening off as soon as his ships had watered to his rendezvous with Hood, he was to hear of the loss of St Kitts, largely owing to the refusal of its inhabitants to assist the garrison to mount the guns he had left on the shore for its defence.

Meanwhile de Grasse, hearing of Rodney's arrival, had taken his fleet back to Fort Royal, not neglecting to capture the little island of Montserrat as he passed. He was well satisfied with his achievements and now, while he refitted his ships, he waited for the arrival of a convoy from France. Then, as Rodney and Hood well knew, he intended to embark all the troops he could raise, join the Spanish ships lying at Havana and attack Jamaica,

[207

Britain's most important possession in the West Indies. He hoped, somewhat naïvely, to avoid battle with Rodney.

The first task for Rodney's fleet was to intercept de Grasse's reinforcements. Before this could be attended to, however, it was urgently necessary to relieve Hood's ships as far as possible of the distresses they had been labouring under. This was accomplished at St Lucia.

On 15th March he wrote to inform the Admiralty:

'As most of the fleet under the command of Sir Samuel Hood were in the greatest want of repair, water, stores and provisions, particularly bread, they having been a considerable time without any, as likewise of anchors, the whole fleet, on their departure from St Christopher's, having been obliged to leave them behind, I caused the utmost despatch to be made in dividing the anchors, stores and provisions brought in the squadron under my command from Great Britain amongst the fleet in general, and hastened their refitting and watering; but such has been the severity of the weather, unusual at this season in this climate with so violent a surf on the shore, that many of the long boats of the fleet have been destroyed. However, I have now the pleasure to acquaint their Lordships, that in a few days the whole will be complete and ready for service, except the *Intrepid* which has been found unserviceable, and must be sent to Great Britain with the May convoy.'

A light-hearted letter from Lord Robert Manners at this time tells us much of the condition of Hood's veteran ships.

'The *Resolution* is ordered to sea this morning, and not in the most pleasant condition, being entirely destitute of stores, and all our rigging condemned as unserviceable. To say the truth she herself complains a little. I am administering to her the most salutary and efficacious remedies that can be applied in this country and there is soon to be a consultation of carpenters upon her, as it is generally supposed a change of climate will be found the only means of restoring her health which has been lately very much impaired; and as her disorder is chiefly a violent relaxation in all her parts, so as to admit of the free ingress and egress of water—the reverse of a diabetes—I opine a northern climate is the most proper to brace her up, and restore many of her faculties which she has now, I grieve to say, entirely lost.

'It is remarked that copper-bottom ships, when once they begin to show their defects, drop all at once.'

The condition of de Grasse's ships can have been little better. In one important matter the British fleet held a great advantage. In spite of the cheerless condition of their leaky ships, the health of the ships' companies was infinitely better than it had been a year ago. Gilbert Blane's recommendations had been given heed to. Scurvy had almost vanished, particularly in those ships which had been longest in the West Indies and so had benefited from Blane's theories. Other diseases too were enormously reduced through following his advice as to hygiene, cleanliness and proper care for the sick. Hospital ships had been fitted out to augment the inadequate accommodation in hospitals ashore. These latter were equipped and supplied by contractors who, even when honest by the standards of the day, fulfilled the exact letter of their contracts and not an iota more. For instance, shortly before Rodney assumed command in the West Indies in 1780, his predecessor Hyde Parker had reported that: 'On my surveying the Hospitals in October last, I found between five and six hundred Patients, amongst whom not one who had ever been allowed what is called full diet in the Contract . . . nor any, except the hundred specified in the Contract, that had Cradles, Beds or Sheets; the rest, which were five-sixths of the Number, were laying about on the floors of a Room in their nasty Cloaths or more nasty Hammocks.'

Before leaving England in January 1782, Rodney had had Blane made Commissioner for the Sick and Hurt. This appointment had not previously existed, commanders-in-chief having been expected to attend to the business amongst their many other preoccupations. 'My time and attention being occupied with the other arrangements of so great a fleet,' Rodney told the Admiralty, 'as well as the general objects of war, I had no leisure to examine and settle the particulars referred to me. A want of order therefore unavoidably took place in the management and accommodation of the sick, to which I cannot but ascribe a part of the mortality that prevailed.'

All these improvements added up to present a picture vastly different from the previous year, and Gilbert Blane was to record with justifiable pride that in Hood's squadron, out of twenty-

[209

two ships of the line there were not twenty-two men who could not come to quarters. The French fleet was by no means so healthy and Blane was later to lament that epidemic disease was contracted by the working parties cleaning out the captured French ships. Like Hood, de Grasse was in pressing need of provisions and stores, without which he could not embark on the projected expedition against Jamaica. It was all the more important therefore for Rodney to ensure the interception of the convoy known to be on its way to Martinique from France.

Hood, who had been refitting with his squadron in the Grand Cul de Sac, rejoined the main fleet at Gros Islet Bay on 7th March. He at once began to press his commander-in-chief to get to sea. Weather conditions in the Atlantic were favourable to fast passages from Europe. The February packet had already arrived. A Danish ship had made St Lucia in twenty-nine days from Spithead; the French convoy might arrive any day. Rodney was understandably desirous of completing the refit of his whole force and unwilling to divide it too widely with de Grasse concentrated at Fort Royal; he was perhaps the victim of wishful thinking, therefore, when he argued that de Grasse's reinforcements would not sail before the beginning of March. Hood gave in to the probability of it, but 'thought it very possible to happen otherwise'.

He was to be proved right. When the fleet at last sailed, thirty-six of the line by now, the French convoy was only a few days' sail from its destination. All might yet have been well if Rodney had heeded the counsel of his able second-in-command. Hood thought it possible that the French would make their landfall at the northern end of the chain of islands before running south to Fort Royal. Rodney was certain that they would follow their invariable custom of making for Point Salines, Martinique.

Hood 'took the liberty of giving him two or three instances to the contrary and added that admitting there was the greatest probability that the expected convoy would make Salines Point and but a bare possibility of its making Deseada (Desirade), humbly submitted whether it would not be prudent to guard against that possibility; for allow the enemy to come here fourteen sail of the line strong, you can have two squadrons of eighteen sail of the line which will admit of four sail to play upon the transports and storeships and still have ship for ship, and the destruction of the transports seems to me an object deserving attention. Sir George was perfectly silent to this.'

Thus wrote Hood to George Jackson on 31st March, after events had proved him to be right. Rodney, with de Grasse's powerful fleet 'snug in Fort Royal', preferred to keep his fleet concentrated to the windward of Martinique. The French convoy, with an escort of only two sail of the line did, in fact, make their landfall at Desirade and, passing between Dominica and Martinique, safely reached Fort Royal on the 20th. Rodney has been condemned for the faulty disposition which robbed him of a great opportunity. Hood was scathing in his criticism.

'We may from *luck* (of which we have not hitherto had a common share) yet do something to retrieve our country's misfortunes; but (I) am afraid we cannot expect it from judgement or by acting by any rational well-digested plan, which the present situation of things here makes absolutely necessary. . . . How Sir George Rodney could keep his whole force to guard one path, when half of it was fully equal to the service, and to leave *another* (which appeared to me the most probable the enemy would take) without any guard at all, is matter of the atmost astonishment to me. I have really fretted myself ill, for nothing short of a miracle can now retrieve the King's affairs in this country.'

No doubt the crusty, gout-ridden and undoubtedly self-opinionated commander-in-chief was infuriating to Hood, himself by no means lacking in self-esteem and a sufferer from his liver. Nevertheless there was something to be said for Rodney's wish to keep his fleet concentrated. Following Hood's plan, if de Grasse had slipped away from Fort Royal and gone to leeward to join the Spaniards in an attack on Jamaica, or even gone to attack St Lucia or Barbados, there might have been a fatal delay before the scattered British squadrons could have concentrated again.

Events showed Hood right and Rodney wrong; but in Rodney's defence, he was very conscious that the salvation of the dwindling empire was in his hands. He dared not take his eye off de Grasse for too long. By maintaining a position from which he could instantly latch himself on to the tail of the French when they left Fort Royal, he made sure that de Grasse could not achieve his object without fighting. There was little element of luck in such a strategy. The incubus of a valuable convoy which must sail with him made it certain that de Grasse must accept battle to protect it.

Rodney now brought the whole of his fleet to Gros Islet Bay, therefore, leaving frigates between his anchorages and Fort Royal. That 'the great events which must decide the empire of the ocean' were impending, he knew. The enemy's plans to capture Jamaica were about to be put in motion. While he watched and waited, Rodney evidently encouraged his subordinates to speak their mind as to their views on the strategy to be pursued. Hood considered that a regiment and five or six ships of the line should be sent at once to Jamaica. Rodney, ever courteous, allowed that Hood might be right; but he still determined on keeping his force concentrated. When the advice was not acted upon, Hood was piqued. Writing to Middleton he sneered: 'What Sir George Rodney proposes I cannot say, but from what I hear from those who have the goodness to come to me (for I have been confined to my cabin for some days) he seems to have no plan.'

Rodney was evidently as voluble and capricious in his talk as ever. 'He told Admiral Drake yesterday,' Hood went on, 'he would go to windward, that de Grasse might not know where he was; and to others almost in the same breath that he would push to Jamaica directly. "Well, but, Sir George," says a pretty shrewd captain of my division then present, "suppose de Grasse should think the force already in the neighbourhood of Jamaica equal to the conquest of the island, aided by a body of troops he very possibly has sent, or may send, and remains in force at Fort Royal; what will become of all these islands?" His answer was in his accustomed off-hand strain: "Oh, damn these islands, Jamaica is of ten times more consequence than all of them put together." His manner of talking, is to be sure, very extravagant and extraordinary, but without much meaning.'

Rodney's eccentric manner of speech is confirmed by as firm an admirer as Gilbert Blane, who was one day to write:

'It must be admitted by his most sincere friends and admirers and those who lived most in his society, that he had a peculiar, desultory and declamatory style of conversation, whether in private company or in business.'

For all Rodney's erratic talk—talk which was more properly

thinking aloud—he knew very well that to regain 'the empire of the ocean' he must bring de Grasse to action in a decisive battle. He had but to wait for the French expedition to set out, when, to protect his transports and store ships, de Grasse must bring out his fleet. Rodney realised, as de Grasse did not, that for the French expedition to succeed the British fleet would have first to be eliminated. To fend it off in an indecisive skirmish as at the Chesapeake and other encounters would not be sufficient.

While Hood was penning his letter to Middleton, Rodney paid his sick subordinate a visit of two hours on board the *Barfleur*. 'I never found him more rational. . . .' Hood wrote as soon as had gone. 'But there is, I am sorry to say it, no great reliance to be placed in a man who is so governed by whim and caprice.'

What whim or caprice there was in Rodney's strategic planning can only have taken the shape of considering the various ways of inducing de Grasse, with his inferior force, to put to sea. Once he left the shelter of Fort Royal, encumbered with his convoy, he could with certainty be brought to action, an event which Rodney knew would decide the outcome of the naval war and to which he looked forward with confidence and impatience. Hence Rodney's alternating suggestions for hastening the event by taking the fleet away from St Lucia to encourage the enemy out.

Such a move proved unnecessary, however. De Grasse was being pressed to carry out the grandiose scheme for the capture of Jamaica which had been agreed with the Spaniards waiting for him at Cap François. He allowed himself to believe that by sailing along the chain of islands running north and then west from Martinique, and mostly French or Spanish possessions, he could always avoid action by sending the convoy into harbour while his fleet, keeping to windward, could fend off its opponent as he had succeeded in doing on previous occasions. On 5th April some deserters from Martinique brought Rodney the intelligence that troops were being embarked in transports at Fort Royal and that sailing orders for the 8th had been issued.

This was excellent news. Rodney did nothing to discourage the enemy's plans. His fleet was kept at anchor in Gros Islet Bay, the ships pressing on with the endless repairs needed to keep ships of the line seaworthy and battleworthy. The tedious business of topping up the water casks was kept in full swing so that ships should have full supplies when the moment came to weigh anchor. On Sunday, 7th April, the commander-in-chief was being entertained to dinner at the house of the Agent Victualler on Pigeon Island. This official was none other than Mr Marr whom we saw being given his start in life by Rodney at Jamaica in 1771 and who had since been of service as the admiral's agent during the difficult days of his exile. He was no doubt reaping a rich reward now. Also at the table were General Matthew, commanding the garrison, Rear-Admiral Drake, Captain Alan Gardner of the *Duke* and Captain 'Billy-go-tight' Cornwallis of the *Canada* and a number of others. From a letter of Cornwallis we get a revealing picture of Rodney as seen through the eyes of one who disliked and ever afterwards disparaged him.

'As the dinner was near over the Captain of one of the frigates which had been watching the enemy came to the Admiral, who was sitting at table, to inform him that part of the French fleet had sailed that morning and that the remainder were ready to go out with the land wind.' (This was young George Anson Byron of the frigate *Andromache*). 'Instead of being much pleased at the information, he asked him how he dared to quit his station, and talked to him in such a style that the clerks, doctors, mates at the bottom of the table thought it high time for them to go, and the captain was obliged to plead a sprung bowsprit as an excuse for having brought him the news that an inferior fleet, clogged with a convoy, if he chose to sail immediately, would be in his power the next morning.

'The captain, who from the suddenness of the attack could not be asked to sit down by the master of the house, nor was he in any way treated like a gentleman, went away; and the Admiral, observing my astonishment and indignation, got up and, coming over to me, said, "He is one of my own making, I never spare them, by God." Without entering at all into the matter, I said, "You know, sir, the *Canada* has artificers on board from other ships—that we are heeling and caulking and coppering between wind and water." "I shall sail in the morning," was the answer, and I went on board—but as I did not believe they would wait until morning to sail from that open bay, we went to work immediately, and had the launch hoisted in and all was ready in the middle watch . . . but there was no occasion to have been in such a hurry for though the Admiral sent some ships out, he suffered a punishment to go through the fleet in the morning' (a flogging round the fleet), 'and did not weigh until twelve o'clock; as the *Canada* had gone as far up the bay to get smooth water for heeling and was within the Admiral's ship, she did not weigh before the *Formidable*.'

The facts given in this strange indictment have been checked as far as possible by reference to ships' logs from which it is ascertained that the *Andromache* which had been on patrol off Fort Royal did anchor in Gros Islet Bay during the afternoon of the 7th but returned to her station in time to bring the news next morning that the whole French fleet was out. A general signal to the fleet for all officers and men to repair on board their own ships was made at 7.15 p.m. on 7th April. The *Canada*'s log records on the same evening, 'Finished coppering the starboard side. Righted ship.' The log for the morning of the 8th records the flogging of one man for disobedience of orders and two others for quarrelling. At 8 o'clock 'two men from the *Hercules* came alongside and received twenty lashes each, sentence of a Court Martial, for being concerned in burning the town of Choc' (Choque). 'At nine a signal was made in the offing for a fleet, the Admiral made the signal to prepare for action. At half past eleven weighed and came to sail in company with the fleet.'

Thus Cornwallis's facts are, in general, borne out. His indignation is understandable and would have been less severe if Rodney had had the ability or desire to take his subordinates into his confidence. The admiral's refusal to rush the fleet to sea at the first signs of a move by de Grasse is explainable by his unwillingness to do anything which might send the French back into harbour. He wanted them well at sea and thoroughly committed. If he had valued more the good opinion of his captains he might have explained this to Cornwallis; but that was not Rodney's way, nor was it the Navy's way until Nelson taught it to be a 'band of brothers' for a time. The treatment of young Byron, the son of his old friend 'Foul-weather Jack', was not without reason. The frigate captain had, indeed, abandoned his station without orders. He could have passed his intelligence by signal. Being a protégé of the admiral he could expect to be roughly treated for such a betrayal of the trust given to him. The system of favouritism, for all its defects, impelled a patron to demand a high standard of conduct of his protégés.

By noon on 8th April the British fleet, thirty-six sail of the line, was clear of the harbour and streaming northwards under a press of canvas after the enemy. By 2.30 p.m. the advanced look-out frigate was signalling 'Enemy in sight', and at 6, masthead look-outs in the battleships could see the swarm of sails on the northern horizon. Dawn revealed the French widely scattered, the main body of their fleet barely moving in the calms and catspaws of wind in the lee of the island of Dominica. Their van, however, and a few of their centre division, fourteen ships in all, had won clear of the northern point of the island and, in the channel, between Dominica and the little group of islets called Les Saintes, had their sails filled by the steady trade wind. Two French ships of the line, the *Auguste* (80), flagship of de Bougainville, commanding the rear squadron, and the *Zélé* (74), also of the rear, had somehow lost touch with the fleet during the night and could be seen to the north-west far to leeward of the van. The British fleet was suffering the same disability as de Grasse and it was not until 7 a.m. that some of the van squadron under Hood caught the breeze. Eight of them began to draw ahead, leaving the remainder of the fleet becalmed. The result was two-fold. The *Auguste* and *Zélé* were in danger of being cut off; but Hood's eight were faced by fourteen of the enemy until the centre and rear could come up to their support. Nevertheless Hood formed line of battle and boldly pressed ahead, his course converging with that of the *Auguste* and *Zélé*, beating northwards to join the detached French van. The *Auguste* safely weathered the British squadron but the *Zélé*'s course was leading her towards a collision with Hood's leading ship, the *Alfred* (74)—an apparently suicidal course of action. A collision would in fact have occurred had the *Alfred* not borne up.

The two ships passed, a stone's throw apart. The crews stood to gaze in an astonished silence and not a gun was fired. No signal from the commander-in-chief to engage having been hoisted, Hood would not give the order on his own initiative. The *Zélé* sailed on unharmed to join her comrades.

Her escape was fraught with incalculable consequences to the

French fleet; for she was indeed to prove de Grasse's undoing in the days to come. Her loss at this stage might even have been an eventual advantage to him. Hood's inaction was at no time criticised by Rodney and it has been suggested that Hood feared to bring on a battle prematurely. If so, his forbearance failed in its object, for the French van under de Vaudreuil now hoisted their battle colours and bore down, fourteen strong, to attack Hood's small squadron.

An opportunity to defeat the British fleet in detail had been given to the French by the vagaries of the wind and by Hood's overbold, even foolhardy advance out of reach of support. Hood saw his danger and, to avoid further separation, ordered his ships to bring to. But the main body of the British were still far astern and only at a snail's pace working their way out of the area of calms. De Vaudreuil, however, was well indoctrinated with the French strategical concept of avoiding decisive battle. The aim of the French fleet was to cripple their opponents and shake off pursuit so that they could proceed with their ulterior object of carrying their own fleet and convoy to join the Spaniards at Cap François. De Vaudreuil had a healthy respect for the carronades mounted in the British ships, the 'smashers'—so deadly and destructive at really short range, but useless otherwise. His ships therefore hauled their wind while still at long shot. With Hood's ships hove-to, they were able then to sail along his line in succession, each ship, as it reached the end of the British line, tacking and sailing round in an ellipse to join up again in the rear to repeat the operation. It was performed with admirable precision and the French broadsides, aimed high as usual, worked considerable havoc with their opponents' rigging. (*see page 222*) A golden opportunity to sink or capture the majority of Hood's squadron was missed, nevertheless. As Hood was to write to George Jackson, 'Had de Grasse known his duty, he might have cut us up by pouring a succession of fresh ships upon us as long as he pleased.'

Meanwhile the British centre and rear had at last won clear of the area of calms. As the trade wind filled their sails, Rodney led them close-hauled on the starboard tack to the northward, a course which, if they were left free to follow it, would take them between the French van and the remainder of their fleet and would gain them the weather gage. The French saw the danger. De Vaudreuil's squadron hauled their wind and ceased fire, then tacked on to a southerly course to rejoin the rear. They thus headed Rodney off; but he had managed to gain so much distance to windward that when the French all wore round on to the starboard tack—the same tack as Rodney was on—they were almost brought to a general action, an eventuality they were determined to avoid. Some desultory exchanges of fire in fact took place but, as Rodney told Hood that night, 'Except the two rear ships, the others fired at such a distance that I returned none.'

The immediate danger past, de Grasse once again ordered his van to attack Hood's still isolated squadron. It had been reinforced by the rejoining of the *Royal Oak* who resumed her rightful place leading the line. The *Barfleur's* log records that 'at twenty minutes past eleven o'clock the *Royal Oak* passed and cheered us. Sir Samuel Hood hailed her and desired to know the reason why they had not sooner got into their station'. She had evidently gone considerably astray during the night for Captain Burnett replied that she had been becalmed until then which would hardly have been the case if she had been in the lead. She was to atone for her laggardly ways now. When the French van bore down to resume their cautious assault, the *Royal Oak*, with the *Warrior*, bore the brunt, the former's main topmast being shot down, the latter's falling two days later.

This second engagement of the van lasted from 12.14 to 1.45 p.m. when the British centre and rear at last coming up, the French hauled off. The French efforts to cripple their opponents had been not unsuccessful, a number of Hood's ships being considerably damaged aloft; so that when the French made off, close-hauled, to windward, it was beyond the capacity of the British fleet to follow them. Hood's squadron having so far borne more than their fair share of the heat and burden of the day, Rodney assigned it to the rear position, making Drake's squadron the van. Nevertheless, as Hood claimed, 'we handled them very roughly.' One of them, the *Caton* (64), was so damaged that she was detached for repairs to Guadeloupe. There, too, de Grasse had sent his convoy, under escort of two 50-gun ships, to seek the protection of the batteries guarding the anchorage of Basseterre.

De Grasse's hopes of holding off his enemy to allow the convoy to proceed had been proved false. He can never have had much faith in such a possibility, but to accomplish the difficult task set him he had been forced to try it. He concentrated now on the more immediately attainable goal of outsailing his opponent to wind-ward and shaking off pursuit. The damage done aloft to a number of the British ships forced Rodney to lie-to for repairs during the ensuing night. At daybreak on the 10th the French were seen to have got away some twelve to fifteen miles to windward and were only just in sight from the deck of Rodney's ships.

With his ships already repaired under the magical touch of the wonderfully skilled men of the age of sail, Rodney beat doggedly to windward throughout the 10th, only to have his efforts defeated by a mistake on the part of his staff. It was one of the happenings on which Hood based his indictment of Sir Charles Douglas as a Chief of Staff. As he described it to Jackson:

'Sir George carried a stiff sail all day, neared them very much by sunset, and intended to have carried a plain sail all night, but by a strange blunder in Sir Charles Douglas, by making the signal for the leading ship to shorten sail, which was then under her topsails only, with her mizzen topsails aback, the fleet lay-to all night. . . . At daybreak only a few of the leeward-most part of the French fleet could be seen from the masthead.'

The error might have been fatal, but during the night de Grasse's scourge, the *Zélé*, delivered the first blow to his hopes by colliding with another seventy-four, the *Jason*. From evidence culled later from Swedish naval officers who were on board several of the French ships as observers, it is clear that the French fleet was already suffering from a shortage of trained officers of the watch, a shortage inevitable, under their system of re-cruitment, as a war progressed. The evil effects were to be sorely felt in this campaign. So damaged was the *Jason* that she was sent limping away to Basseterre. Added to the loss of the *Caton*, this reduced the French fleet to thirty-one of the line. The *Zélé* had come off more lightly than the *Jason*, but she had lost her fore topmast. During the day, therefore, she inevitably dropped away to leeward.

Rodney, discovering how much the enemy had gained on him during the night, had ordered a General Chase to windward, which was kept up all day; and though this did little to bring him up on the French main body, it posed a threat to the *Zélé*. Towards sunset, therefore, the exasperated de Grasse was forced to bear down with his fleet to cover her; this, as Rodney was to record 'brought him so near that I flattered myself he would give me an opportunity to engage him the next day.' In this Rodney was over-optimistic. His situation was still the same, with the enemy well to windward. Dogged persistence might prevent de Grasse from shaking him off, but luck or a mistake on the enemy's part would be needed before he could force an action. His most sanguine hopes could not have envisaged that both these were about to strike a decisive blow in his favour.

Once again it was the luckless *Zélé* which was to be the primary cause of the enemy's discomfiture. Rejoining the fleet after dark and approaching it on the opposite tack she ran headlong into the *Ville de Paris*, de Grasse's huge flagship. The *Zélé*'s foremast and bowsprit fell in a tangle of wreckage; helpless, she drifted away again to leeward.

The British fleet, since dark on a tack to the southward, went about at 2 a.m. on 12th April on to the starboard tack, which with the wind at south-east, allowed them to head east-north-east. They were still on this course as day broke shortly after 5 o'clock, grey with overcast, a light trade wind ruffling the surface of a calm sea. They were grouped, as was the normal procedure, not in a single line but in a more compact 'order of sailing'. With the first light, however, the order to form line of battle was given. By the standing orders Hood's squadron should have led on the starboard tack; but on account of the damage on the 9th Rodney had reversed the normal order and he now ordered Drake's squadron to take the lead.

As the visibility grew the French fleet was revealed, spread out in great confusion from the north-north-west to north-north-east, at distances between six and fifteen miles, the majority standing south on the larboard tack. The nearest ship, in the north-westerly quarter, could be seen to have lost her foremast and to be in tow of a frigate. It was the *Zélé* towed by the *Astrée*; since 5 a.m., after much delay in passing the tow rope in the dark, they had been heading north for Gaudeloupe. Once again, therefore, de Grasse had to decide whether to desert his wayward cripple or to bear down in her support. If he chose the latter he must lose all he had gained to windward. If he came too far he might lose the weather gage. To sharpen the horns of his opponent's dilemma, Rodney signalled Hood to send ships away in chase. Hood despatched his four rearmost ships. *(see page 223)*

The next move was with the enemy. While waiting to see what it would be, on board the ships of the British fleet the hands were piped to breakfast. Rodney himself, anxious days and sleepless nights taking their toll, went back to bed to await the outcome. On the quarter-deck Sir Charles Douglas remained to watch the slow unfolding of the situation, gauging the relative positions of the two fleets, checking the strength and direction of the fluky, early morning wind. His excitement mounted as he watched. At 7 o'clock he snapped shut his long spy-glass and strode aft to the admiral's quarters under the poop. Entering, he swept off his gold-laced cocked hat with a dramatic flourish and addressed his chief. 'I give you joy, Sir George. Providence has given you your enemy broad on the lee bow.'

The moment was, indeed, worthy of the conscious touch of drama in Douglas's behaviour, and Rodney realised it at once. The long doubts and maddening frustrations of the past days seemed at an end. Unless something unexpected happened the chance was at last being given him to seize the weather gage. Whatever happened de Grasse must now be forced to fight. Hurrying on deck he saw at a glance that Douglas had judged correctly.

As Rodney had hoped, de Grasse had refused to abandon the *Zélé*. Signalling for his scattered force to concentrate, he himself in the *Ville de Paris* had crowded on sail and borne down to the rescue. Now, as Rodney could see, he had come so far to leeward as to make battle inevitable. The repeated mishaps which had dogged the Frenchman's steps and frustrated his careful strategy had fogged his judgement and led him into a trap.

Three alternatives were open to him. He could, of course, continue down the wind, in flight, which would for the time being postpone a clash. Rodney would, however, follow and, holding the weather gage, must eventually force him to turn at bay. Such a course of action was therefore unthinkable. Instead, de Grasse could haul his wind on either the starboard or larboard

5. *The Saintes. 1782 April 9th, 10 a.m.* Rodney's vanguard (eight ships under Hood) engaged with the fifteen ships of de Grasse's vanguard, while the main fleets lie becalmed under the lee of Dominica. Hood's ships are hove-to to retain contact with Rodney.

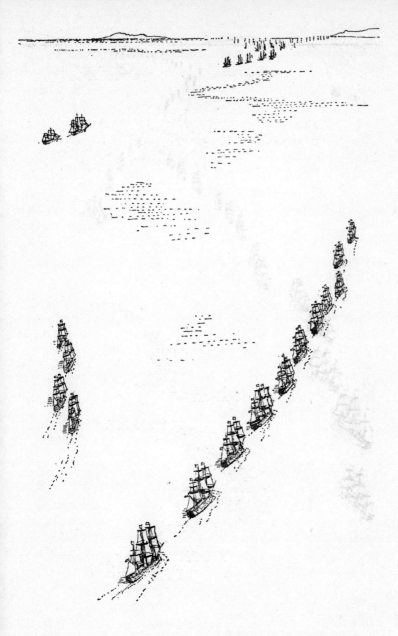

6. *The Saintes. April 12th, 6 a.m.* Rodney (his leaders in foreground) finds de Grasse under his lee bow and can therefore offer battle. De Grasse runs down to protect the *Zélé* in tow of *Astrée* and four of Hood's ships are detached to attack these two.

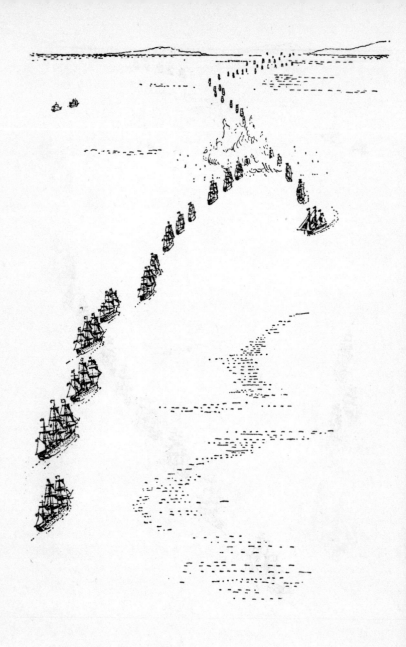

7.   *The Saintes. April 12th, 8 a.m.* Rodney (in foreground) fails to weather the French van and makes contact with the sixth ship in the French line. As the fleets pass on opposite courses, the action becomes general.

8. *The Saintes. April 12th, 9 a.m.* A veer of wind heads off the
French fleet (four in the foreground) and enables Rodney (in the
middle distance) to push through the French line. His example is
copied by Affleck resulting in great damage to the French and
the loss to them of the weather gage.

tack. The latter would take him on a track crossing that of the British at an obtuse angle. The fleet whose leading ship reached the point of intersection first would gain the weather gage. The former would set the two fleets on parallel tracks to the northwards towards the Saintes with the French ahead but to leeward of the British. On approaching the islets the French would in any case have to go about on to the larboard tack, thus bringing about an encounter; but the postponement would give time for the confusion in their ranks to be resolved.

Either way, a clash could not now be long delayed. Signals broke out at the *Formidable*'s masthead, to be repeated by the flanking frigates and down the line of battleships—to recall the ships in chase of the *Zélé*, to call in all cruisers, to shake out all reefs, to close the line of battle to one cable's length asunder, to prepare for battle.

The news spread like wildfire through the ship's companies. Excitement seized them as they set about the familiar routine of clearing ship for action—the precautions against fire by strewing the decks with wet sand and rigging wet blankets, cloths and frieze-screens round the hatchways and the magazine hatches; the sousing of sails and boats; the dousing of the galley fire; the dismantling of the cabin bulkheads; the rigging of the cockpits as casualty stations; the supply of cartridges and shot; and finally the thunderous rumble as the great guns were run out, to be followed by a strange silence as seven hundred men with suddenly nothing more to do waited, cold hands kneading their entrails, for what was to come, and wished there was not so long to wait.

As Hood's chasers turned back in obedience to their recall, de Grasse, his anxiety for the *Zélé* allayed, made his choice. He signalled for line of battle on the larboard tack; a race for the windward gage thus immediately began. The French ships, some of which had been as much as seven miles to the windward of their flagships at dawn, were still in the process of forming their line. They must still be in disorder when the two fleets met. 'What evil genius is inspiring our Admiral?' exclaimed de Vaudreuil's flag-captain, du Pauillon, who was to lose his life an hour later.

In the British fleet, in sharp contrast, perfect order reigned. There was nothing more for the admiral to do for the time being.

Rodney, with Douglas, Blane, Symonds and the secretary sat down with calm satisfaction at the breakfast table. Lord Cranstoun, who had joined the *Formidable* a few hours before sailing from Gros Islet Bay as supernumerary captain preparatory to relieving Symonds, remained on deck to keep them informed of developments. For a time the race for the weather gage hung in the balance; but as the British fleet ran north and out of the influence of the high land of Dominica, it met the more easterly breeze then blowing out in the channel between the islands. The leading ships were forced away to larboard to keep their sails full and it became clear that the French must pass across ahead of them to win the race.

Cranstoun brought the news to the breakfast table. It was a disappointment. It meant that the battle must now develop as a mutual cannonade between the two fleets passing on opposite courses, an action not likely to produce decisive results. Nevertheless the direction of the wind was such as to allow the British ships to force a really close action. Given that, Rodney had no doubts of the outcome. Going on deck he gave the order for the signal to 'Engage the Enemy Closely' to be made. A cheer went up as the familiar flags were recognised and the huge Red Ensign of battle was hoisted. Then the heart-stirring throb of the drums beating to quarters began.

At three minutes to eight o'clock on the morning of 12th April, 1782, the *Marlborough* (74), leading the British line, reached the French line at its ninth ship from the van, the *Brave* (74), and the first broadsides thundered out in the last major action to be fought against a fleet wearing the white battle flag of Royal France. *(see page 224)*

XV

THE battle which now followed was to be called the Battle of the Saintes by the British, the Battle of Dominica by the French. The strength of the two fleets in line-of-battle ships gave the British a superiority of thirty-six to thirty-one. As the battle was fought this had little bearing on the outcome. On the other hand it can safely be said that the British had a very real superiority in morale, in fighting spirit and skill. The difficulties under which the French laboured to keep their fighting ships manned during a war have been discussed in an earlier chapter. By 1782 the war had been in progress for five years and they were feeling the pinch of a shortage of trained personnel both on the quarter-deck and on the lower deck. In contrast the British who started a war with lubberly crews swept up from the streets and alehouses by the press gang, had had time and opportunity to train their men into highly-skilled, incredibly tough 'prime seamen'. Similarly their officers, continuously at sea since their teens, disciplined with calculated severity, had had to develop both skill and hardihood to survive.

It was perhaps in fighting spirit that the greatest advantage lay with the British. The French were second to none in courage; but the principles under which they fought, the avoidance of decisive action and the concentration on crippling an enemy rather than crushing him, inevitably engendered a feeling of inferiority. The British on the other hand were unquestioning in their belief that they were superior in every way to their enemy. That one Englishman was worth several 'Frog-eaters' went without saying. When the enemy held off at long-shot and aimed high to destroy their rigging, they were contemptuous and furious at being prevented from an all-out trial of strength. The sailors on each side were unwilling conscripts, ready to desert at the first opportunity: but whereas the British sailor in action would fight with the demoniac fury of one who never doubted the outcome, the French had little heart for it and were apt to lose their heads in the chaos and confusion of a close, hard-fought fight. This was the sort of battle they had to face on 12th April, 1782.

After receiving the first broadside of the *Brave*, the *Marlborough* put her helm up to turn parallel to the enemy line and bring her own guns to bear. Then in the gentle breeze she led the line past the French ships, on an opposite course to them, engaging each one as it glided slowly by. The signal for Close Action was up in the flagship; but Captain Taylor Penny had no need of its urging to take his ship into point-blank range. This was what every British captain had been waiting for, an opportunity to bring his devastating carronades into action, to hammer the enemy who preferred to play 'long bowls'. Now it was at pistol range and every shot told in the French ships. Twenty-two times the scene repeated itself for the *Marlborough* before she found she had passed the rear French ship. Astern of her the whole British line was following in her wake, cannonading and slowly passing ship after ship of the French centre and rear.

A scene typifying the eighteenth-century Navy was played out in the *Hercules* (74), thirteenth in the line. Captain Savage was a fair sample of the type of rough, tough, hard-swearing naval officer that made up the majority. A martyr to gout, he normally controlled his ship from a chair on the quarter-deck; but now he limped to the bulwarks on the engaged side, whence between the broadsides he hurled scorching abuse at each French ship as it came abreast of him. Wounded, he was carried to the cockpit for the surgeon's rough ministrations, but was soon back to continue his verbal assaults through his speaking trumpet.

In the *Russell*, commanded by James Saumarez, the conduct of the captain of the maintop was recorded as an example of the fighting spirit of the lower deck. A shot smashed one of his arms, whereupon, refusing all assistance, he slid down a backstay to the deck and walked to the cockpit where the mangled limb was amputated. He returned on deck and remained there encouraging his shipmates for the rest of the battle.

[229

The ships of the French van ahead of the *Brave* if they had continued close-hauled would have had no opponents and the British rear would have come into action completely fresh against French ships which had already suffered a prolonged cannonade. De Grasse therefore ordered them to bear up parallel to the British rear. This they did and Hood's squadron came into action with them though not at such point-blank range as the remainder of the fleet.

The battle had assumed the form of a passing cannonade on opposite tacks, a replica of the Battle of Ushant and likely to be equally indecisive. Nevertheless de Grasse now realised that his fleet was getting much the worst of the exchange at the point-blank range which suited the British methods and armament and on account of the ragged state of his line. Furthermore his van was heading for the area of calms in the lee of Dominica. Desperately he tried to break off the action. Twice he signalled for his fleet to wear on to the opposite tack, first by wearing all ships together and then by wearing in succession. With the enemy a bare pistol-shot to leeward, either of these manœuvres was palpably impossible and his signals were ignored. All control of the situation was out of his hands, indeed, by now. At 9 o'clock the leading French ship had come abreast the last of the British line. At the other end the first six ships of Drake's division had drawn clear of the enemy line and had hove-to to repair rigging preparatory to working back into action. Other ships were joining them one by one. If nothing happened to change conditions the two fleets would, in another hour or so, draw clear of each other, leaving the British too crippled to be able to renew the engagement from their leeward position.

In the centre, the *Formidable* had been in action since 8.23 a.m. Next astern of her was another three-decker, the 90-gun *Namur*, while immediately ahead was the *Duke* (98). The latter and the *Formidable*, their guns equipped in the style devised by Douglas, had been pouring broadsides into their successive opponents at a rate almost to silence the opposition. So close were they passing that a midshipman of the flagship averred that he 'could have thrown cold shot aboard them, they were so near'.

Rodney, his gout temporarily forgotten, had alternated between the quarter-deck and the great cabin to which he had

230]

limped from time to time to watch from the stern gallery the progress of the ships astern. On one such excursion the sight of a dish of lemons on the cabin table reminded him how dry-throated the breathing of powder-smoke had made him. A midshipman, Charles Dashwood, attending on him was told to make a lemonade. Amidst the thunder and confusion of battle Dashwood saw no harm in using his dirk to stir the drink; but the admiral, fastidious even at such a moment would have none of it. 'That kind of thing is all very well for the midshipmens' mess,' he protested. 'Drink that yourself and send my steward here.' Meanwhile he quartered a lemon and stood sucking it as he contemplated the tremendous spectacle.

The tall mass of the *Ville de Paris* and her flanking three-deckers the *Couronne* and *Languedoc* had been engaged and passed. A shot from the *Ville de Paris* had smashed a hen-coop on the deck of the *Formidable*. From it had flown a bantam-cock which perched itself on the rail of the poop. At each broadside it flapped its wings and lustily crowed defiance. Rodney was delighted at the episode and gave orders that the bird should be protected and petted for the rest of its life. The whole scene was shrouded in a dense, impenetrable cloud of smoke out of which ships loomed briefly, to be veiled again as the guns belched forth afresh. The *Sceptre*, next astern of the *Languedoc*, had melted into the smother. Now on the starboard bow the next seventy-four hove into sight, the *Glorieux*. She had just suffered the hammer blows of the mighty *Duke*. Her rigging hung in a crazy tangle. Rodney was on the quarter-deck standing with Gilbert Blane. As they watched they saw the Frenchmen manning the upper deck guns throwing down their sponges and rammers and running for shelter. She was ripe for the *coup de grâce*. Rodney turned to Blane: 'Run below and tell them to elevate their metal,' he said, a phrase which Blane correctly interpreted after cogitating it on his way to the gun-deck, as an order to raise the breeches and so depress the gun-muzzles to aim at the water-line.

Blane, a penetrating and accurate recorder of events of the battle, was thus unfortunately absent from the quarter-deck during the crucial happening which now took place and about which there has been great controversy. For at this moment there was a sudden change of wind. It had earlier shifted, it will be remembered, from south-east to east-south-east, robbing the British of any chance of weathering the French line during the approach. It now veered back again to south-east. The French ships, which had been close-hauled were at once taken aback and forced to turn to starboard—towards their enemy—if they wished to keep their sails full. Thus from a line ahead they were transformed into a quarter-line-in *échelon*, in other words. The British ships on the other hand were free to luff up, to starboard, or keep away, to port—and so to leeward—as they wished.

In the rolling smoke which enveloped everything, this was not immediately apparent in the British ships. What did appear to Sir Charles Douglas, on the quarter-deck of the *Formidable*, was an unaccountable gap between the *Glorieux* and her next astern, which had not come into view when she should have done. Immediately afterwards Douglas realised that by luffing—which had always been possible even before the change of wind as the British ships were not close-hauled—the *Formidable* could lead through the gap in the French line and seize the weather gage. Rodney was off the quarter-deck at the time, on one of his visits to the stern gallery. Douglas turned aft to go to him and they met as the admiral stepped out on deck. Sweeping off his hat, Sir Charles exclaimed: 'Sir George, I give you joy of the victory.' Rodney was used to Douglas's flowery turns of speech. From the stern gallery the new situation had not been so apparent. 'Pooh,' he replied, irritably, 'the day is not half won yet.'

'Break the line, Sir George,' Douglas declaimed, still without pointing out the new state of affairs which had been clear to him from his station on the quarter-deck. 'Break the line and the day is your own and I will ensure you the victory.'

Rodney's reply shows that he still did not grasp his chief of staff's meaning. 'No, I will not break *my* line,' he said.

In his excitement and frustration, Douglas now ordered the helm to be put down, an order which Rodney at once counter-manded, with a stern reminder to the chief of staff as to their respective positions. The admiral then strode away to the weather rail and for the first time could see the situation for himself. Turning back to Douglas, still standing, exasperated, by the wheel, he gracefully conceded: 'Very well, Sir Charles, you may do as you please,' he said. Thus the decision was taken which turned the Battle of the Saintes from a passing encounter into a decisive victory.

The order was given to luff and the *Formidable* led the way through the gap between the *Glorieux* and the *Diadème*, engaging both as she passed close between them. To port, indeed, she found an immobilised group of four French ships foul of each other and able to make only a feeble reply to the broadsides poured into them. The gap had been formed, in fact, by the *Diadème* being taken aback. At the shift of wind she had borne up to keep her sails full, but out of the smoke had appeared the *Duke* on a collision course. In both ships the helm was put a-weather to pass to leeward, but the Frenchman had then reversed his helm to avoid collision and had thus been taken aback. The three ships astern of the *Diadème* closed up on her to form a close, conglomerate group.

To one side of them filed past the *Formidable* followed by the next five ships, each firing larboard broadsides into them while completing the destruction of the *Glorieux* with their starboard guns. The Journal of the *Formidable* recorded that 'not a single shot missed and dreadful must have been the slaughter'. To leeward passed the *Duke* which, after raking them with her powerful armament, followed the *Formidable*'s example in luffing up to cut through the French line to windward.

Rodney can have known little of what was happening in other parts of the battle while the smoke of continuous gunfire enveloped his flagship. To starboard, the ill-fated *Glorieux* could be seen as the last of her masts went by the board under the fire of the *Canada*, third ship astern of the *Formidable*. There was admiration for a gallant foe as the white battle flag was nailed to the stump of a mast by her first lieutenant, de Kerlessi, after her captain had been killed. To larboard the sickening slaughter in the group of ships round the *Diadème* could be estimated from the number of sharks boiling round them as bodies were thrown overboard.

Suddenly, as the *Formidable* ran clear to windward of the smoke, the whole picture became clear. To the southward could be seen the British rear squadron, led by Commodore Affleck in the *Bedford*, and Rodney could see that Affleck too, thrusting forward through the blinding smoke, had passed (though unintentionally) through the French line, leading the whole of Hood's squadron in the rear to windward (*see page 225*). He could see, also, though not hear over the continuing roar of battle, the men of the *Barfleur* and other ships cheering as they saw the flagship's bow emerging to windward out of the smoke. The *Bedford* had actually cut through astern of the *César*, twelfth ship of the French line. Both the *César* and her next ahead, the *Hector*, had been torn asunder as ship after ship of the British rear luffed up and cut close across the *César*'s stern.

To the northward the last of the British van ships were running clear of the French rear. Both fleets were cut into three separate divisions. But whereas Rodney's centre and rear were still in good order ready to renew the fight, and in a position to do so now that they held the windward gage, the French had been thrown into the greatest confusion, first by the shift of wind and then by the fearful cannonade many of them had suffered while, single-handed and unsupported, they suffered the successive broadsides of the British rear and centre filing by. The British manœuvre had left the way clear for them to fly to leeward; and this they proceeded to do, hoisting every stitch of canvas that damaged masts and rigging allowed them. De Grasse signalled frantically for them to re-form on de Vaudreuil's rear squadron which was the leewardmost. But no heed was paid to him. The French had had enough.

The Battle of the Saintes had been won; but the fruits of victory had still to be gathered. Rodney hoisted the signal to tack and for close action. In Drake's division, in the van, in spite of having exchanged broadsides with a score of enemy ships each, the casualties had been amazingly light. The *Marlborough*, for example, which had led the line and engaged twenty-two ships in succession, had only three men killed and sixteen wounded. The *Prince George*, sixth in the line, had the heaviest casualty list with nine killed and twenty-four wounded. These figures are accountable partly to the feebleness of the French fire—Gilbert Blane was to record that 'I can aver from my own observation that the French fire slackens as we approach and is totally silent when we are close alongside'. It must also have been a result of the French custom of firing high to cripple the enemy ships, as the damage aloft shows: the *Marlborough* 'found four main shrouds, five fore

234]

ditto, main and fore topmast spring stays, all the fore topmast backstays, main top-gallant stays and rigging shot away; all the sails much shattered; the fore and main top-masts and top-gallant masts wounded in several places; the foremast cross-tree shot away and main yard wounded, also mizen and cross-jack yard. . . .'

Other ships in the van recorded similar damage aloft. The *Princessa*, indeed, had the trucks, at the very summit of all three masts shot away, which indicates some very wild aiming indeed. So much damage was received aloft by the ships of Drake's division that it was impossible for his ships to tack. With what sails they could spread, however, they wore round and limped slowly after the retreating enemy. Only the *Russell*, which had anticipated the orders and had wore on her own initiative, had any immediate prospect of being in at the kill.

The wind had been falling light as the day wore on. Rodney's own division in the centre was just able to tack and drift slowly in pursuit of the group of ships round the *Ville de Paris*. In the rear, Hood's squadron was almost becalmed, but by dint of hoisting out his boats to tow his bow round, he was able to set the *Barfleur* on a course down wind towards the fleeing enemy.

By 1 p.m. the smoke had drifted away and dispersed, revealing the situation in its entirety. To leeward the French could be seen making off in three separate and confused groups. Less damaged aloft than the British, the majority were drawing away. Between the two fleets could be seen the dismasted *Glorieux* in tow of the French frigate *Richmond*, a recent capture from the British. What British ships had any wind in their sails turned in her direction as though drawn by a magnet. On the *Formidable*'s quarter-deck, Douglas, ever ready with classical reference, declaimed:

'Behold, Sir George, the Greeks and Trojans contending for the body of Patroclus.'

Not unreasonably, Rodney snarled in reply: 'Damn the Greeks and damn the Trojans. I have other things to think of.' A little later, however, when the full extent of the enemy's discomfiture became clear, he made a characteristic *amende*:

'Now, my dear friend, I am at the service of your Greeks and Trojans,' he cried, 'and the whole of Homer's Ilead, or as much of it as you please, for the enemy is in confusion and our victory is secure.'

A little later the *Richmond* cast off the tow, Lieutenant de Kerlessi of the *Glorieux* refusing to let her be risked in a hopeless effort on his behalf. The *Glorieux* was left immobile, awaiting her doom. Rodney now hauled down the signal for line of battle, hoisting in its place that for Close Action so that ships were left free to decide their own actions. Half an hour later, however, this was hauled down. Hood, his squadron the least crippled in the British fleet, looked for 'General Chase' to replace it; but in vain. Astonished and furious, he did what he could to achieve the same result by signalling to the ships of his own squadron to make more sail. The *Formidable*'s log shows that Rodney made similar signals to laggards; but as the flagship herself remained under easy sail, these were evidently aimed at keeping the fleet together rather than urging them on in chase. In the *Barfleur* Hood set the example of spreading every stitch of canvas his wounded spars would carry. His log recorded, 'Employed making sail and repairing rigging. Main topsail yard being shot in two, got it down and another up. Two o'clock set the main topsail and studding sails. In hoisting the main top-gallant sail carried away the main top-gallant mast, it being wounded.'

Thus it was ships from the British rear that first came up with the French cripples. To the *Royal Oak* the shattered *Glorieux* surrendered, the last surviving officer tearing down the flag nailed to the stump of a mast. The next to be overtaken was the *César*, between one and two in the afternoon. Attacked by the *Bedford* and *Centaur* and in little condition to fight after the pounding she had suffered earlier, she surrendered when the *Centaur* was laid alongside for boarding. As the *Centaur*'s crew poured in upon the *César*'s deck, many of the Frenchmen, fearing their ship was about to founder, crept into the *Centaur*'s lower deck through the gun-ports. It was a strange experience for the boatswain of the French ship, for in 1759 he had been one of the crew of the *Centaur* when she had been captured by the British.

For all the efforts of Hood's squadron to crowd sail, it was not until 4 p.m. that the next French cripple was overtaken. This was the *Hector*. She had fought gallantly in the main action; but now, as Cornwallis's *Canada* ranged up alongside and round-shot began again to send the tearing, mangling splinters flying, the gunners dropped their handspikes and rammers and ran. Her

236]

captain, de la Vicomté, sword in hand, succeeded in rallying them for a time; but when the *Alcide* came up and he himself was killed by a shot from her, the colours were struck and Captain Thompson took possession of her.

In the meantime neither Hood's ships nor those of Drake were having any success in overhauling any others of Bougainville's or de Vaudreuil's squadrons. The main interest was now transferred, therefore, to the centre of the three detached bodies into which the French had been split, the five ships gathered round the *Ville de Paris*. Excitement rose as it was seen that the French flagship was lagging. De Grasse's signals to his fleet to re-form had been ignored. His van and rear were fleeing down the wind, all else forgotten. Even the ships of his own squadron, fine three-deckers such as the *Couronne* and *Languedoc*, his immediate seconds, would not wait to stand by their chief. One French ship only, the little *Ardent*, a sixty-four captured from the British in 1779, reached across the front of the enemy pursuers to go to the support of the flagship. But singly she could do nothing. Brought to action by two British sixty-fours, the *Belliqueux* and *Prince William*, she was hammered into subjection in twenty minutes.

The prow of every British ship in the vicinity was now directed towards the *Ville de Paris*. The *Torbay, Canada, Monarch, Marlborough* and *Russell* each exchanged broadsides with her, but it was not until the *Barfleur* came up that she was finally brought to bay. Slaughter on her decks had been appalling. Ammunition was running low. Deliberately de Grasse sheered away from his tormentors to make his last stand opposed to a first-rate and a flagship. 'Observing the *Ville de Paris* to edge towards the *Barfleur*,' wrote Samuel Hood, 'I concluded the Count de Grasse had a mind to be my prisoner, as an old acquaintance, and therefore met his wishes, by looking towards him. As soon as I got within random shot he began to fire upon me, which I totally disregarded till I had proved by firing a single gun from the quarter-deck that I was *well* within *point blank* when I opened so heavy a fire against him that in ten minutes he *struck*.'

There was nothing else that de Grasse could do, indeed, with his rigging cut to pieces, his hull smashed from end to end by raking broadsides to which he could only reply feebly and at long intervals. Three hundred of his crew had been killed and there were not enough unwounded left to throw the corpses to the waiting sharks. On the upper deck there were but two men besides himself still standing. With his own hand he hauled down the flag as the sun set beyond his flying fleet. For the first time in naval history a first-rate had been surrendered to an enemy.

The *Formidable* came up soon after the *Barfleur* and Rodney was a witness of the surrender. Gilbert Blane described the scene:

'The ships immediately engaged with her at that moment were the *Barfleur*, flagship of Sir Samuel Hood, and the *Russell*, Captain Saumarez. The *Formidable* was right astern and having come within shot, was yawing in order to give the enemy a raking broadside, when Sir Charles Douglas and I, standing together on the quarter-deck, the position of our ship thereby opened a view of the enemy's stern, between the foresail, and jib-boom, through which we saw the French flag hauled down; upon which we, forgetful of what was due to decorum in that place, stupefied as it were by an ecstasy of joy, rushed into each other's arms in a hearty embrace.'

Rodney himself must have been equally moved at the dramatic climax of the momentous day. The long anxious months with the fate of the Empire in his hands were over at last. Victory had crowned his patient efforts to bring his wary enemy to battle. The French fleet was fleeing in confusion. Five ships of the line had been captured, one of them the biggest battleship in the world. Aboard them was found the greater part of the siege train of heavy artillery intended for the assault on Jamaica. As Rodney had promised, the French commander-in-chief was his prisoner. As darkness fell over the calm sea, Rodney brought the fleet to for the night. In his cabin he penned the opening words of his despatch:

'It has pleased God, out of His Divine Providence, to grant to his Majesty's arms a most complete victory over the fleet of his enemy, commanded by the Count de Grasse'. . . .

XVI

THE stresses of the last four days and sleepless nights, bodily fatigue and ceaseless anxiety had left the ailing sexagenarian in a state near exhaustion. The emotional shock coming at the end of the long day of battle brought him close to collapse. The securing of his matchless prize and preparations for the reception of his illustrious captive occupied his attention to the exclusion of all else. Hood, about to make sail to resume the pursuit, was flabbergasted to see the signal for the fleet to lie-to for the night. 'So soon as the *Ville de Paris* had struck,' he wrote to Jackson, 'Sir George's faculties seem to have been benumbed, further than respected that ship *alone*.'

That the shattering defeat which had been inflicted on the French was not carried through as it should have been is undoubted. Years later, writing to Cornwallis, Nelson was to refer to it. 'On the score of fighting, I believe, my dear friend,' he wrote, 'that you have had your full share, and in obtaining the greatest victory, if it had been followed up, that our Country ever saw.'

Hood, too, must have been near the end of his endurance—he was fifty-eight years of age, had fought two fierce actions in the last four days and can have had little sleep or rest since putting to sea. But it did not blind him to the necessity for a relentless pursuit if full advantage of the victory was to be reaped. Bitterly he complained to Middleton: 'My boat had scarcely got on board' (the *Ville de Paris*) 'when Sir George made the signal and brought-to and continued to lay to the whole night. After the glorious business of yesterday, I was most exceedingly disappointed and mortified in the commander-in-chief. In the first instance for not making the signal for a general chase the moment he hauled that down for the line of battle, which was about one o'clock; had he so done, I am confident we should have had twenty sail of the line before dark; instead of that he pursued under his topsails all the afternoon, though the flying enemy had all their sails set their very shattered state would allow. In the next that he did not continue to pursue under that easy sail, so as never to have lost sight of the enemy in the night. . . . Had I, my dear Sir Charles, had the honour of commanding His Majesty's noble fleet yesterday, I may, without the imputation of vanity, say the flag of England should at this hour have graced the sterns of upwards of twenty sail of the enemy's ships of the line.'

Two accusations are thus made which must be considered separately. That the *Formidable* did not pursue under a press of sail can be attributed to Rodney's desire to keep his fleet in some measure concentrated. A number of Drake's division and the five ships of the centre which had followed it along the lee side of the enemy had suffered severely. The *Prince George* had lost her foremast and several others had lost topmasts. The *Fame* was for a time in danger of sinking. Furthermore Hood's own flagship, though she crowded sail, had only come up with the *Ville de Paris* late in the evening and a bare half hour before the *Formidable*. It is not clear, therefore, how fifteen further prizes could have been taken before dark.

Some understandable exaggeration on the part of the exasperated second-in-command must be allowed, for he was undoubtedly right in condemning the inactivity which came with nightfall. Every effort to follow and harry the demoralised enemy should have been made. How much a General Chase during the night would have immediately achieved is not so certain, however. A few ships either did not see or chose to disregard the signal to heave-to. Amongst them was the *Anson* whose log for the next morning reads: 'At 6 a.m. saw our fleet from the mast-head bearing E.N.E., but no sight of the French fleet.' Thus the immediate results of the failure to pursue were perhaps unimportant. Nevertheless it must be said that Rodney's strategical grasp failed from the moment de Grasse's white flag came fluttering down. The failure was to cost many of the fruits of one of the most decisive naval victories of history.

While the fleet lay-to in the calm quiet of the tropical night, repairs to hulls and rigging were pressed on against the probable resumption of the pursuit on the morrow. In the captured prizes there were more grisly duties to perform. Dr Blane was there to record the scene.

'The carnage on board the prizes is dreadful,' he wrote, 'and the damages of the enemy are in every respect greater than ours. By the best accounts that could be obtained, the *Ville de Paris* had near three hundred men killed and wounded. . . . The *Glorieux*, when boarded, presented a scene of complete horror. The numbers killed were so great that the surviving, either from want of leisure, or through dismay, had not thrown the bodies of the killed overboard, so that the decks were covered with the blood and mangled limbs of the dead, as well as the wounded and dying, now forlorn and helpless in their sufferings.'

An even more appalling tragedy was played out, after the battle was over, in the *César*. The French sailors, battened down below by the prize crew, dissolved into disorder and broke into the spirit room. A naked light carried by one of them accidentally set fire to a cask of liquor. In a short while the ship was ablaze from end to end. Boats dared not approach. When the flames reached the magazine, she blew up. Everyone aboard, English and French, died in the flames or met death amongst the sharks.

British casualties in the battle had been astonishingly light—243 killed and 816 wounded in thirty-six ships all closely engaged. The heaviest list came from the *Duke* where there had been thirteen killed and sixty wounded. Amongst the killed was Captain Blair of the *Anson*. Bayne of the *Alfred* had been mortally wounded in the engagement on 9th April. Hearing that it was owing to loss of blood from a shattered leg while being carried to the cockpit that Bayne had died, Blane devised simple tourniquets, —'pieces of leather, about the breadth of a hand, long enough to embrace a limb, with slits to admit a piece of broad tape; a piece of linen or calico rolled so as to act as a compress to an artery, and a cylindrical piece of wood to twist the tape'. He recommended that warrant and petty officers should carry such tourniquets in action.

Nothing yet existed to combat infection of wounds, however. That gallant young captain of the *Resolution*, Lord Robert Manners—the 'young man of fashion' concerning whom Lord Sandwich had been 'tormented to death' and whom Rodney had given post rank at the age of twenty-two—lost a leg, besides receiving splinter wounds in the arm and breast. Put aboard the frigate taking Rodney's despatches, with apparently a good chance of recovery, he developed tetanus and died before reaching England.

Blane recounted how 'it was with difficulty we could make the French officers believe that the returns of killed and wounded made by our ships to the admiral, were true; and one of them flatly contradicted me, saying we always gave the world a false account of our loss. I then walked with him over the decks of the *Formidable*, and bid him remark what number of shot holes there were, and also how little her rigging had suffered, and asked if that degree of damage was likely to be connected with the loss of more than fourteen men, which was our number killed, and the greatest of any in the fleet except the *Royal Oak* and *Monarch*. He . . . owned our fire must have been much better kept up and directed than their's.'

Rodney courteously permitted de Grasse to remain in his own ship for the night, but in the morning he was brought on board the *Formidable*. Hood was also aboard the fleet flagship at first light to 'pay my compliments, and to try if it was possible to recover the mistake that had unfortunately been made, and so far prevailed upon Sir George to leave the ships of his own fleet, which were most disabled, to take care of the prizes and carry them to Jamaica, and to push on in search of the enemy with the rest. . . .'

'I lamented to Sir George on the 13th that the signal for a general chase was not made when that for the line was hauled down, and that he did not continue to pursue, so as to keep sight of the enemy all night, to which he only answered, "Come, we have done very handsomely as it is." I could, therefore, say no more upon the subject. I said the same afterwards to Sir Charles Douglas upon his paying me compliments on the management of my division. His answer was, "Sir George chose to pursue in a body." '

In this Douglas proved himself at least a much more loyal subordinate than Hood. For he, too, had tried to persuade Rodney to continue the pursuit through the night. He was bitterly hurt by the snub he had received and for a time was determined to resign his position as first captain. His affection for his chief prevailed, however, and when in years to come criticism of Rodney was raised in his presence he would have none of it. 'We had a great deal to do, Sir, and I think you will allow we did a great deal' was his usual reply on such occasions. Nor would he countenance compliments on his share in the victory at Rodney's expense. At Gilbert Blane's dinner table he reproved one such bearer of tittle-tattle on the subject, advising him to tell his informant 'to keep his breath to cool his porridge'. Such disinterested loyalty is almost unique in the navy of that day, and Douglas's character gains an added lustre from it. Rodney was only too justified when he wrote, 'Sea officers in general are too apt to be censorious.' In Douglas he found a welcome exception.

Hood, in comparison, justified as his criticisms of Rodney's inertia after the battle may have been, shows up badly. Not only to Middleton, the Controller, and to George Jackson, second secretary at the Admiralty, did he send his bitter accusations, but he repeated them in letters to Lord Robert Manners, a junior post-captain of twenty-four—but, of course, a young nobleman with influential relations. Nothing could be better calculated to undermine discipline, the loss of which Hood himself bewailed at other times. Lord Robert died before the letters could reach him and they ended up in the hands of his brother, the Duke of Rutland, as Hood probably realised they would in any case.

Nevertheless sympathy must go to him in his frustration at seeing what he regarded as a glorious opportunity of annihilating the French fleet slip away. Rodney's concurrence in the resumption of the pursuit on the morning of the 13th lasted for only four hours, when he brought the fleet to once again. 'Good God,' Hood raved, 'not to avail himself of the manifest advantage his most *complete* victory gave him is not to be thought of with any degree of temper! We might as easily have taken the whole of the French fleet as we did the five sail (probably a ship or two might have got off, but I am confident not more than three of the line could have escaped had they been properly pursued), which would most effectually and substantially have retrieved all the misfortunes of old England, have set her on tip-toe, and have humbled France in the extreme . . . how shamefully was the opportunity neglected.'

By mid-day on the 13th, however, the propriety of going away to leeward after a vanished enemy had become very doubtful. The wind was never more than 'light airs, inclinable to calm'. Since dropping out of sight the previous evening, the French fleet might have gone anywhere. Ever in Rodney's mind must have been the danger of being carried away to leeward. He decided that his first care must be to make sure that the enemy had not doubled back to the islands—for once he himself had gone to leeward he would be committed, by the damaged state of most of his ships' rigging, to carrying on to Jamaica. The Windward Islands would then have been at the enemy's mercy.

This was one of the reasons Rodney brought forward long afterwards for not having pursued during the night, but it serves as an answer equally to criticisms of his subsequent actions. He also feared that had the least damaged of his ships come up during the night with the enemy who had gone off 'in a close connected body' they might have been overcome, one by one. He went on to conjure up a picture of the French luring his ships away to leeward by means of false lights in fast-sailing frigates. None of these arguments can really be said to hold water. The enemy, far from going off in a close connected body, had fled in confusion. The next morning de Vaudreuil had only ten ships in company. Six others with Bougainville never halted their flight to leeward until they reached Curaçao on the mainland of South America. All had been so mauled during the battle that they were almost as incapable of beating to windward as were Rodney's own ships. That Rodney at the time cannot seriously have entertained the ideas he thus put forward later is clear from his letter to Lady Rodney on the morrow of the battle in which he said:

'I am of opinion that the French will not face us again this war, for the ships which have escaped are so shattered, and their loss of men so great, that I am sure they will not be able to repair or replace either in the West Indies.'

Thus Hood's contention would seem to be right—that the capture of the *Ville de Paris* and of the person of the enemy commander-in-chief so satiated the ambitions of the tired-out Rodney that he could not rouse himself to do more.

De Grasse was brought to the *Formidable* on the morning of the 13th and remained as Rodney's guest for the next two days. He

244]

showed no shame or embarrassment at the crushing defeat he had suffered and which he indignantly blamed on his subordinate admirals and captains whom he accused—not entirely without justification—of having deserted him. Hood, visiting the *Formidable*, was astonished to see him so far from being down-cast at his ignominious position as to take part with the thought-less glee of a boy in the capture of a shark. De Grasse maintained 'that he thought his fleet superior to mine', Rodney wrote to his wife, 'and does so still, though I had two more in number; and I am of this opinion, as his was composed of all large ships, and ten of mine only sixty-fours.'

From the pen of Gilbert Blane we have a revealing picture of the French admiral. 'After the surrender of the *Ville de Paris* the Admiral sent Lord Cranstoun, one of the captains of the *Formid-able*, on board of that ship, to beg the Comte de Grasse to remain there at his ease, if he chose. He came voluntarily on board the *Formidable* next morning, and remained there for two days, during which time I had a great deal of conversation with him and his officers. Sir Charles Douglas did me the honour to introduce me thus: '*C'est le médecin de nos armées navales, qui est presque assez habile pour faire revivre les morts;*' to which the Comte, humouring the badinage, answered, '*Et peutêtre pour faire mourir les vivants.*'

'He bears his reverse of fortune, with equanimity, conscious, as he says, that he has done his duty, and I found him very affable and communicative. I told him that the people of England had begun to despair of the safety of Jamaica, fearing that he was to complete his career of success by taking it. He said he would have done so, had his Court kept their word, by sending him twelve ships of the line in November, as they promised. . . . He attributes his misfortune, not to the inferiority of his force, but to the base desertion of his officers in the other ships, to whom he made the signal to rally, and even hailed them to abide by him, but was abandoned. They all blame Bougainville in particular, whom they cannot hear mentioned with patience; and they represent him as a mere charlatan who, by a knowledge of the world and a plausibility of tongue, has persuaded some favourites of the Court that he is a man of talents, though without a grain of spirit or professional ability. . . . The Comte de Grasse said they were a hundred years behind us, and added that were we not enemies, he should have been charmed with the superior discipline, neatness and order that prevailed in our ships of war.'

For the sake of his reputation in France de Grasse would have done better to have reserved some of this generosity and tolerance for the conduct of his own people. Already, while on board the *Formidable*, he was composing an indictment of many of his captains for the misfortunes of the day. Some had disobeyed his signals; others, and notably the captains of his two seconds, the *Languedoc* and the *Couronne*, had abandoned him. When he eventually reached England as a prisoner on board the *Sandwich*, the flattering and kindly treatment which the English customarily give to a vanquished foe encouraged him in his self-esteem. When crowds assembled outside his lodging in London calling for the brave Frenchman, he readily and affably appeared on the balcony to receive their acclaims. While still a prisoner he had pamphlets published setting out his accusations against his subordinates.

The French Government naturally supposed that only for very genuine reasons would an admiral thus publicly sully the honour of his service. They set out to investigate and, if necessary, to punish the culprits. While all the relevant documents and log-books were being gathered together and witnesses collected, the captains of the *Languedoc* and *Couronne* were held in prison. In 1784 the court martial was ready to sit. Its findings were uniformly against de Grasse and cleared everyone whom he attacked. Furthermore the court criticised the admiral for having borne down too far to leeward on the morning of 12th April in support of the *Zélé*, which, having a fresh breeze not shared by the English, was in no immediate danger. On his return to France de Grasse was disgraced, forbidden to present himself at court and was on one occasion in danger of his life at the hands of an infuriated mob.

We have run ahead of our story, however. From 13th to 17th April, Rodney lay with his fleet to the leeward of Guadeloupe, becalmed, more or less—though Hood claimed that they could have made 'more than twenty leagues farther to the westward'— while refitting and repair of ships and prizes went on.

The admiral's despatches and letters announcing the victory were sent on their way in the care of Lord Cranstoun in the frigate

Andromache. He gave a full mead of praise to Admirals Hood and Drake, to Commodore Affleck and to Sir Charles Douglas. In addition 'The gallant behaviour of the officers and men of the fleet I have the honour to command,' he said, 'has been such as must for ever endear them to all lovers of their King and Country. . . . In short I want words to express how sensible I am of the meritorious conduct of all the captains, officers and men who had a share in this glorious victory obtained by their exertions.'

Rodney also found time for a typical transaction. When storm-bound in Plymouth the previous January he had gone ashore to lodge with the Admiralty Commissioner, Paul Ourry. After one of the admiral's fiery statements as to the drubbing he was going to give the enemy, to which he was somewhat addicted when the wine was in him, Ourry, half jesting, half serious, said: 'Sir George, if what you so vainly anticipate should come to pass, will you make my friend, Hancock Kelly, a captain?' Rodney laughingly agreed. With his despatches went a laconic message to the commissioner:

'My dear Paul,

'Tis done—the battle's o'er and Britain's flag victorious. I have made your friend Kelly a captain. My compliments to the amiable Caroline.'

Frigates were sent, 'the moment we had a breeze,' to re-connoitre the islands; they returned with the information that all was quiet and the harbours empty. John Rodney's *Sybil* was not amongst them, incidentally. Having sprung a bowsprit he was under repair at Barbados at the time of the battle. 'I am extremely sorry for it,' the admiral told John's mother, 'for if he lives a hundred years he never may have such another opportunity.' The battle was to benefit him nevertheless, his father transferring him to command of the *Anson*, his first ship of the line, in place the dead Captain Blair.

By the 17th Rodney, assured of the safety of the Windward Islands and of Antigua, was ready to proceed to Jamaica. Hood, stamping with impatience, was at last to be let off the leash. With ten of the line he was instructed to 'go as far ahead as hull down . . . but if you think otherwise, which I submit to your better judgment, please to make sail till you get abreast Altavela' (about half-way along the south coast of San Domingo). Even now he railed at being given only ten ships while Rodney kept twenty to protect his precious prizes. Nevertheless he took advantage of the discretionary powers given him. 'Judging the only chance I had of intercepting any stragglers of the *flying enemy*,' he reported to Rodney, 'was to be off the Mona Passage as soon as possible, I carried studding sails below and aloft night and day, and on the 19th at daylight made the west end of Porto Rico.'

He was rewarded by the sight of sails to the north-west. Giving chase he overtook and captured the two French sixty-fours, the *Caton* and the *Jason*, which it will be remembered had been sent to Basseterre, damaged, on the 10th and 11th April, and the frigates *L'Aimable* and *Ceres*. They were found to be loaded with shells and other ordnance stores, amongst which were forges for red-hot balls for a siege. An even more notable capture was missed in the escape of the frigate *Astrée* on board which was the redoubtable old Marquis de Bouillé. From the prizes Hood gleaned information which set the final seal on his searing disappointment. With a sick heart he told his chief:

'It is a very mortifying circumstance to relate to you, Sir, that the French fleet which you put to flight on the 12th (twenty-six in number including frigates) went through the Mona Channel on the 18th, only the day before I was in it.'

The story of Rodney's active life draws to a close on this disappointing note. On 29th April he arrived at Port Royal, Jamaica, with his prizes and those of his own ships most needing refit, having left Hood with twenty-five of the line to cruise off Cap François and watch the enemy. For all Rodney's victory, the Franco-Spanish combined strength was considerably superior to the British and a Spanish army of 13,000 men was available to attack Jamaica. Hood made the most of the unfavourable position to back his criticisms of Rodney's past inertia. 'We might have done just as we pleased,' he wrote to Jackson, 'and instead of being at this hour on the defensive, a force might have been preparing to return to the Windward Islands for the purpose of attacking the enemy's possessions there.' To Middleton he complained, 'Had Sir George done what he might and ought, we

248]

should all most probably have been peaceably at home by our firesides in the course of another year. . . . Now, the whole business will be to come over again.'

Nevertheless the Battle of the Saintes had taken the heart out of the French Navy and Rodney had prophesied correctly when he said that they would not face the British again in the West Indies. The Spaniards had never had any heart to fight in alliance with the French. In May Hood was telling Middleton that there was not 'even the appearance of any cordiality or scarce any intercourse between the French and Spanish officers and seamen'. Furthermore disease was making great inroads in the strength of the troops. Rodney was content that the situation was well in hand. On arrival in Jamaica he occupied himself with the administration of the fleet and station and with the business of repairing and refitting his much-damaged ships and prizes, while Hood commanded at sea. He found 'the King's Dockyard suffered to go to almost total ruin . . . and that no repairs whatsoever had been done since I left it in 1774'. He set about the indolent officials in his usual spirited fashion and, as he told his wife, 'I have roused them and made them active in spite of themselves, or out they must go'; while to their Lordships of the Admiralty he reported that 'everything belonging to the naval department is in so ruinous a condition and so extremely inconvenient, that unless their Lordships will please to give directions to put things in proper order, his Majesty's and the public service must be extremely retarded and that briskness and activity so necessary towards defeating the designs of the enemy, greatly discouraged.'

By 19th May the first of the season's trade convoys was ready. It sailed under the command of Sir Peter Parker, the retiring port admiral, his flag in the *Sandwich*. A passenger in the flagship was the Comte de Grasse.

Rodney's health soon deteriorated again, as it so often did after a period of great exertion. When Hood returned to Port Royal on 21st May, Rodney was glad to turn the work over to him. Hood poured gentle scorn on his chief's claim to be unwell. He was relying in this upon information from Symonds, the late captain of the *Formidable*, for whom Rodney had at last found a vacancy in the *Warrior* and who was nothing loth to malign the admiral with whom he had got on so badly. Hood, however, found himself in complete agreement with Rodney's views on the deplorable condition of the naval establishments of Port Royal, and he was equally voluble in his indictment of the dockyard officials.

Meanwhile Rodney had received no news from London since sailing from St Lucia and no orders as to what was expected of him during the approaching hurricane season. On 9th July, 1782, he wrote to the Admiralty, 'Their Lordships may imagine my concern in not having received any despatches from Great Britain since sailing from St Lucia, and no orders whatever relative to the great and important fleet I have the honour to command, whose situation in this climate, and so near the hurricane months, they may be sure gives me the utmost anxiety. At all events I am determined (unless ordered to the contrary) that his Majesty and the nation shall not run the risk of almost half the fleet of Britain experiencing destruction, but that I shall proceed with the greatest part to the coast of America . . .'

The following day, a veritable bolt from the blue, there arrived at Port Royal His Majesty's ship *Jupiter* flying at the main the blue flag of Admiral Hugh Pigot carrying the order for Rodney's recall and his own succession to the command.

XVII

No news of political events at home had reached Rodney since he had put to sea from St Lucia in pursuit of de Grasse on 8th April. Thus he did not know that in the middle of March the Tory Government of Lord North had been forced to resign on account of growing criticisms of the conduct of the war. It had been replaced by a Whig administration under Lord Rockingham, whose faction had taken the lead in censuring Rodney's conduct at St Eustatius. Rodney's patron, Lord Sandwich, was out of office. The King himself—Rodney's faithful supporter—was shorn of much of his power by the defeat of his 'Friends' in Parliament. In the absence of pressing reasons to the contrary, therefore, it was inevitable that an admiral of the Whig persuasion should be sent to replace Rodney from whose enemies in the fleet—and they were many—malicious whispers about his conduct had been flowing to members of the erstwhile Opposition.

The new First Lord was Rodney's old friend, but ardent Whig, Admiral Viscount Keppel. Though he protested against the supersession of Rodney, he was not prepared to risk his new-found position to gain the point, even when the successor selected was an admiral who had been virtually retired since 1770 and had never previously flown his flag at sea. Promoted to Admiral of the Blue, Pigot sailed from Plymouth in the *Jupiter* on 17th May, the very day that the *Andromache* arrived bringing Lord Cranstoun and Rodney's despatches.

Keppel was roused from his bed at 2 a.m. on the 18th to read them. The appalling blunder the Government had made was at once plain. What he could do to retrieve it, he did. A messenger galloped through the night to Plymouth, averaging eight miles an hour on the journey, to stop Pigot. He was too late. The *Jupiter* had sailed out of sight and beyond recall.

When the news of the victory was given out, London went wild. 'All London was in an uproar,' Rodney's daughter Jane wrote to him. 'We were at the play. When we went in the whole house testified by their claps and huzzas the joy they felt at the news, and their love for you; their acclamations lasted for, I am sure, five minutes. You may judge how happy we were.'

England indeed had been starved of excuses to celebrate during what had, until now, been a depressing and almost continuously disastrous war. Only once before had London rung its bells and fired the Tower guns in salute and that had also been on account of a Rodney victory. With 'brave Rodney' facing the enemy all would be well, had ever been the belief of the man in the street. Now he had been proved right. The Government's too hasty super-session of the nation's hero raised a storm of protest. Lampoons and cartoons lauding Rodney and ridiculing Pigot and the Government flowed from the presses. How Rodney 'broke the enemy's line' was the dramatic phrase on everyone's lips.

The deeply embarrassed Government hastened to make generous amends. On 22nd May, 1782, both Houses of Parliament voted their thanks to Rodney, his officers and men. During the debate Burke buried the hatchet, declaring wryly that if there was a bald spot on the admiral's head he would gladly cover it with laurels. The committee which had been appointed to investigate the irregularities of the St Eustatius affair was discharged and the matter officially closed. The following day Parliament voted to confer on Rodney a barony of Great Britain. The Opposition, led by Lord Sandwich, who quoted the instance of his own ancestor, the victor of the Battle of Solebay, argued for an earldom, but unsuccessfully. Rodney took his title from the family estate of Rodney Stoke, though he refused the Duke of Chandos's offer to sell it to him; Lady Rodney did not like Somerset and there was no house remaining on the estate. A few days later a pension of £2,000 a year was voted for the lifetime of Rodney and his wife and children. (In the following year it was to be granted in perpetuity.) At the same time Sir Samuel Hood was given an Irish barony, and Drake and Affleck were made baronets of Great Britain.

None of this was, of course, known to Rodney when Pigot

arrived so unexpectedly to relieve him of his command; nor can he have yet known how the news of his victory had been received by the new administration when he sailed for home on 23rd July in the *Montagu* (74), accompanied by the frigate *Flora*. The two ships arrived in the Bristol Channel on 21st September and, having shifted to the *Flora* for the last part of the journey, Rodney landed the next night at Bristol. When the news of his arrival got around, torchlit crowds assembled outside the house of Mr Tindal, in the fort, where he was to pass the night. Their enthuastic welcome and acclamations were a taste of similar festivities which were to be staged in his honour wherever he went for the next several months. At last the people of England were able to honour the heroes of the 12th April in the person of their favourite admiral. Freedoms of cities and boroughs were showered upon him, the first to honour him being the Society of Merchants of Bristol. On 15th November, 1782, he was conducted through the city by a procession, comprising, amongst a number of allegorical and heraldic figures, 'Britannia', a vessel named 'The Rodney', manned by eight gentlemen in sailors' habit, 'Mars, supported by four javelin men', 'Minerva', similarly supported, colours and laurels, bands, drums and fifes; and finally, behind a large banner inscribed to 'The gallant and victorious Lord Rodney, saviour of his country, protector of its islands and scourge of its perfidious foes', himself in 'an open carriage drawn by six horses, the drivers in the habit of British sailors'. Cannons fired and bells rang. At 'a very elegant dinner', the 'Society of Merchants presented his Lordship with the freedom of the society, embellished by a curious drawing of the position of the two fleets in the engagement of 12th April with the *Formidable* and her associates breaking the French line.'

The freedom of the City of Bristol followed in the next month. London paid its homage when 'six aldermen and twelve commoners, preceded by the City Marshal, waited on Lord Rodney at his house in Hertford Street, who might be said to have made his public entry into the City, being met by a body of sailors, who took out the horses and drew his Lordship's carriage to the London Tavern, where a sumptuous entertainment was provided, at which were present many of his Lordship's friends. In the evening, a great many houses in the City were illuminated.'

The cities of Edinburgh and Cork followed the example of London and Bristol in conferring their freedom, as did Huntingdon, Liverpool, Northampton, Exeter, Great Yarmouth, Poole, Dundee, Leicester and Winchester. While they lasted, the adulation and applause must have been balm to the soul of Rodney with his memories of other times, of the days of crushing debt and fear of prosecution, of penurious exile and of cruel attacks on his financial probity and military competence. One feels that he must have enjoyed the part he had to play in the ceremonies, the toasts, the speeches and processions and that he played the part to perfection.

While the enthusiasm lasted the West India merchants who had suffered at St Eustatius held their hand; but with the end of the war in 1783 and the passage of time men's thoughts turned elsewhere and the old business was resurrected to dim the evening of Rodney's life. Though Parliament had washed its hands of the matter, the merchants were able to bring suits against him in the Admiralty court. In some cases orders for restitution were made. In all of them—sixty-four in number—the legal costs which he had to defray were more than enough to absorb the large sums of prize money due to him. A number were still outstanding at the time of his death. He was soon reduced to an 'honourable poverty'. A memorial he addressed to the King for protection from his persecutors makes clear the desperate straits to which he was driven. Another from his son and heir, Colonel George Rodney, petitioned for permission to retain his military rank although he had been forced to 'sell his company'. He had borrowed to purchase it, on the strength of his father's golden prospects after the capture of St Eustatius. Now he could not raise the money to repay the debt.

Such were the harassments which tormented Rodney in his declining years. They were spent mostly at Purbeck Park near Portsmouth, which house had been taken for him prior to his return from the West Indies. He did not care for it and always hankered for Southwick House.* From the West Indies he had written:

'I have long had a great inclination for Southwick. I could wish

* *In recent years the Navigation School of the Royal Navy, and famous in the Second World War as the headquarters of General Eisenhower at the time of the invasion of Normandy.*

it was taken, and I shall write to Thistlethwaite, the gentleman with a hard name, to let me have it immediately.'

But Purbeck had already been bespoke. In November 1782 Rodney complained in a letter to Hood that it was 'too cold and too fine' for him and that he preferred Southwick.

The faithful and conscientious Dr Blane was not forgotten. He had remained in the West Indies under Admiral Pigot, pursuing his efforts to bring health and hygiene to the fleet, and returned to England in 1783. On Rodney's recommendations he was appointed physician to St Thomas's Hospital where he carried on his great work, for which he was later knighted, and which entitled him to be honoured as one of the fathers of naval medicine.

Year by year Rodney's agonising attacks of gout became more frequent and more violent. He visited Bath regularly in search of an easement if not a cure. Early in 1782 he was writing to a friend:

'I have at last been able to get down stairs; but I find myself so very weak after the severe fit of sickness I have lately undergone, and my spirits so low, as to convince me that my hour-glass is almost run out; but it is what I must expect from my years and infirmities; however I have no cause to complain on that score, as my days have been multiplied beyond what I imagined or my constitution promised. . . .'

His old friend and associate through so many eventful years, Lord Sandwich, born in the same year as Rodney, was also near the end of his course, and died on 30th April 1792. Rodney survived him by less than a month. In May he was staying at the house of Colonel Rodney at the corner of Hanover Square and Princess Street. His gout had been unusually bad. On the 23rd he was seized by spasms in his stomach. Sir Walter Farquhar, the family physician, was sent for. He found the admiral unconscious. When presently he came to, Sir Walter said, 'I hope, my dear Lord, you feel yourself better?'

'I am very ill, indeed,' came the reply; and George Brydges Rodney sank back, dead.

So died an English admiral who must be granted his place in the halls of fame not far behind Blake and Nelson and with his great exemplar and early chief, Hawke. But for a weakening of his faculties and spirit owing to the advanced age at which the great moment of his life came, there is no doubt that his place

[255

would have been as high as any. In spite of the physical handicaps under which he laboured, he had achieved by noon on 12th April, 1782, all that was necessary to ensure the greatest naval victory of the age of sail to that date. He had done so by seizing the opportunity offered him in all the heat and confusion of a great battle. To grasp it had entailed breaking at great risk with the century of hide-bound tradition that had robbed the Navy of victory again and again in the past. Luck of course had played its part, as it always has in successful commanders' careers. His decision was made easier by the firmness and tactical vision of his chief of staff. The decision, nevertheless, was his alone to make. That he failed to follow up his victory is undeniable and culpable. Nevertheless he had done enough to revive the wilting fame and prestige of his country and his service and so lower the pride and morale of the enemy as to reverse the previously disastrous trend of the war.

Dramatic as were the events of the Battle of the Saintes, however, Rodney himself said that he preferred to rest his reputation on that other encounter with a greater opponent than de Grasse: the clash with de Guichen at the Battle of Martinique. In this he stands justified; for Martinique was the fruit of Rodney's success in raising the efficiency and discipline of the fleet from the low level at which he had found it. Unremitting drive at the cost of popularity and in defiance of open animosity had given him the flexible, manageable force with which he outmanœuvred the foremost naval tactician of France.

After the Saintes, the mortified French officers taken prisoner conceded that the discipline and training of their opponents put the British '100 years ahead'. Whatever material benefits of his victory Rodney failed to reap, the moral effect was to confer upon the Royal Navy a vital advantage which was to continue to the end of the age of sail.

In the autumn of 1782, Lord Howe's fleet returning from the relief of Gibraltar found itself to leeward of a Franco-Spanish fleet superior to it by ten ships of the line. For a whole day it lay-to inviting attack; but the enemy contented himself with a distant cannonade before making off. A French historian sadly commented that 'Quantity disappeared before quality'. When war with France came again eleven years after the Saintes, Britain's navy faced that of revolutionary France with a vast fund of moral superiority which would not have existed but for Rodney's victory. Nelson's genius flowered in the rich soil of the Navy bequeathed by Rodney, Hood and Kempenfelt and later St Vincent, cleansed of the indiscipline of its officers yet liberated from its unreasoning subservience to the letter of the Fighting Instructions, though it still had to rid itself of eighteenth-century callous disregard of the elementary rights of the men of the lower deck before it could enter on its golden age.

Rodney was an eighteenth-century aristocrat to his fingertips. With many of the faults of his class, he possessed also the great virtues in full measure. It should not be forgotten that at a time when the Navy was suffering harsh adversity and, ill-equipped and neglected, was facing—alone—a world in arms against it, when Keppel and Howe would not, for political reasons, risk their reputations to serve their country at war, Rodney shouldered the burden of responsibility. Had he failed, the populace which cheered 'Brave Rodney' would have been equally vociferous in demanding his blood, as it had done with Byng twenty-five years earlier. Some human imperfections of character can be forgiven such a man.

> 'No farther seek his merits to disclose
> Or draw his frailties from their dread abode,
> (There they alike in trembling hope repose,)
> The bosom of his Father and his God.'

George Brydges Rodney was buried in the little church of Old Alresford where he lies beside his first wife, Jane. A memorial to them adorns the nave of the church. The nation's homage to one of its greatest sea officers is represented by the memorial in St Paul's Cathedral.

Naval Gunnery in the Eighteenth Century

I N Rodney's time, naval guns had changed very little for the last 150 years. They were simple masses of iron cast in a single piece, thick at one end which would comprise the breech, and tapering away at the other, the muzzle. They became guns when they were bored out to the required calibre and a touch-hole drilled at the breech end. On either side of the gun, at the point of balance, were cylindrical projections known as trunnions. Upon these the gun rested on its carriage. This was a stout oaken structure with vertical sides, cut away at the breech end in steps, and mounted on wooden wheels called trucks.

Pivoted on its trunnions, the gun could be elevated or depressed to aim high or low and increase or decrease the range, fine adjustment being managed by a wedge or quoin inserted between the breech and the floor or bed of the carriage. To raise the massive breech for this purpose, heavy ironshod poles (handspikes) were used, the cut-away steps forming the fulcrum.

No attempt was made to alter the horizontal aim or training of ship-mounted guns. The ship itself was pointed so as to bring the guns to bear on the target. In ship to ship actions the order to fire was given when every gun was bearing, the resultant salvo being known as a broadside.

Guns were classified according to the weight of ball they fired, the largest naval gun being the forty-two-pounder, found on the lowest deck of a three-decker. A forty-two-pounder ball was, about the size of an Association football. The other two decks of a first-rate would mount twenty-four- and twelve-pounders. A 'seventy-four' would mount thirty-two- and eighteen-pounders on their gun decks. On the upper works—poop, quarter-deck and forecastle—the first-rate would have twelve-pounders, the 'seventy-four' nine-pounders. Towards the end of Rodney's career the forty-two-pounder was being replaced by the thirty-two-pounder as the heaviest naval gun, its handiness and better rate of fire being held to outweigh the disadvantage of a lighter projectile. In his last campaign his newest ships had been given carronades on their upper works. These were short-barrelled, close-range weapons, sometimes known as 'smashers'. Their weight and recoil being less, carronades of greater calibre than the standard guns could be mounted. They could only be used at point-blank range but their destructive power was then enormous. The French did not adopt this type of gun until a later date.

Besides solid iron cannon balls, guns could be loaded with other types of shot.

(a) *Canister or Case*—a number of small balls packed in a cylindrical metal case, for use at close quarters.

(b) *Grape.* Nine small shot (larger than in Case) the size varying with the calibre of the gun, in a thick canvas bag tightly corded to make a cylinder. The shot in a thirty-two-pounder grape weighed three pounds each.

(c) *Langridge.* Scrap-iron used instead of shot to destroy sails.

(d) *Chain.* Two cannon balls connected by a chain.

(e) *Bar shot.* Two cannon balls connected by an iron rod.

To load the gun, it had first to be hauled inboard by means of tackles secured to ring-bolts in the deck amidships and to the carriage. After the first shot this was not again necessary as the recoil did the work. It was necessary indeed to limit the run-back of the gun carriage by means of a heavy rope breeching secured to the ship's sides and to the pommelion, a solid knob at the breech end of the gun. Before reloading it was first necessary to clean the bore of the smouldering material left by the previous cartridge. This was done with a corkscrew-like object on the end of a pole, known as a 'worm', and followed up with a wet sponge. A cartridge made of specially treated paper and containing black powder was then fed into the barrel by a ladle, followed by the wad and the shot and the whole rammed home.

The gun's crew then manned the two tackles rigged for hauling the carriage into its firing position with the gun muzzle protruding beyond the square gun-ports in the ship's side. The gun-captain would clear out the touch-hole or vent with a priming iron, which would also prick a hole in the cartridge, and fill the touch-hole with powder from his powder flask. At the order to fire he would apply the glowing end of the slow-match fixed to the end of his linstock. With a vicious spurt of flame from the vent, a convulsive leap backwards against the breeching, a shower of sparks and burning debris and a dense cloud of smoke, the gun would fire with a deafening explosion.

Rodney's 'First Captain' in his last campaign, Sir Charles Douglas, was an enthusiastic gunnery innovator. In his previous ship, the three-decker *Duke*, he had directed his inventive genius to doing away with some of the limitations and shortcomings of guns of the day. The first of these was the danger to the guns' crews on account of the hideous violence of the recoil. Time and again the breechings would be parted and the three-and-a-half tons or more of gun and carriage would career destructively across the deck, killing or maiming any who came in its way. Douglas inserted a strong steel spring into the breeching to take the first shock of recoil. Behind the back wheels he set inclined planes with corrugated surfaces. These modifications effectively prevented any further broken breechings.

The spray of sparks which were blown back on board when firing to windward constituted another great danger, being liable to fall amongst cartridges waiting to be fed into the guns. Explosions from this cause were by no means rare. Douglas instituted the simple expedient of wetted wads; and there was no more trouble. The process of loading and firing the gun was slow, cumbrous and dangerous until Douglas modified it. To eliminate the necessity of worming, he gave cartridges flannel bottoms. To speed up and make safer the priming and firing, he procured goose quills and filled them with powder kneaded in spirits of wine. All the gunner had to do to prime was to slip one of these into the vent. Finally, to do away with the awkward slow match and linstock, he adapted a flintlock actuated by the pull of a lanyard.

The rate of fire was greatly increased by these improvements; but the full value of this could not be applied while the guns were limited to firing exactly on the beam only. Often the guns would be loaded and ready but owing to a sheer of the ship they would not be pointed at the target. Douglas devised a system of tackles and fittings by means of which the guns could be swivelled so as to fire as much as forty-five degrees before or abaft the beam. Thus not only could a broadside be concentrated on a small target, but when passing an enemy the guns of a ship so fitted could fire a broadside on the bow, another when the enemy came abeam and again on the quarter, as compared with the single broadside previously possible.

Douglas's gunnery reforms did not come into general use until after the period covered by this book. But at the Battle of the Saintes they were tested in action in both the *Duke* and in Rodney's flagship the *Formidable*. Writing after the battle, Douglas reported:

'Sir George had so much confidence in the obliquity and quickness of the fire of this his Majesty's ship, her guns fitted and appointed as the now approvedly tremendous *Duke*'s are, as far as time would permit, that the *Formidable* penetrated the enemy's line of battle between the second and third ship astern of the gallant de Grasse, almost totally silencing their fire by pointing the guns—where the untoward knees called standards do not interfere with the tackles—as far forward as possible, according to the new exercise, before they got so far aft as to be upon her beam. Of 2,600 goose quill tubes, not one failed. Nor did a single gun require worming until our twenty-two rounds of flannel-bottomed cartridges were all expended. Not a single lock ever once missed-fire on board the *Duke*. Some of our men on board here, not having been thereto so well trained, cut off theirs and repented thereof. In both actions we used wetted wads, nor did a single spark of fire ever return upon us.'

APPENDIX B

Glossary of terms in use in Rodney's day

Aback
: A ship or a sail is taken *aback* when the wind strikes the sail on its forward side, forcing the sail against the mast, taking the forward way off the ship.

Abeam
: At right angles to the ship's length.

Abreast
: In a position abeam (see above).

Admiral
: Vice-Admiral, Rear-Admiral of the Red, White and Blue, etc. See Flag.

Admiralty
: The office of Lord High Admiral, discharged by the Lords Commissioners for executing the office of Lord High Admiral or, in short, the Board of Admiralty. Comprised the First Lord and a number of Naval Lords.

Back, to
: To brace a sail round so that the wind strikes its front surface, thus taking way off a ship. The wind 'backs' when it changes direction by moving in an anti-clockwise direction.

Beam
: The width of a ship.
: On the beam, the same as Abeam.

Bear up or down
: Refers strictly to the movement of the helm to alter the course of a ship. Thus bearing up means putting the helm up (to the weather side) and so turning away from the wind. To bear down is the reverse. The expression 'to bear down' was used loosely, however, to mean to go towards (the enemy) and was actually done in most cases by 'bearing-up'.

Beat
: To tack to and fro to gain distance to windward.

Boatswain	The Warrant Office responsible for the sails, rigging, anchors, cables, cordage, etc.
Bomb-Ketch	A two-masted vessel, mounting mortars. Sometimes called, for short, a 'bomb'.
Braces	Tackles attached to the ends of yards to haul them round and so adjust the angle of the sails to the wind.
Bring-to	To take the way off a ship by turning up into the wind or by backing some of the sails.
Broadside	The simultaneous discharge of all the guns on one side of a ship.
Bulkhead	Partitions or walls between one part of a ship and another.
Capital Ship	A ship of the line.
Captain	The commanding officer of a ship of war. The leader of a party or seamen made up for a special purpose. Thus Captain of a Gun (Gun's Crew) Captain of a top, Captain of the Hold, etc.
Careen, to	To heel a ship over so that work can be done on parts of her hull normally under water. Done by shifting weights, such as guns, or hanging them high up the masts.
Carpenter	The warrant officer responsible for the fabric of a ship and her boats.
Caulk, to	To drive oakum between a ship's planks and cover it with tar to prevent entrance of water.
Close-hauled	Sailing as close to the wind as possible.
Commissioner	An officer appointed by the Admiralty to supervise on their behalf. Thus dockyards each had a Commissioner and there might be a Commissioner for Sick and Hurt to supervise medical arrangements on a station.
Commodore	In the absence of an admiral, a captain could be given the temporary rank of commodore which gave him authority over any other captains met with even if they were senior on the captain's list. A commodore flew a Broad Pendant to indicate his status.

[263

Comptroller	The most important officer of the Navy Board. Responsible for all the Navy's material.
Corvette	A term used only by the French in the eighteenth century to indicate a ship of war smaller than a frigate. Equivalent to a sloop in the British Navy.
Counter	That part of a ship's stern immediately above the waterline.
Cross-trees	Timbers at the head of a lower mast supporting the platform of the 'top'.
Crowd Sail, to	To spread every possible sail.
Ensign	The national flag of a ship.
	The Red, White and Blue Ensigns were all used by British ships of war until after the Battle of Trafalgar. Originally used to distinguish the three squadrons, van, centre and rear, the system lapsed in the eighteenth century and ships then wore Red, White or Blue Ensigns according to the rank of their admiral (see *Flag*).
	The French ensign before the Revolution was plain white.
First-rate	A ship of the line of the largest size—a three-decker.
Flag	The banner flown at the masthead by an admiral. The eight grades of admiral—Admiral of the Blue or White, Vice-Admiral and Rear-Admiral of the Blue, White or Red, were distinguished by the colour of the flag, and the mast on which it was flown, an admiral's at the main, vice-admiral's at the fore, rear-admiral's at the mizen. There was no Admiral of the Red, this rank being reserved for the (non-existent) Lord High Admiral.
Flag-captain	The captain of a flagship, the ship in which an admiral sailed and flew his flag.
Flag List	The list of admirals in their order of seniority.
Flag Officer	Synonymous with admiral, though sometimes including commodore.

Foretop	The platform at the top of the foremast. Above it rose the fore topmast.
Frigate	A small fast-sailing warship with a single tier of guns. Employed on scouting duties, as a signal repeating ship for a fleet or as a despatch-vessel, carrying messages between ships and squadrons or from port to port.
Ginger-bread	The carved ornamental woodwork on the sterns of sailing ships of war. Often gilded, hence the expression 'the gilt is off the ginger-bread'.
Go about, to	To go from one tack to the other. The opposite of wearing.
Guardship	A warship stationed in a harbour to super-intend marine affairs. In times of war supplied press gangs and accommodated 'pressed' men.
Gunner	The warrant officer responsible for the guns, ammunition and magazines.
Hand, to	When a sail was furled, it was first clewed up, that is to say the lower portion was hauled up to the yard by means of the clew-lines. It was then neatly parcelled up and secured by the gaskets by men working on the yard. This latter operation was known as 'handing'.
Handspike	An ash pole rounded at the handle end and squared and metalled at the other. Used in elevating and depressing a gun and also for heaving round the capstan.
Haul the wind, to	When sailing free (or large) to alter course so as to sail as close to the wind as possible.
Heave down, to	To careen a ship to make repairs to her hull.
Heave-to, to	To bring a ship to a standstill by putting some sails aback while others are left drawing. A ship will then 'lie-to' in the most comfortable position.
Helm	The tiller of a ship, the wooden beam inserted in the rudder-head and to which the wheel ropes were attached, a turn of the wheel thus moving the rudder one way or the other.

[265

	Thus starboard helm turned a ship to port, weather helm, or helm 'up' turned a ship away from the wind and vice-versa (see *Bear-up*).
Hull down	At a distance at which the hull of a ship is beyond the horizon but the masts and sails are still visible above it.
Landfall	The first land sighted after an ocean voyage.
Landsmen	Untrained members of a ship's company.
Larboard	The left-hand side of a ship when looking forward.
Lee Gage	The leeward position as opposed to the weather gage or position when two fleets are in each other's presence.
Lee Shore	A shore line on to which the wind is blowing.
Leeward	The direction opposite to that from which the wind is blowing.
Leeway	The lateral drift of a ship to leeward.
Lie-to, to *Lay-to*	See *Heave-to*.
Line Abreast	Ships in a line abeam of one another.
Line ahead	Ships in a line ahead and astern of one another.
Line of battle	A fleet or squadron drawn up in line in a pre-arranged order.
Line-of-battle ship	See *Ship of the line*.
Lower Deck	Properly, the lower gun deck. The deck on which the lowest tier of great guns was mounted. The living space for the majority of a ship's company.
Main-top	The platform at the top of the (lower) main-mast.
Master	The warrant officer responsible for the navigation and handling of a ship-of-war. Also responsible for the stowage of the hold.
Master's Mates	The master's assistants, qualifying for a master's warrant, usually midshipmen unlucky in getting a commission who had accepted the rank of master as the limit of their ambitions.

Mates	Warrant officers' assistants. Masters and surgeon's mates ranked as officers. Boatswain's gunners' and carpenters' mates were ratings.
Midshipman	A 'young gentleman' entitled to 'walk the quarter-deck' while qualifying for a lieutenant's commission. They will have completed two years at sea as 'captain's servant' before being rated. They were neither commissioned, warrant, nor, in all cases, even petty officers, but they had some of the privileges of officers. In the eighteenth century there were also midshipmen of mature age who had been raised to the quarter-deck from 'before the mast'. They might remain midshipmen all their days.
Mizen	The aftermost mast of a three-masted ship.
Navy Board	The administrative board of the Navy, consisting of the treasurer, surveyor, comptroller, master of the ordnance and clerk of the ships. They were quite separate from the Board of Admiralty and functioned at their own Navy office. Their responsibilities often cut across those of the Admiralty and in the nineteenth century the Navy Board was abolished and its functions taken over by the Board of Admiralty.
Oakum	Old tarred rope, untwisted and teased out for use in caulking.
Ordinary	Ships 'in ordinary' were those in reserve kept in a state of preservation.
Pendant	Pronounced 'pennant'. A long narrow banner worn at the masthead by a man-of-war in commission. A 'Broad Pendant' is the square, swallow-tailed flag flown by a commodore.
Poop	The raised deck forming the aftermost portion of a ship's upper works.
Port	The left-hand side of a ship when looking forward. The same as 'larboard', the term used in the eighteenth century.

Post-captain	The rank which entitled an officer to command warships above a certain size, or 'post-ships'.
Press Gang	A party of seamen authorised under a 'press warrant' to kidnap seamen for service in the Navy. They did not in practice confine themselves to seamen, however.
Privateer	An armed private ship authorised by a Government's Letter of Marque to prey upon an enemy's shipping.
Purser	The warrant officer responsible for provisions, stores and accounts.
Quarter	That part of a ship's side between mainmast and stern.
Quarter-deck	The uppermost deck between the mainmast and break of the poop. Only officers might linger on it.
Quarter line	The formation of ships in *échelon*. Intermediate between line-ahead and line abreast. In the eighteenth century called 'bow and quarter line'.
Rake, to	To fire a broadside into the stern or stem of a ship, thus sweeping the whole length of its decks.
Reef, to	To reduce sail area by bunching up some of it and tying the fold with reef points, lengths of rope sewn on to the sail for the purpose.
Rigging	The ropes which support the masts (standing rigging) and manage the sails (running rigging).
Run free, to	To sail other than close-hauled. To sail down wind.
Sail or Ship of the line	A ship with an armament powerful enough for her to take her place in the line of battle. From Anson's time, a 'sixty-four' or bigger.
Schooner	A small, fast, despatch vessel with fore and aft lower sails, square-rigged top sails.
Scurvy	A disease caused by a deficiency of certain vitamins. Its symptoms are mainly a general debility and muscular weakness accompanied

	by bleeding gums, loosening of teeth and subcutaneous hæmorrhages leading eventually to death.
Seventy-four	A two-decked ship of the line mounting twenty-eight thirty-two-pounders, twenty-eight eighteen-pounders and eighteen nine-pounders.
Shake, to	To take to pieces, as with removable bulkheads when clearing for action.
Sheet	The tackle by which the lower lee corner of a sail was hauled down to spread the sail fully (see *Tack*).
Shot plugs	Wooden plugs which with the aid of canvas and oakum were used to repair shot-holes in a ship's side planking.
Sixty-four	The smallest ship of the line, mounting twenty-six twenty-four-pounders, twenty-six twelve-pounders and twelve six-pounders.
Sloop	The smallest ship used for fighting purposes during the eighteenth century.
Spring, a	A hawser attached to a ship's cable when at anchor and brought aboard at the stern, by hauling on which a ship could be slewed round to bring her guns to bear.
Spring, to	To split a mast or yard through over-straining it.
Starboard	The right-hand side of a ship when looking forward.
Studding-sails	Additional sails spread on booms attached to the end of the yards for use in light winds. Also called steering-sails.
Strike, to	To haul down or to lower an object. Thus, to strike one's colours or to strike something down into the hold.
Tack	The tackle which hauled down the lower weather clew or corner of a sail to spread it fully. Each lower corner had a sheet and a tack (see *Sheet*). When close-hauled the tack would be hauling the weather clew down inside the

[269

	gunwale. Thus the expression 'on the starboard tack' was short for 'close-hauled with the starboard tack on board'.
Tack, to	To go about. To turn a ship through the wind from one tack to the other. The opposite of 'wearing'.
Tarpaulin	A sheet of tarred canvas. Used to make foul-weather clothes and hats. The rough, uncultured type of naval officer who scorned to wear smart clothes or uniform.
Top	The platform at the top of each lower mast.
Topmen	Selected smart seamen stationed in the tops to attend to the spreading and furling of the upper sails.
Truck	The circular wooden cap on the upper masthead. A wheel of a gun-carriage.
Veer	The wind veers when it changes direction by moving in a clockwise direction. The opposite to backing (see also *Wear*).
Vent	The touch-hole in the breech of a gun.
Waister	The least skilful or active of the sailors theoretically stationed in the waist where the work was unexacting.
Warrant officer	An officer of a grade junior to any commissioned officer and whose authority derived from a warrant issued to him by the Navy Office. They superintended particular departments of a ship. The principal warrant officers were the master, surgeon, purser, boatswain, gunner and carpenter.
Wear, to	To turn a ship from one tack to the other by turning initially away from the wind. The opposite of 'tacking' or 'going-about'. Sometimes called 'veering'.
Weather	The side from which the wind is blowing. The opposite of 'lee'.
Weather, to	To get to windward of a piece of land or another ship.
Wind & Water	'Between wind and water', the area of a ship's

bottom exposed to damage by enemy gunfire through the ship heeling over to the
wind.

Windward The direction from which the wind is blowing.

BIBLIOGRAPHY

The British Navy in Adversity, Captain W. M. James, C.B., R.N. (Longmans Green, 1926.)

Flights of Naval Genius, N. C. Brian Tunstall (Philip Allan & Co., London, 1930.)

Histoire de la Marine Française, E. Chevalier (Librairie Hachette, Paris, 1877.)

Letters of Lord Barham, edited by Sir John Laughton (Navy Records Society, 1911.)

Letters of Sir Samuel Hood, edited by David Hannay (Navy Records Society, 1895.)

The Life and Letters of Admiral Cornwallis, G. Cornwallis-West (Robert Holden & Co., 1927.)

The Life of Augustus Viscount Keppel, Rev. Thomas Keppel (Henry Colburn, 1842.)

The Life and Correspondence of Admiral Lord Rodney, 2 vols., Major General Mundy (John Murray, 1830.)

La Marine Militaire de la France, G. Lacour-Gayet (Librairie Ancienne Honoré Champion, Paris, 1910.)

Memoirs and Correspondence of Admiral Lord de Saumarez Sir John Ross (Richard Bentley, London, 1838.)

Naval and Military Memoirs, Robert Beatson (Longman, Hurst, Rees & Orme, 1804.)

Rodney, David Hannay (Macmillan, 1891.)

The Royal Navy, Wm. Laird Clowes (Sampson Low, Marston & Co., London, 1898.)

The Sandwich Papers, 4 vols., edited by J. H. Owen and G. R. Barnes (Navy Records Society, 1932.)

INDEX

274]

278]

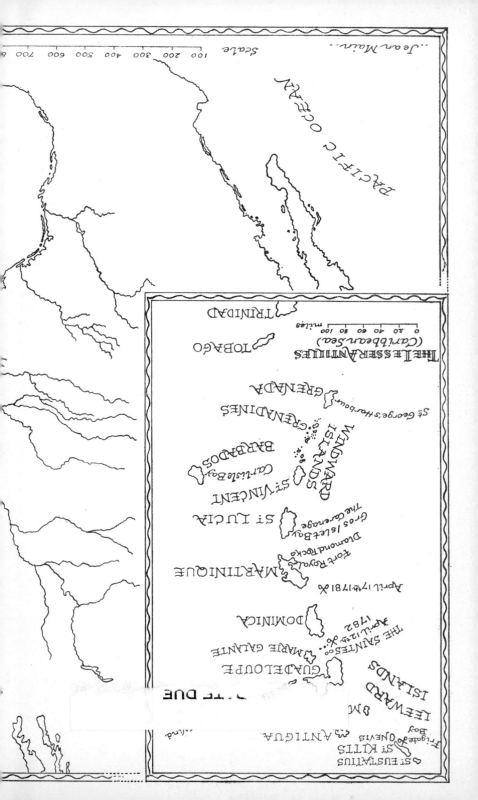

PACIFIC OCEAN

Scale
100 200 300 400 500 600 700 8...

...Jean Marie...

THE LESSER ANTILLES
(Caribbean Sea)
miles
0 20 40 60 80 100

TRINIDAD
TOBAGO
GRENADA
St George's Harbour
GRENADINES
WINDWARD ISLANDS
BARBADOS
St VINCENT Carlisle Bay
St LUCIA
Gros Islet Bay
The Carenage
Diamond Rock
Fort Royal
MARTINIQUE
April 17ᵗʰ 1781 ✕
DOMINICA
THE SAINTES ✕ MARIE GALANTE
April 12ᵗʰ &
1782
GUADELOUPE
LEEWARD ISLANDS
8M
DATE DUE
ANTIGUA
Frigate Bay NEVIS
St KITTS
St EUSTATIUS
Wind...